Ten Seasons

Recent Titles in
Contributions in Drama and Theatre Studies
Series Editor: Joseph Donohue

TEN SEASONS
New York Theatre in the Seventies

SAMUEL L. LEITER

CONTRIBUTIONS IN DRAMA AND THEATRE STUDIES, NUMBER 21

GREENWOOD PRESS
NEW YORK • WESTPORT, CONNECTICUT • LONDON

Library of Congress Cataloging-in-Publication Data

Leiter, Samuel L.
Ten seasons.

  (Contributions in drama and theatre studies,
ISSN 0163-3821 ; no. 21)
  Bibliography: p.
  Includes index.
  1. Theater—New York (N.Y.)—History—20th century.
I. Title. II. Series.
PN2277.N5L37   1986   792'.09747'1   86-369
ISBN 0-313-24994-6 (lib. bdg. : alk. paper)

Library of Congress Catalog Card Number: 86-369
ISBN: 0-313-24994-6
ISSN: 0163-3821

First published in 1986

Greenwood Press, Inc.
88 Post Road West
Westport, Connecticut 06881

Printed in the United States of America

The paper used in this book complies with the
Permanent Paper Standard issued by the National
Information Standards Organization (Z39.48-1984).

10 9 8 7 6 5 4 3 2 1

For Jack, Catherine, and Miles

★ ★ CONTENTS

★ ★
TABLES

★ ★

PREFACE

This book was originally intended as a comprehensive account of every facet of New York theatre in the seventies. The period was enormously rich in controversies, developments, and talents. The avant-garde was stretching the boundaries of the theatre to places it had rarely been before; new theatres were being built on Broadway for the first time in half a century, and venerable ones were being threatened with destruction; the musical theatre was being redefined; the city's production loci were being expanded; widespread institutionalization and subsidization were replacing the traditional producing methods; the commercial theatre was experiencing a startling turnaround from near death to vibrant life; numerous new ideas for selling shows were being created; with the rise of regional theatres, New York was becoming a showcase for new works rather than an originator of them; exciting young actors, directors, and designers were lighting up stages in every corner of the city; and fascinating and important changes were being made in every corner of the profession. The period seemed ripe for a thorough account of each of its myriad manifestations.

As the book took shape, practical considerations of length and scope began to arise, and it became evident that I would have to exercise much greater selectivity than I had initially realized. Thus, I have chosen to concentrate on representative areas and to leave the rest for future chroniclers. Another book will have to provide an overview of each of New York's major institutional theatres; of the era's numerous outstanding designers; of innovations such as the Theatre Hall of Fame and the New York Theatre Museum; of the squabbles and problems surrounding the presentation of the theatre's various awards; of the city's annual theatre festivals; of the difficulties of producing repertory in New York; of the various legal hassles—many of them with box-office treasurers—with which the theatre was involved; of the most significant producers; and so on. As for details of all the Broadway, Off-Broadway, and many Off Off-Broadway works of the seventies, interested readers will find them in my forthcoming *Encyclopedia of the New York Stage, 1970-1980*, part of a multivolume series for Greenwood Press.

What *Ten Seasons* does include will, I hope, compensate for its necessary omissions. The state of Broadway, Off-Broadway, and Off Off-Broadway production is surveyed in Chapters 1 and 2; the latter chapter also includes concise histories and descriptions of the contributions of the leading experimental theatre artists and companies of the decade. Chapter 3 discusses such areas as the growing significance of America's non-profit institutional theatres as a source of New York's plays; the diminishing role of non-English-language countries as providers of new material for local production; and the principal plays and playwrights of the decade, arranged under the rubric of national origin, with special sections on black playwrights and women playwrights. The musical theatre, including revues, is examined in Chapter 4. In Chapter 5 representative patterns into which plays of the period fall are discussed, including plays about women, biographical plays, plays about homosexuals, plays about blacks, plays about show business, plays about politics, and so on. Chapter 6 looks at the pattern of revivals, dramatic and musical, that formed so dominant a part of seventies production. The new ticket-selling ploys of the period are explained in Chapter 7, as are audience patterns and the changing fortunes of New York's playhouses, old and new. Finally, in Chapter 8 a selective account is given of the decade's top acting talents, of the directors who made an impact, and of the critics who told us what to see and what to miss.

For their consistently helpful attitude I would like to thank the staffs at the Lincoln Center Library for the Performing Arts and at Brooklyn College, the two institutions where the bulk of the research for this book was done. And, as I have done in the past and hope to do in the future, I express my deep gratitude to my wife, Marcia, for her assistance in all the nitty-gritty details that accompany the writing, typing, editing, and indexing of a book.

Ten Seasons

★ 1 ★
BROADWAY

"SLIME SQUARE"

At the onset of the 1970s the Broadway theatre district was rapidly sliding into the mire of despair. Broadway, wrote *New York Times* critic Walter Kerr, was like a ghost town the streets of which were so silent "you could put your ear to the ground and hear only the subway."[1] Theatres were empty and marquees were dark. When, in 1973, a national energy crisis forced theatre landlords to cut back their marquee and display case lighting by 25 percent, a palpable cloud of gloom pervaded the entire neighborhood.

Times Square was the blighted symbol of the putrid mess into which the Broadway district was evolving. Garbage was piled high on Broadway's once fabled streets; pornography, prostitution, and drugs were easily available on sidewalks and in doorways; and muggings were commonplace. At one point in 1970 seven members of the Lyceum Theatre production of *Borstal Boy* were mugged within a three-week period, six right near the old Forty-fifth Street playhouse.Well-known actress Barbara Barrie never went anywhere without her trusty umbrella with which to bash would-be assailants over the head. Brazen thieves came right up to the box office to snatch the cash out of ticket-buying hands.

Broadway's leading powers sought every means to stem the wave of crime and to control the spread of smut, but their efforts proved as futile as spitting into the wind. More police, better garbage pickups, improved street lighting, and all sorts of zoning ordinances and licensing laws were proposed and, often, put into effect. Producer Alexander H. Cohen, a major force in the attempt to clean up what theatrical publisher Leo H.

Shull called "Slime Square," even asked for a special committee to approve all new businesses planning to open in the district. For all its questionable overtones, Cohen's was a poignant plea in the wilderness for some sort of government intervention to prevent Broadway from sinking in the muck of shoddiness surrounding it.

Actors demonstrated, rallied, and signed petitions to make the area safe and respectable once more. In 1972, after being propositioned by a teenage girl and hearing of another actress who was urinated on by a stagedoor wino, actress Joan Hackett circulated a petition asking the city to set up a separate red-light district in which the sex merchants could ply their trade. In 1975, a crew of 200 Broadway celebrities manned brooms in a massive street-cleaning demonstration to point up the area's deterioration. Two years later, the casts of twenty-five Broadway shows, many in full costume, took part in a massive anti-pornography rally attended by about 8,000 people. Yet, despite these and other efforts, and the periodic "cosmetic corrections," as the *New York Times* liked to call them, Times Square's smut remained consistently visible. A *New York Times* editorial observed in 1977, "The city appears unable to protect its theatregoers from the psychic shocks of drama's present environs."[2]

Some signs of improvement were beginning to appear by the end of the decade. Two Broadway theatres had been reclaimed from their fate as movie grind houses, and the promise was that more conversions would come as new productions proliferated and the possibility of a theatre shortage grew. Theatre Row, a group of Off and Off Off-Broadway playhouses, successfully abolished the porno elements from Forty-second Street west of Tenth Avenue. Across the street from Theatre Row was the new Manhattan Plaza, an apartment complex for show people. Big money was being invested in area hotels, housing, and business, with various plans in the air for developing the district as an enormous entertainment and cultural center.

Times Square continued to present a sleazy, dangerous face to the public through the end of the decade, but the Broadway theatre by then had experienced a great surge of commercial popularity; in contrast to the early part of the period, large crowds of eager playgoers were turning out and keeping local theatres open. The recently moribund Broadway theatre had made an economic comeback that was nothing short of astounding.

SPLIT PERSONALITY

The story of the New York theatre in the seventies, especially that of Broadway, reveals a case of split personality. The first four years were disastrous. Broadway's first new full-scale playhouses since the late 1920s were turning out to be white elephants. The failure rate in the commercial theatre, never very encouraging, grew depressingly worse. One show after another found it impossible to muster up enough critical or audience interest to give a second performance. In those first four years, seventeen Broadway "turkeys" gobbled their way into oblivion after a single showing. At one point, ten shows closed in a two-week period.

But in 1974 something happened, something that demonstrated that indomitable will to live that has caused the theatre to be dubbed the "fabulous invalid." Blood began to pump in Broadway's veins, its lungs inflated, and color rose to its pallid cheeks. People returned to its theatres, there were more new blockbuster hits, summer business—which usually suffered box-office doldrums—boomed, and grosses started climbing. Theatres which recently had gone begging for shows with which to open their seasons were experiencing the rare elation of booking jams. Producers with shows on their hands were like pilots circling Kennedy waiting for an open runway. And there was no relapse, as season after season through the latter part of the decade witnessed new records set in attendance and income figures, making the period the richest in history for those with successful shows. A spirit of euphoria filled Times Square's air.

Broadway's economic revival, however, was no reason for adventurous producers with unusual properties to feel elated. As Alexander H. Cohen told a group of arts management students, "Broadway is dedicated to continuing commercial theatre. If you're going to ask anything about why Sam Shepard isn't produced on Broadway, we'll cut the crap from the beginning! Broadway is a commercial institution—it has nothing to do with pretentious notions. It's there to make money."[3] Only in the protected environment of the subsidized theatre can the producer or artistic director afford to take risks without fear that his institution will disappear following a failure. But even in grant-supported institutions, this picture too had begun to change well before the eighties rolled into view.

Broadway producers had reason to bite their fingernails from 1970 to 1974. The average number of shows produced during these years—about 56 per annum—did not show any startling changes, but the more telling statistics—annual number of weeks played and annual grosses earned—caused sleepless nights. In 1970-71 all shows running tallied a combined total of 1,099 playing weeks;[4] in 1973-74 the number had declined to 852. Similarly, the annual gross for all Broadway shows in 1970-71 was $55 million; in 1973-74 it was $46 million, down 18 percent. The major reason for the dropoff in playing weeks, despite the stable number of annual productions, was that more shows were closing quickly rather than trying to hold on in the face of bad reviews or poor attendance. Most were not sufficiently insured by "overcall" or contingency provisions for extra funds in their financing arrangements.

A total of 500 performances, once the sign of hit status, was no longer always sufficient to guarantee success, especially for musicals. For example, *The Rothschilds*, a 1970 musical, managed to survive for 507 performances but lost $650,000 in the process. *Follies*, a Stephen Sondheim musical, was an epochal award-winning, lavishly praised show that sank after 521 performances to the tune of $700,000.

Broadway flops were taking ever greater drubbings at the box office. As the years went by, the amounts wasted on some catastrophes crept closer and closer to $1 million. In a few cases, these sums—and more—were lost without the show's ever making it to Broadway after its out-of-town tryout. Among those that did manage to open in 1972, *Dude* and *Via Galactica* were shot down with debits of almost $900,000 each. In fact, in 1972-73 nearly $6 million was lost on a string of musical duds, one of them, the attractive *Seesaw*, parting with $1.25 million.

During these years, all was not bleak. Some shows *were* making money or breaking even; there were simply not enough of them. The biggest hits included several revivals such as *No, No, Nanette*, *Irene*, and *Man of La Mancha* among the musicals, and *Emperor Henry IV* and *A Moon for the Misbegotten* among plays. New American hit plays were few; two of them—*The Prisoner of Second Avenue* and *The Sunshine Boys*—were by America's golden boy of comedy, Neil Simon; others included *That Championship Season* and *The River Niger*. Not a single American play of 1973-74 was a commercial success. The biggest money-makers among foreign plays were all from Britain—*Sleuth*, *Home*, and *Butley*. Musicals achieving hit status were *The Me Nobody Knows*, *Two Gentlemen of Verona*, *Grease*, *Sugar*, *Jesus Christ Superstar*, *Pippin*, *A Little Night Music*, and *The Magic Show*. A few revue-type and specialty shows like *Bob and Ray, The Two and Only; Don't Bother Me, I Can't Cope; Will Rogers U.S.A.; Liza;* and *Good Evening* also did nicely, especially those with small casts and simple scenic requirements. These represent almost all the hits of the four-year period, during which 224 shows were produced; an awesome number were flops. (Actually, between 30 and 40 of those 224 were produced by such non-profit institutions as the Circle in the Square, Lincoln Center, the Phoenix Theatre, and the City Center Acting Company. On the other hand, several, including a couple of hits, were done on Broadway in hopes of recouping substantial sums to plow back into the furrows of the non-profit theatres that originally gave them life.)

From 1974 to 1980 the figures representing annual playing weeks and annual gross made staggering leaps. Part of the reason for the skyrocketing grosses was an annual rise in ticket prices during these inflationary years; still, attendance was on the upswing and it did not require statistics to point this out. Anyone who remembered Broadway's dreary side streets in the early seventies could see the changes all around. Streets at showtime were filled with crowds, lights were on in most theatres, and long lines formed outside of ticket windows and at the TKTS half-price ticket booth in Duffy Square (established in 1973) every day of the week, regardless of the weather.

In 1974-75 there were 1,101 playing weeks for Broadway shows (as compared with 852 for the previous season). In the decade's final year, there were 1,540 weeks, up 40 percent from its first season. Even more amazing were the figures for the annual gross. In 1974-75 Broadway's gross income was $57.5 million. Five years later it was $158 million, an increase of 187 percent over 1970-71. The number of annual productions did not make unusual progress, although there were three seasons during which 62 (1974-75), 65 (1976-77), and 66 (1979-80) shows were produced. One season (1977-78) offered only 46 new works, but that was because so many theatres were filled with long-running shows that new ones had nowhere to go. For the first time in years, theatre owners could pick and choose what shows they would allow upon their stages.

Whereas seventeen shows had collapsed instantly in 1970-74, only ten went so quickly in the 1974-80 period (and none at all in 1979-80). But, as before, even shows with impressive runs or reviews were not necessarily making profits. The ever-spiralling inflation rate forced costs so high that longer and longer runs were increasingly poor risks, even when, like Edward Albee's *Seascape*, the piece won the Pulitzer Prize. A classic example of a show that had the notices, the awards, and, for a time, the audience, was the musical *Sweeney Todd*. This show gave plenty of evidence during its early days of Standing Room Only that it would be a blockbuster. It ran for over a year and chalked up 526 performances by June 1980, but still succumbed like one of its anti-hero's victims, with a $400,000 slit in its throat.

Hit plays may have been harder to bring off in an economic whirlpool requiring many shows to wait two years to go from the red to the black, but hits did continue to appear in varying shapes and sizes. Straight plays hoped to emulate the over $4 million in profits of *Same Time, Next Year* or the $1 million-plus of *Deathtrap*. Musicals vied to hit home runs that would travel as far as *Grease, A Chorus Line,* and *Annie* with their untold millions at the box office and further millions from road shows, albums, and other sources.

A sign of the period's prosperity was the ad business done by *Playbill*, the free monthly program/magazine distributed by all Broadway theatres. Back in 1973 *Playbill* was $400,000 in the red and was even considering charging patrons for copies. Judging by the difference in the number of advertisements between a March 1973 issue of *Playbill* and one for March 1980, the magazine increased its ad revenue by approximately 60 percent during the period.

The ripple effect on *Playbill* indicates how important the theatre's grosses were to the city's economy in general. Broadway emerged as one of New York's strong growth industries; consequently, the city and state governments began to take a new and enlightened attitude toward theatre's economic significance. An unparalleled surge in tourism to the city further underlined the theatre's place as the Big Apple's foremost tourist attraction.

In 1974-75, during a twenty-five-day musicians' strike that closed down Broadway's musicals, a study was made of the theatre's impact on theatre-related business.[5] It was determined that the theatre was responsible for generating $45 million in restaurant grosses, $10.3 million for the cab industry, $4.3 million for garages and parking lots, $2.5 million for hotels and shopping, $1.8 million for one-day bus tours, and $3.9 million for air tours connected to hotel stays—a $127 million bonanza from which the city collected $5.6 million in taxes. Another $168 million spent in the metropolitan area was traceable to the theatre's presence as well. The study concluded: "The commercial theatre in New York City stimulates income and employment amounting to more than a quarter of a billion dollars annually."[6] When Broadway's musicals were forced by the strike to close down, the city lost $30 million in revenues.

As the theatre boomed, the economic impact on New York soared. In 1977-78 the theatre generated $381 million for the economy, in 1978-79 the figure was $455 million, and in 1979-80 the total reached $480 million, or almost half a billion dollars.

TICKET PRICES

It cost up to $15 to see a Broadway musical from orchestra seats on a Saturday night in 1970, while $8.50 to $9 was charged for desirable plays. Comparable seating at Off-Broadway theatres cost about half as much. The figures went up only slightly, in the cheaper ranges, through 1975. Then, in that year, heart-stopping price increments began to appear, with *Chicago* leading the musicals with a $17.50 top. *Equus*, taking on the burden of Richard Burton's star salary, moved up to $15. Prices kept bouncing up a dollar or two each year so that the high price for a musical in 1977-78 was generally $22.50. Then Liza Minnelli's piece of the gross for *The Act* boosted that show to a maximum of $25 a ducat. Meanwhile, plays cost theatregoers up to $17.50 or $18 for good seats on the weekend. Soon a $20 high was common for most plays. By 1979-80 $27.50 for a musical was not unusual and people were paying $22.50 to $25 for the best seats at comedies and dramas. The $30-plus ticket was waiting around the corner as the summer of 1980 got under way. Although it had taken the previous four decades for the price of a ticket to double, the single decade of the seventies saw them double again. What the next decade would hold in store seemed frightening to contemplate.

Throughout the decade economists noted that, despite the sharp rise in prices, show tickets were still a bargain when compared with the general cost-of-living increases for New York residents. Thus a 66 percent ticket hike from 1968 to 1978 compared favorably to an 88.3 percent rise in the cost of living. A 1977 study noted that the best seats on Broadway had averaged $7.81 in 1965.[7] In 1976 they averaged $14.66, an 88 percent jump that trailed behind the overall 89 percent increase during the period. Therefore, in terms of inflation, a ticket costing $7.81 in 1965 was worth $7.73 in 1976. Musicals were an even better buy, went the argument, as the $9.04 ticket to a 1965 musical cost only $8.42 in 1976, when adjusted for inflation. In 1980 (shortly before the $30 ticket arrived), tickets to top musicals cost 83 percent more than they did in 1970. Compared to the 99 percent rise in New York's cost of living during the same period, theatre tickets were still worth the expense. However, economist William Baumol cautioned that, while it was true that theatre prices actually had decreased during the preceding century when adjusted for inflation, "now . . . prices are rising in real terms for the first time."[8]

The top prices quoted above were the most dramatic signs of inflationary price hikes. When the *average* cost of all seating is taken into consideration, the figures are not quite as fearsome, though certainly far from comfortable. For the five seasons of 1975-80 *Variety* presents the following averages:

1975-76	$9.86
1976-77	10.80
1977-78	12.05
1978-79	14.05
1979-80	15.29[9]

The rise of the average cost of tickets for *all* shows was "only" 61 percent, instead of the obscene 83 percent leap in the price for the best seats to musicals.

PRODUCTION COSTS AND LABOR PROBLEMS

Increases in ticket prices were the most visible results of the awesome ascension of production costs. Prices were not rising in a vacuum. Few outside of the theatre profession are aware of the complex budgets and high costs associated with putting on a show. The sets, costumes, and stars are only the most obvious of a long list of expenses producers must carry as they wait for a show to pay off. Burdened with crushing real estate taxes, advertising expenses, and trade union featherbedding (producers have to deal with eighteen trade unions, from actors to stagehands to press agents to ushers), Broadway's showmen have many additional expenses to bear. They frequently must pay for new costumes, sets, actors, directors, or designers when the original choices are scrapped in mid-rehearsal. Sometimes a new writer is brought in to "doctor" the script. Any number of unexpected financial obstacles may arise before a show ever gets to New York. On top of this, a superstar may be paid as much as 12.5 percent of the weekly gross (Jack Lemmon broke the long-standing 10 percent barrier in *Tribute*). A producer of a musical in 1980 had to do a good deal more than $200,000 a week to keep his show plugged in.

At the beginning of the decade it cost slightly over half a million dollars to produce a musical and around $140,000 to do a play. It was up to $600,000 for musicals in 1976-77 and over $200,000 for plays. By 1980 the average musical cost $1 million, almost twice as much, and plays were up, on the average, to $500,000. Off-Broadway the story was similar, except that the figures were about a tenth as high. Nevertheless, Off-Broadway ticket prices in the higher ranges were double those charged for the same seats ten years earlier.

Aside from the usual 25 to 30 percent for rent, 2 to 5 percent for royalties to authors, composers, and lyricists, and 10 to 12.5 percent for the star (when there is one), the producer must pay out widely varying sums from his weekly grosses. Salaries can be one of the most expensive factors. *A Chorus Line* reportedly had to distribute 70 percent of its operating costs in company paychecks.[10] Over a five-year period from 1976 to 1980 its weekly payment to musicians climbed from $9,000 to $14,000 and its cast members' total earnings per week went from $15,000 to $22,000. With its total of 120 people on the payroll, one can see part of the reason for its costly tickets.

Expenses for all theatre expenditures rose dramatically in the decade's second half; in addition to wage increases, there were dizzying escalations in fuel bills (producers are responsible for heat and electricity in the theatres they rent) and advertising (television commercials have become an increasingly crucial element in selling a show). And in the personnel area, union featherbedding did little to keep costs in bounds. Unless a special arrangement is worked out with the union, each show must hire a minimum of four stagehands, no matter what the show's actual demands. Sixteen, at least, are used on big musicals. *Annie* employed thirty; its total outlay for backstage crew was about $13,000 a week at the end of the decade. Similarly, the musicians' union demands that a minimum number of its members be employed on every musical, regardless of the needs of the score. During the decade, six of Broadway's theatres had to use at least twenty-six musicians. If there was no need for them in the pit, they only had to walk to the theatre to pick up their checks—thus, their designation, "walkers."

Producer-director Hal Prince experienced a particularly painful encounter with the union in the matter of walkers. Prince's revival of *Candide* had been received with great enthusiasm in its Off-Broadway production at the 180-seat Chelsea Theatre in Brooklyn. Prince and the Chelsea's directors agreed to move the show to Manhattan, in search of a larger audience and, they hoped, much-needed revenue for the constantly struggling Chelsea (which has since become defunct). *Candide* had been staged in an "environmental" setting that threw actors and audiences together in a shared space. There were several "stages," providing an unusual multifocus style to the show. When a suitable Manhattan space for recreating the Brooklyn show on a larger scale failed to materialize, Prince opted for the Broadway Theatre, the interior of which he proceeded to have converted to the environmental concept. The new arrangement allowed for 900 seats in the normally 1,800-seat house.

The Broadway's contract with the musicians' union called for it to employ a minimum of twenty-five musicians, but *Candide's* score required only thirteen. Realizing that a twenty-five man complement would seriously increase his costs and make it much more difficult to recoup in a reasonable time, especially with only 900 people when the house was full, Prince petitioned the union for a concession; he was rejected. At a second hearing, various cogent reasons for reducing the orchestra were put forth, including the fact that this theatre had been dark for over a year; with a hit it might be open for years, providing secure employment for the musicians involved. More employment, it was noted, would come from additional companies on the road. This and yet another hearing resulted in negative union actions, aside from a concession to allow the musicians to perform in costume without extra pay. In the end, Prince had to hire twenty-five musicians and stew in his ire as twelve were taken on as walkers.

Some of the issues raised by Prince came to public attention on September 18, 1975, when Local 802 of the American Federation of Musicians went on strike, closing down nine Broadway musicals and putting over 750 theatre people out of work. For twenty-five days the union haggled with the League of New York Theatre Owners and Producers (LNYTP) and other theatre owners as 300 striking musicians awaited the outcome. The city lost vast sums as theatre-related businesses suffered from the absence of playgoers.

The union was exceedingly reluctant to give up its thirty-year tradition of using walkers. It argued that the average Broadway musician worked only ten weeks a year and was therefore not even entitled to unemployment benefits; the walker provision gave these players a chance to earn a decent living. The producers argued back that the cost of paying these artists made production on Broadway increasingly riskier for them and would, in the long run, produce fewer jobs, rather than more, as fewer shows were mounted. Prince observed that during *Candide's* eighty-week run, he had had to pay twelve walkers $343,585 in wages for work they did not perform. The LNYTP asserted that the thirty-four walkers currently employed on Broadway were costing a total of $632,172 a year. All agreed that if they were forced to pay these non-playing musicians at the new salary rates being asked for, their shows would be seriously jeopardized. In fact, the death of two shows, *Candide* and *Raisin*, soon after the strike ended was partly attributable to the strike.

When the dust finally settled, the new contract, in addition to salary increases, did make slight headway in the walker controversy. For the next six years, eight of the thirty theatres under LNYTP jurisdiction would be entitled to employ a maximum of thirteen fewer musicians than were formerly required—about a 10 percent reduction. Also, although the number of walkers already employed was not reduced, the union agreed to their remaining at the current pay scales and not getting the raises being paid to those who performed. Another change was that the old rule calling for four walkers to be hired for straight plays using taped music could be scrapped in favor of a new regulation allowing up to four minutes of tape to be played before hiring them.

A strike by its own personnel was hard enough to digest, but the theatre also suffered dyspepsia from strikes outside its immediate sphere. The walkout that least hurt business, despite producers' initial fears to the contrary, was the newspaper strike of 1978 in which New York's three dailies ceased publication. This deprived the theatre of ad space and reviews for a couple of months, but the broadcast media did their best to keep the public informed through paid commercials and expanded news coverage. Only one major show, *Wings*, chose to postpone its opening until the strike was over.

The other important strike was that of mass transit, in the spring of 1980. Off Off-Broadway's La Mama was forced to cancel a projected work to be written and directed by Italian filmmaker Lina Wertmüller when producer Ellen Stewart grew fearful there would be no audience. The Off Off-Broadway Alliance later claimed that its theatres dropped 75 percent in ticket sales during the eleven-day strike, yet no show was forced to shut down. On the Main Stem, the effects were not so dire, as long lines queued up for the big hits. Few cancellations were received, according to one report.[11] Business did drop heavily for some works when the traditionally active Passover and Easter weekends arrived, but other shows like *Sugar Babies*, *Evita*, and *A Chorus Line* did their strongest business yet. No generalization concerning the strike's effect could be made other than that it was not as bad as it might have been.

TECHNICAL OVERLOAD

Incompetence is no stranger to the world of theatrical production. Its too-common presence has often led to outlandish financial expenditures completely unjustified by the needs of a specific show. Everyone has heard of the wealthy backer who finances a show to give his girlfriend a chance to be a star, or of the producer who puts on a production to gain a tax write-off when it fails. But even seriously intentioned shows, when burdened by carelessly conceived technical requirements, can instantaneously wipe out a healthy bankroll. The pressures to succeed on Broadway in the seventies convinced some producers that elaborate special effects were one way to draw audiences to their shows. Lavish expenditures on computerized scenery and lighting systems, hydraulic stage lifts, and other technical advances were a principal component of many Broadway musicals, but the results led more often to embarrassment than to pride.

One such show was *Dude*, a musical that called for the area normally used as orchestra seating to be replaced by an environmental scenic plan with a circular garden floating in mid-air and covered with tons of turf. The audience was to be seated on earthen banks surrounding and within the acting area. To suggest "the highway of life" a track-like path was to circumnavigate the space. This egregiously cost-generating scheme was agreed to by producers Peter and Adela Holzer. Furthermore, as the show took shape, one mistake after another was made in the selection of the creative staff, cast members, and production concept.

The hapless Broadway Theatre (later to be torn apart for *Candide*) had its orchestra seating ripped out for the installation of the earth environment, but when the dirt was hauled in there was no way to prevent it from seriously despoiling the playhouse's interior. As revolt among the actors brewed (one cast member, the late William Redfield, said the show never was completely blocked), plastic "dirt" was brought in as a solution. When the show began previewing, acoustical problems prevented audiences from hearing the lyrics to Galt McDermott's rock score. The show was already in its third preview when a new director, Tom O'Horgan, was brought in. Three weeks of reworking ensued, during which the set and costumes were completely redesigned and cast changes were made. New developments were going on right up to opening night. The show by this time had spent close to $900,000. The Holzers were sharply criticized by the theatre community for their poor judgment throughout the production process.[12]

Another, even more catastrophic, calamity, *Got Tu Go Disco*, arrived in 1979. It had perhaps the longest and costliest "take-in" in Broadway records. The take-in (or "load-in") is the period required to set up a show's technical components, from lights, sets, sound, and the stage floor itself to any special effects required. A typical one-set take-in on Broadway requires about one and a half days, a heavy musical about three to four. *Got Tu Go Disco* took nearly ten weeks. A source close to the show asserts that the inexperienced producer's incompetence was the major reason for the show's problems.[13] Scenic elements arrived badly built or behind schedule. The planning for the heavy special effects was disastrous. The show was to have motion picture screens affixed to the side walls of the theatre, and the ceiling was to be covered by an enormous curved screen as well as an elaborate pleated curtain (called an "Austrian curtain"). These devices were extremely difficult to set up and work properly. Also hoped-for was a cove built into the area above the rear of the theatre for a rocket ship in which the stars would make their entrance, flying onto the stage. This prop never worked properly and was scrapped without ever being used. Another contrivance insisted on by the producer was a transparent dance floor that rose on a hydraulic lift. Through transparent pipes affixed to the floor colored dyes were to be circulated, but the effect was difficult to achieve. Danger existed from the possibility of leaking fluids coming in contact with nearby high-voltage wiring. The effect was cut. According to the source of this information, the producer, apparently in anguish over the money he had spent on such lavish but impractical effects, secretly instructed a technician to operate the illuminated dance floor on opening night. Seeing this hazardous and unrehearsed device in operation with a crowd of dancers on it, the production stage manager, who had not been informed it would be used, nearly had an apoplectic fit.

Got Tu Go Disco was one of the biggest losers of the decade, costing a reported $2 million, although rumor has it that the price tag was nearly twice that sum.

SHUBERT BREAKDOWN

In April 1978, disturbed by the flak it was receiving after charging $25 a seat for the small-scale musical *The Act* and $17.50 for the two-character, one-set *The Gin Game*, the Shuberts, Broadway's most powerful real estate and production firm, agreed to disclose their budgets to Tom Buckley of the *New York Times*.[14] A look at these figures explains why ticket buyers were being assessed such steep prices. *The Act*, projected to come in at $800,000, actually rose to well over a million when shovelfuls of extra money were poured over its out-of-town defects in an attempt to cover or eradicate them before the show hit New York. These flaws led to the hiring of a new director and costume designer, and the creation of new sets, lights, costumes, lyrics, and music.

The Act was a relatively small show with only two leading players and twelve dancers. Its principal performer, Liza Minnelli, was considered such a draw that she earned a percentage (undisclosed, but apparently over 10 percent) that would have netted her up to $25,000 a week of the gross if the playhouse was filled to capacity (the capacity gross was $238,135). A large expense account was also paid her.

In addition to the heavy costs for visuals and cast and crew earnings, costly items on the budget included transportation for the company to its tryout cities and back to New York (totaling about $350,000), plus salaries for arrangers, composers, copyists, accompanists, and fees for insurance, lawyers, and pension and welfare funds.

To break even each week a $155,000 gross was needed. The Majestic Theatre, which housed *The Act*, seats 1,655. Twenty-five to thirty weeks of playing to $200,000 average grosses would have paid off handsomely enough to snare a $1 million profit by the end of Minnelli's contracted run. The producers might have made it, since the show, which opened October 29,

1977, did good business in the face of mediocre reviews. What no one counted on was the star's coming down with the flu, a subsequent three-week cancellation of the show, and a loss of at least $600,000 in potential grosses. Insurance paid back only a little more than a third of that. Moreover, the star now negotiated to reduce her appearances from eight to seven a week, a Broadway first. She had to make up the drop in the grosses from her salary. By late April 1978 *The Act* was down $200,000 with two months left before Minnelli's contract expired.

The Gin Game's experience was more comforting, but its story is similarly instructive. It boasted two respected actors, Hume Cronyn and Jessica Tandy, a popular director, Mike Nichols, but an unknown playwright, D. L. Coburn. Its main setback was the loss of three days' playing time in Boston when Cronyn's illness forced a temporary shutdown. This cost the show $60,000, forcing the budget up from $210,000 to $270,000. The stars, author, and director earned an aggregate of over 30 percent of the weekly grosses. Sets, props, wigs, costumes, lights, and sound for this relatively simple show came to almost $169,000 while rehearsals, publicity, legal fees, managerial fees, insurance, and cartage from Boston to New York made up the remainder of the budget (cartage alone cost $24,000). *The Gin Game* paid off its investment in two months and settled back to enjoy nice profits.

BOMBS AND BONANZAS

During the last six years of the seventies, there was a marked downturn in the number of one-night flops, on and off Broadway. Broadway suffered only ten such headaches in these years, while Off-Broadway, now almost entirely subsidized or on subscription plans, witnessed seven such misadventures. (All the latter, of course, were in the non-subsidized sector.) Table 1.1 lists all the one-performance Broadway shows of the decade.

This list is not meant to deny the existence of similar if not worse debacles that nevertheless managed to eke out an additional few performances from equally depressing circumstances. There is, however, a special significance to being on this list. It shows that these producers, whatever their artistic aspirations, realized full well that the only way to handle the economic agony promised by negative reviews and empty houses was to end it all as soon as possible.

A good example is Norman Kean, co-producer of *A Broadway Musical*. Kean, of course, had no notion that his show would end up such a turkey. Difficulties in the tryout period prepared him for mixed reviews at best, but, he revealed, "We did not foresee at all in any of our cards or crystal balls the notices we got."[15] He could easily have gotten more cash from his eager backers to keep the show around a bit longer, he admits, but he did not feel it was fair to risk their money on such a heavily panned work. In his view, the critics on the second-night list either would have been unduly influenced

Table 1.1
One-Night Flops on Broadway

1970-71	*Father's Day*
	Johnny Johnson
	Frank Merriwell
	Gandhi
	The Candyapple
1971-72	*Wild and Wonderful*
	Ring Round the Bathtub
	Tough to Get Help
	Heathen
	Children! Children
1972-73	*Status Quo Vadis*
	The Enemy Is Dead
	Let Me Hear You Smile
	Look Away
	42 Seconds from Broadway
	No Hard Feelings
1973-1974	*Rainbow Jones*
1974-75	*Don't Call Back*
	Fame
	Medea and Jason
	Mourning Pictures
1975-76	*Home Sweet Homer*
1976-77	*Something Old, Something New*
1977-78	*The November People*
	Stages
1978-79	*Gorey Stories*
	The Meeting by the River
	The Goodbye People
	A Broadway Musical
1979-80	none

by the first nighters and repeated their pans, or would simply have failed to attend the performance.

Sometimes a one-night loser develops a reputation for having been better than its critical reception would warrant one to believe. In such cases, the producer gets blamed for bailing out too soon. The most well-known of such shows in the decade was Oliver Hailey's *Father's Day*. Producer Joe Kipness recalled having been censured for his decision to close the show. He explained, however, that "If you're losing $40,000 a week, $30,000 a week, there's not enough money. You can't fight it. But we had no business whatsoever; we lost a fortune. I found there's no sense fighting if you get lousy critical reviews."[16]

To Bernard Jacobs of the Shubert Organization, one-night flops "are either inadequately budgeted or have spent monies in excess of what they've budgeted to the opening night. If a show is properly financed it will have enough money to survive for at least a few weeks to see if it will catch on."[17] The classic example of a show which turned from possible fiasco to smash-hit fame because of the money spent to promote it following weak reviews was *The Wiz*.

There are those like Ira Bilowit, theatre journalist, who find one-night stands terribly unfair to the theatre community and to those second-night critics who invariably do come, no matter what the reviews of the first-nighters claimed.[18] To deny them the chance to see the show, he avers, is to harm the chances of some artists of receiving awards for which they might be nominated by those attending the opening. Second-nighters cannot vote if they have not seen a show. The situation is rare, but does occur, as when Marian Seldes was nominated for a Tony for her performance in *Father's Day*. Bilowit's argument presumes, however, that a show which, for whatever reason, folds after one performance should be entitled to award consideration. The point is arguable at the very least and suggests the questionable validity of Broadway awards in general—especially in sparsely represented seasons.

LONG RUN RECORDS

The decade witnessed new long run records broken on Broadway. Off-Broadway, *The Fantasticks* claimed 8,350 performances by May 31, 1980, making it far and away the longest-running show in American theatre history; it had opened twenty years earlier. It was scheduled to close in June 1986, however. *Grease*'s 3,388 made it the longest Broadway run of any type of show, beating out the runners-up, *Fiddler on the Roof* with its 3,242, *Life with Father*'s 3,224 (this was a straight play), *Tobacco Road*'s 3,182 (another straight play), and *Hello, Dolly!*'s by now "mere" 2,884. All of these would be surpassed in September 1984 when *A Chorus Line*, which opened in 1975, became the all-time leader; it was still going strong in mid-1986.

Hello, Dolly! moved ahead of its closest musical competitor, *My Fair Lady* (2,717), on September 9, 1970, with Ethel Merman playing the title role. Among the celebratory events marking the day was a 14.2-mile marathon run from Yonkers with the runner bearing a torch to City Hall. When the curtain fell on performance number 2,718, the 1,404 spectators rose and gave the show a seven-minute ovation, followed by a cake-cutting ceremony on stage. On December 28, 1970, *Hello, Dolly!* closed, having grossed $27 million during its six years, eleven months, one week, and five days at the St. James theatre. Seven stars had played Dolly Levi, beginning with Carol Channing, who returned in one of the show's two revivals during the decade.

Fiddler soon made history when on July 21, 1971, it reached performance number 2,845. It had opened September 22, 1964, at the Imperial, moved on February 27, 1966, to the Majestic, and then to the Broadway on December 16, 1970. Six of the original male cast members were still with the show. When the curtain descended a shower of balloons floated down onto the audience; Mayor John V. Lindsay, speaking alongside a birthday cake, joked that when his term expired in two years he'd be back to play Tevye. On May 11, 1972, *Fiddler on the Roof* became Broadway's second longest-running hit, passing *Tobacco Road*, but still in the shadow of *Life with Father*. The show's final curtain fell on June 17, 1972. Its $375,000 investment had been turned into a net profit of $8,347,500 and productions of the show had been staged throughout the world in sixteen languages. It returned to Broadway with the original Tevye, Zero Mostel, in the 1976-77 season.

Grease became Broadway's long run champion on December 8, 1979. To celebrate the occasion, 255 actors from its many casts came back to town for a reunion on the stage of the Royale Theatre. For each $10,000 invested in *Grease*, backers had received over $400,000. The film version had raked in a $200 million gross, and other spinoff sources proved highly lucrative as well. All this from a show that Clive Barnes, then the most powerful reviewer in New York, had casually dismissed. *Grease* had opened at the Eden Theatre Off-Broadway (though with a Broadway-scale contract) in February 1972, moved to the Broadhurst on Broadway in June, and then, in November, to the Royale, where it remained for nearly seven and a half years.

This phenomenally popular rock n' roll musical about "greasy" teenagers of the fifties had as many as eight touring companies, as well as productions around the globe. Having begun life in a Chicago basement in 1971, it came to New York with a capitalization of only $100,000 and ten investors. By the time the show closed, one of these had earned $1.5 million from his $37,500 roll of the dice.

ANGELS

It was just such long-running shows that, despite their relative rarity, kept attracting investors to Broadway. Of course, many invested because the theatre was a glamorous place to lose their money. It brought a thrill to be associated with so exciting and risky, yet culturally prestigious, a profession. When the expected first-night parties, backers' auditions, and other celebrity-laden events failed to materialize, backers could be severely disappointed, more so than if they had lost all their money on a flop. No one put money in a Broadway show without complete awareness of the immensity of the odds against their getting back a dime. The Securities and Exchange Commission specifically requires that the formal prospectus inviting investment in a Broadway show state uncategorically that the "angel" be prepared to lose his shirt.

Because of the greater risks involved, Broadway producing and money raising took some unusual turns in the seventies. It is important to understand, first, that each commercial production is registered as an independent company. Partnership in the show's capitalization is represented by general and limited partnerships, though some shows, like those the Shuberts produce or co-produce, have only general partners. In a general/limited partnership arrangement, only the limited partners make the necessary investments. They stand to lose nothing more than what they have put in (except for an "overcall" or contingency fund to which they may have to contribute if their contract calls for it); the general partners, the actual producers and associate producers need put in nothing. A show's budget is broken down into one hundred points of which the general partners get fifty while the limited partners get the remainder, each point of which is worth one-fiftieth of the total capital. Points on a $1 million show go for $20,000 each. One can buy a number of points or fractions of a point.

With escalating production costs and the ever greater risk of failure many old-line angels sought other pots than theatre to put their money into. Since an SRO musical smash hit required an average of thirty-two weeks of capacity business in the late seventies before it could break even, investors seeking to make a killing knew better than to try it on the Great White Way. Producers had to search for new investors and they found them among a group the theatre of the past generally had bypassed. These were the small investors, those with a spare $1,000 or two they were willing to wager on an unusual, if chancey, investment. Even Hal Prince, who, with a large number of hits, had a select group of backers who had stayed with him from show to show, began to seek funds from this newly discovered source. Many producers hated the prospect because to have more than thirty-five investors on a show required having to go through a web of red tape in filing with the SEC. But getting thirty-five or fewer people possessing the wherewithal to support a $1 million or $2 million long shot was becoming ever more difficult, whereas it was not so hard to locate small investors just begging to flush their greenbacks away. This change may have meant a loss of the prestige once associated with being an angel. It did, however, serve to democratize the process and open the theatre's doors to many who had never been "backstage" before. These investors were in love with *theatre*, not merely its potential profits. For most, it was enough if the producer sent them friendly newsletters and reports of the show's progress.

These small investors were uncovered early in the decade through ads placed in the *Wall Street Journal*. Later, the *New York Times* was used to reach even more readers. Record numbers of investors began to join the Broadway scene by the end of the period, though they were all probably aware that, at the most, their tiny contributions would result in diminutive returns, even for a hit. When *Sweeney Todd* advertised for capital it received 1,500 requests for prospectuses; 100 of these were returned with money. The show's budget was broken into petite shares of $1,800 each, representing only .02 percent of the pie, but people bought fractions of even such small sums. *Sweeney Todd* ended up with 257 partners; *I Remember Mama* had the biggest family of investors—322 who put up $600,000.

If a show needed to reach more potential investors than its producer was capable of finding alone, associate producers would join the project, bringing a pile of money in their wake. *Sweeney Todd* therefore had as general partners two producers and three associates who in aggregate raised the $1.3 million required for the show. This is the reason the theatre program often has numerous names listed where in the past it might simply have read, "David Merrick Presents."

Only a handful of producers, like Lee Guber and Shelly Gross, the Neder-landers, and the Shuberts actually invest in their own shows. The need for outside capital is imperative, so new avenues are always being explored. A couple of hundred small investors may make it easier to raise money, but producers still prefer to get a limited number of backers who put up large chunks of capital. As the old-line backers disappeared they were gradually replaced by a number of major corporations. Most prominent were corpo-rations in the entertainment and communication industries, but capital from outside corporations such as Coca-Cola and Seagram's was enthusias-tically welcomed.

"Inside" corporations, like those from the film, broadcasting, and record-ing industries, recognized the value of a hit for their own special products. It would all be worth the candle if they could match the luck of CBS, which, in return for its $350,000 support of 1956's *My Fair Lady*, harvested well over $30 million in profits.

Columbia, 20th Century Fox, Paramount, Warner Communications, MCA/Universal, and Marble Arch were some of the film companies look-ing to Broadway as a lab for future film material, as well as for box-office returns. Shows like *The Best Little Whorehouse in Texas*; *Nuts*; *The Wiz*; *I Love My Wife*; *Tribute*; *A Chorus Line*; *Annie*; *Platinum*; *I Remember Mama*; *Loose Ends*; *Dancin'*; *Sugar Babies*; *Clothes for a Summer Hotel*; *Happy New Year*; and *The Roast* had reason to be grateful to Hollywood for their existence.

There had been film company involvement on Broadway for many years, but the old pattern was for a studio to buy a show's rights after it had already been produced. In the seventies there was a new pattern: the film companies wanted to put up the cash while the show was in preparation and exercise some control over the development of the project. They were on uneasy terms with the writers, however, whose Dramatists Guild contracts promised them final say in the changes made in their material. If begging didn't work, the film companies were prepared to find the right price for which the writer was willing to sell his control. As it was, artistic control by the film companies was not so much a fact of life as it was a fragrance on the wind, which one could smell getting gradually stronger.

Critic Marilyn Stasio noted in *New York Magazine* that the pumping of film money into Broadway shows began in 1975 with *The Wiz*, only to be followed very quickly by a stream of other shows.[19] These remained free artistically but *Whorehouse* was born when a film company put up all its capital and produced it as well. Stasio says the authors received considerable largesse for giving the company the right to tinker with their script in the movie version. She describes the fear of producers that film companies will cause the withering of Broadway's last vestiges of the creative impulse and that their huge budgets will so overinflate Broadway costs that the old-time producer will have no place anymore on the Main Stem.

Another significant development in the production of Broadway plays was the decision by the Shubert Organization to produce or co-produce plays for their own theatres, something they had not engaged in for many years. During the decade the Shuberts owned sixteen Broadway playhouses, with a half interest in a seventeenth. Their closest competitors were the Nederlanders, whose seventies assets included seven theatres and a half interest in an eighth. Like the Shuberts, the Nederlanders have been filling their theatres with plays they themselves have backed.

The presence of the Shuberts and Nederlanders as backers has made others fear the eventual disappearance of independent producers. A feeling exists that the landlords' participation in production is harmful because they would do only works that satisfy their notions of what will sell and not what might be artistically important. On the other hand, the role taken by the Shuberts in Broadway producing may be seen as one of the reasons for the business renaissance of the decade. Their encouragement of major talent to return to Broadway, their support of many plays from which others had shied away, their backing of a host of theatre development schemes—including the TKTS discount ticket trailer—and their strengthening of the

LYNTP are among positive factors on their side. Tom McMorrow in the *New York Theatre Review* outlined the extent of their involvement in Broadway shows, including many for which they were not credited on the program.[20] Gerald Schoenfeld, who, together with Bernard Jacobs, has headed the Shubert Organization since 1972, declared, "We do not demand billing unless it's actually our production, like *Sly Fox*, *Your Arms Too Short to Box With God*, or *Sherlock Holmes*."[21] From 1972 to 1977, the Shuberts funnelled $4.5 million into Broadway shows, says Schoenfeld, and much more has been invested since then. They pride themselves on their active role in having helped develop a younger, more ethnically diverse Broadway audience than ever before by their production of plays appealing to both youthful and non-white spectators.

The Shuberts do not care to have investors aside from themselves involved in a show but will occasionally co-produce with other major producers or corporations. There are no limited partnerships in their shows. Some of their straight plays of the seventies were not merely "pandering to the audience," and did attempt meaningful statements (*Zoot Suit*, for instance), but such ventures largely failed. Michiko Kakutani wrote in the *Times*, moreover, that the Shuberts, unpopular with producers because of the high rents they charged, had mitigated some of the backlash by their occasional practice of lowering their fees so that marginal shows of serious intent (like *Wings*) could operate at a break-even level.[22]

A debate in which the Shuberts and others have been participating for several years concerns the desirability of government funding for Broadway shows. It has become painfully clear that serious theatre cannot survive on Broadway under the present economic circumstances. *Variety* said recently, "Your show has to be a '9' or '10' . . . or you better leave town."[23] In the mid-seventies a Broadway season might support four or five dramas. By 1980 one or two a year was deemed possible. To producers like Richard Barr only subsidy could make it feasible to do major new plays on Broadway.[24] Otherwise, he suggests, anyone with pretentions to artistry wishing to make a career of the theatre is whistling in the wind. Off-Broadway has become the production arena for most good new plays because subsidy there allows for creative, relatively risk-free growth. Why, questions Barr, cannot work created in the subsidized sector continue its life for larger audiences and greater exposure in commercial Broadway production with subsidy making up the potential losses?

James Nederlander, President of Nederlander Enterprises, also takes a positive view of subsidy for Broadway. In *Producers on Producing*, he says:

I think there should be more subsidy for the arts. The economics of the Broadway theatre don't make sense. I mean, here [in 1974] we have thirty-four [*sic*] theatres on Broadway and maybe twenty of them are lit. . . . You produce a play and two nights later it's out of business after you've spent a year putting it together. So what the future is I don't know. I think it's coming more and more to subsidization.[25]

Some would say that the Shuberts are Broadway's real subsidizers, considering the vast amounts they have put into numerous shows. Such subsidy is the only acceptable kind to Bernard Jacobs, who shivers at the thought of government involvement in Broadway shows.[26] All he wants from the government is relief from some of the unfair tax burdens and legislation affecting producers and investors. Jacobs' main fear is of possible government interference in the theatres it assists. He notes that theatres backed by government sources like the National Endowment for the Arts (NEA) have been prevented by the terms of their grants from using foreign actors. To him this is proof of artistic meddling on the part of the granting agency. Other examples of such indirect involvement exist as well. One of the most upsetting came at the end of the decade when the NEA refused a $150,000 grant to the city's most respected Off Off-Broadway experimental playhouse, La Mama ETC, because of its recent emphasis on foreign productions at the expense of American ones.

Although the Shuberts say they are reluctant to accept public subsidy, such subsidy has indeed been accepted by them and by nearly all aspects of the commercial (and non-commercial) theatre since 1967 when the Theatre Development Fund (TDF) was established by a combination of public and private foundations. TDF came into existence with the aim of helping out deserving works by buying blocks of seats and selling them at low rates to selected groups, such as students and teachers. This practice, still a major impetus for bringing large numbers to the theatre, has occasionally been criticized for making questionable choices in the shows whose box offices are thus bolstered, but its value to the New York theatre in general during the seventies was immense. Of equal significance was TDF's operation of several half-price ticket booths instituted in 1973, a development discussed in Chapter 7. But TDF will either have to increase its funding or some other major form of subsidy will have to be created if the New York theatre is not only to survive but to do so with dignity in the future. With the decline in federal arts subsidies that followed when the Reagan administration took office it seems unlikely that meaningful sums will be available from government sources on a national level; however, the enormous importance of theatre to the economic status and cultural position of New York City as demonstrated during the seventies makes it all the more apparent that government funding agencies on the local and state levels, in addition to private sources, will have to become more heavily involved in supporting this great public resource if the New York theatre as it has hitherto been known is not to become merely a nostalgic memory. For all the subsidy that so radically changed the face of the national theatre during the sixties and seventies, this country is still embarrassingly behind the level of public support given the theatre in many other countries, most notably Germany. The prospect of such government aid to the local theatre, aside from what is already available through such sources as the New York State Council on the Arts, seems remote in the mid-eighties. When important New York politicians are more interested in instituting a tax on tickets to entertainment events or denying the purchase of theatre tickets as a tax-deductible business expense, it seems unlikely that they will turn a willing ear to pleas for more government support of the stage. Subsidy brings many headaches, particularly in the area of play selection when theatres begin to feel the need to please the subsidizers more than the spectators; if wisely used, however, it can only help and not hinder the future growth and security of the theatre. Otherwise, the commercial theatre, at least, is sure to dwindle gradually into a handful of big musical hits, surrounded by a wasteland of deserted playhouses. And that is not too exaggerated a picture of what presently exists.

NOTES

1. Walter Kerr, "Can Broadway Move?" *New York Times Magazine*, 3 June 1973, p. 22.

2. "Curtains Up and Down," *New York Times*, 7 June 1977, p. 34.

3. Stephen Langley, ed., *Producers on Producing* (New York: Drama Book Specialists, 1976), p. 153.

4. Otis L. Guernsey defines playing weeks thus: "If ten shows play ten weeks, that's 100 playing weeks," in *The Best Plays of 1973-74* (New York: Dodd, Mead and Co., 1974), p. 5.

5. "In League for a Theatre Stimulated Economy," *Playbill*, June 1977, n.p.

6. Quoted in Michael Sterne, "Broadway Season Gives City a Reason to Applaud," *New York Times*, 2 June 1977, Sec. II, p. 1.

7. "In League to Meet the High Cost of Today's Theatre," *Playbill*, December 1977, n.p.

8. William Baumol, "Why Broadway prices are breaking records," *Business Week*, 7 April 1980, p. 32.

9. Hobe Morrison, "Legit Season Posts New Record," *Variety*, 14 June 1980, p. 1.

10. Baumol, "Why Broadway prices are breaking records."

11. Richard F. Shepherd, "Box Offices Give Strike So-So Review," *New York Times*, 3 April 1980, Sec. III, p. 11.

12. Patricia Bosworth, "*Dude* . . . an $800,000 Disaster: Where Did They Go Wrong?" *New York Times*, 22 October 1972, Sec. II, p. 1.

13. This source prefers to remain anonymous.

14. Tom Buckley, "Broadway Balance Sheets Divulge Multitude of Costs Behind High Prices," *New York Times*, 5 April 1978, p. 48.

15. Quoted in Jeff Sweet, "Closing a Show on Opening Night: The Instant Flop," *New York Theatre Review* 3 (February 1979): 6.

16. Joe Kipness in an interview with Debbi Wasserman, "What Does a Producer Do?" *New York Theatre Review* 2 (January 1978): 13.

17. Quoted in Sweet, "Closing a Show," p. 7.

18. Ibid., p. 6.

19. Marilyn Stasio, "Broadway's Newest Angel: Hollywood," *New York Magazine*, 4 December 1978, pp. 71-73.

20. Tom McMorrow, "The NEW Shuberts: Schoenfeld and Jacobs," *New York Theatre Review* Preview Issue (Spring/Summer 1977): 14.

21. Ibid.

22. Michiko Kakutani, "Presenting the Amazing Shuberts—'Bernie and Gerry,'" *New York Times*, 1 April 1979, Sec. II, p. 1.

23. Richard Hummler, "Serious Plays in Serious Trouble," *Variety*, 3 December 1980, p. 1.

24. "Government Subsidy for Commercial Theatre," *New York Theatre Review* Preview Issue (Spring/Summer 1977): 4.

25. Langley, *Producers on Producing*, p. 300.

26. "Critics' Roundtable—Producing on Broadway: Subsidy for the Commercial Theatre," *New York Theatre Review* 2 (August/September 1978): 15-21.

★ 2 ★
OFF-BROADWAY
AND
OFF OFF-BROADWAY

Broadway is New York's most visible theatre center, but Off-Broadway has had a long and varied history of its own. Plays of limited appeal had been produced outside the big-time commercial environment of Broadway since the early decades of the century, but only sporadically. Sometimes their impact on American theatre was profound, as witness the work done by the Provincetown Players, the pre-Theatre Guild Washington Square Players, and the Neighborhood Playhouse in the late teens and twenties. Off-Broadway was relatively moribund during the thirties and forties, but it began to flourish as an active, ongoing alternative to Broadway when Off-Broadway's Circle in the Square produced a smashing revival of Tennessee Williams' *Summer and Smoke* in 1952.

Over the next two decades Off-Broadway became increasingly plagued by rising production costs until it began to lose its personality as an area for risk and experimentation, and to take on the attributes of a mini-Broadway, a place where productions with fairly heavy budgets were mounted in hopes of attaining commercial success. Union demands for higher salaries exacerbated these conditions during the 1970s, especially in the wake of two Off-Broadway actor strikes that upped performers' salaries to what they would only a year or two before have earned on Broadway.

The difficulty of making a profit in the union-regulated Off-Broadway theatres (299 or fewer seats until 1974; 499 or fewer thereafter) forced a radical shift in Off-Broadway's essential nature. Beginning in the late sixties, a great portion of its activity was subsumed by subsidized tax-exempt non-profit institutions, many with subscription seasons, allowing them to keep Off-Broadway audiences supplied with both conventional and daring work at a time when it would have been impossible to present such shows independently. Federal, state, and city funds, together with private and corporate contributions, created a welter of top-flight permanent Off-Broadway establishments during the decade, though by the period's close major problems were emerging. Deficits in a deficit-based accounting process were growing excessively unhealthy-looking as the need to cover them became imperative. Subsidies began drying up and many of the non-profit institutions were gradually beginning to seek commercial possibilities in the shows they produced. If this continued they would seriously endanger the original franchise that gave them life. Shortly after the period covered by this book concluded, one of the most respected of Off-Broadway theatres, the Chelsea, succumbed to all the above pressures and was forced to close shop. It was followed a while later by the Classic Stage Company (now known as the City Stage Company; hereafter referred to as the CSC), but that troupe's demise proved to be only temporary.

Meanwhile, a new venue—Off Off-Broadway—born at the turn of the sixties had assumed the alternative theatre role originally belonging to Off-Broadway; during the seventies it became a vital participant in the transfer of plays from the non-profit to the profit-making theatres, while also exploring a broad spectrum of experimental writing and production styles. The period saw a stream of shows originating Off Off-Broadway move on to Off-Broadway production (if not to Broadway), while many works born Off-Broadway moved on. When they were successful in the latter district, a handsome piece of their profits could be returned to the coffers of the original company, provided they owned the appropriate rights. The New York Shakespeare Festival Theatre, for example, was sustained for over a decade by the cash coming in from its monster hit, *A Chorus Line*.

INDEPENDENT PRODUCTION

It seemed at one point in the mid-seventies that the non-profit theatres would push the independent Off-Broadway producers completely out of the picture. There was a sharp decrease in the active membership of the League of Off-Broadway Theatres, and many of the established Off-Broadway playhouses were being run by Off Off companies. A few Off-Broadway shows were making money (one, *Godspell*, made millions), but the chances for a hit were even slimmer than on Broadway. However, Off-Broadway, like Broadway, showed remarkable self-restorative powers. A look at the figures in Table 2.1 discloses the fact that Off-Broadway fought a noble battle to survive, not only as a subsidized arena but as a place for independent production.

These figures are based on the annual listings in Otis L. Guernsey's annual *Best Plays* series. Excluded from them are productions of touring companies from abroad, light opera productions, and children's theatre/ puppet theatre productions. In some cases, productions have been counted if they were originally produced by non-profit companies and then given separate independent production. A few others were produced independently in a theatre normally operated under non-profit auspices, like the American Place Theatre or the Circle in the Square (downtown), but here given over to independent production. Because of the blurry dividing line that occasionally separates Off-Broadway from Off Off, the figures may not be precise in all cases nor might they match those compiled by another method, but they are accurate enough to give a sharp picture of the status of independent production Off-Broadway during the decade.

Table 2.1
Independent Productions Off-Broadway in the Seventies

Year	Number of Productions
1970-71	49
1971-72	48
1972-73	48
1973-74	27
1974-75	31
1975-76	18
1976-77	23
1977-78	29
1978-79	31
1979-80	36

The decade began with three years of nearly identical production totals but then dropped sharply in 1973-74. A valiant attempt to mount a few more shows in 1974-75 was followed by a precipitous falloff to eighteen the next year, thirty fewer than in each of the second and third years. But the final four years presented an optimistic picture of steadily rising totals, the figures for 1979-80 being double those of the period's low point.

Off-Broadway had a fair-sized group of independent hits in the period. Long runs are not the only indication of a show's success, and can sometimes mask what actually was a failure. This was particularly true on Broadway, as seen in Chapter 1, and, in fact, was a distinguishing element of the decade's history. However, in the absence of available statistics regarding Off-Broadway grosses, long runs of 400 performances or more can be assumed to indicate commercial success. This is not to deny that shorter runs may also have resulted in profits. The list in Table 2.2 presents

the titles of Off-Broadway shows that played a minimum of 400 performances. Asterisks (*) denote shows that were still running when the decade
ended (final totals are in parentheses). The totals are only for Off-Broadway. Two of these works were transferred to Broadway where they added
even more performances to those given here.

Table 2.2
Long Runs Off-Broadway in the Seventies

Musicals, Revues, etc.	
Godspell	2,124
Let My People Come	1,327
El Grande de Coca-Cola	1,114
The Proposition	1,109
I'm Getting My Act Together and Taking It on the Road	835
The Club	674
What's a Nice Country Like You Doing in a State Like This?	543
The Dirtiest Show in Town	509
Boy Meets Boy	463
Tuscaloosa's Calling Me	429
Scrambled Feet (831)	388*
One Mo' Time (1,372)	253*
Plays	
Vanities	1,785
The Hot l Baltimore	1,166
One Flew Over the Cuckoo's Nest	1,025
The Passion of Dracula	714
Streamers	478
The Real Inspector Hound & After Magritte	465
Family Business	438
Say Goodnight, Gracie	417
A Coupla White Chicks Sitting Around Talking (440)	39*

When one considers that the vast bulk of Off-Broadway production in
the seventies was in the institutional theatres where subscription seasons
limited most shows to from twenty to forty performances, Off-Broadway's

commercial success totals by the end of the decade were not so depressing as they seemed in the middle of the era when production was in serious decline.

INSTITUTIONAL COMPANIES

The principal institutional companies operating Off-Broadway in the seventies are listed alphabetically in Table 2.3

Table 2.3
Off-Broadway Institutional Theatres

Acting Company

American Place Theatre

Brooklyn Academy of Music Theatre
   Company

Chelsea Theatre Center

Circle in the Square

Circle Repertory Company

Classic Stage Company (CSC)

Colonnades Theatre Lab

Dodger Theatre

Harold Clurman Theatre

Hudson Guild Theatre

Manhattan Theatre Club

Negro Ensemble Company

New Federal Theatre

New York Shakespeare Festival at
   Lincoln Center

New York Shakespeare Festival Theatre

Performance Group

Phoenix Theatre

Production Company

Quaigh Theatre

Repertory Theatre at Lincoln Center

Ridiculous Theatrical Company

Roundabout Theatre Center

T. Schreiber Theatre

A few of these produced for only a year or two at Off-Broadway levels, others produced sporadically throughout the period. Some had their own theatres, others rented whatever theatre was available when preparing a season. A few had Broadway seasons, others were active Off Off. Several combined Off-Broadway and Off Off under the same roof, according to varying contractual arrangements with Equity. All relied on grants from one source or another to keep alive. The nature of their contracts with Actors Equity (a couple were non-Equity) varied according to each theatre's requirements.

These companies operated under a combination of earned and unearned income resources that also varied widely from company to company. The New York Shakespeare Festival's Public Theatre operation, with its several theatre spaces and prolific programming, had a total budget in 1979 of $7,432,000 while playing to an audience of 3,109,000. On the other hand, another Off-Broadway company of repute, the CSC, reported a budget of $215,000 for the same year. It played in a single space to an audience of 24,350.[1]

A fact of life these companies had to deal with in the eighties was the continuing reduction in the amount of aid they could expect from the giant granting agencies. For example, the Ford Foundation's theatre grants in the middle and late seventies averaged three-quarters of what they had contributed in earlier years, while the NEA grants for 1979 came to less than the over $5 million given by the agency four years before. And when the Reagan administration came into power in 1980 far more drastic cuts in NEA funds were instituted.

OFF-BROADWAY ACTOR STRIKES

Off-Broadway's economic suffering was aggravated during the seventies by two distressing actor strikes that helped to boost production costs and ticket prices. The first, and more annoying, was in 1970 when the previous three-year contract expired. The allegedly exorbitant demands for salary increases made by the actors' union led the producers (under the aegis of the League of Off-Broadway Theatres and Producers) to angrily refuse them. Of course, the outcome was bound to be a compromise between Equity's demands and the producers' offerings, but in the Off-Broadway arena where profits are so rare and shows usually survive on marginal levels, any cost increase was bound to imperil the quality of the work done.

About 200 actors and stage managers were affected by the strike, which began November 16. This was Equity's fifth strike since its overwhelmingly successful one in 1919, but it was only Off-Broadway's first. Equity denied that Off-Broadway was any longer an experimental, low-budget environment; it insisted on its actors being compensated in relation to what it viewed as a big business in which actors were exploited while producers grew rich at their expense. The strike killed three shows, and several others claimed that the reason for their ultimate demise or struggling status was their forced closing down.

Off-Broadway's leading lights saw the strike as symbolic of the inevitable eradication of this valuable production locus. The producers argued that Equity failed to recognize that Off-Broadway's function was as a career builder and not as somewhere for actors to earn a living wage. Equity would not buy this argument because all it could see was theatres charging up to $10 a ticket and grosses of over $10,000 a week for hits. (Not all actors were in favor of the union's stance; a group of dissidents, led by playwright Tom Eyen, counterpicketed the strikers, going from theatre to theatre with their placards.) Finally, on December 16, the strike ended with the issues submitted to binding arbitration.

In 1973 another strike loomed on the Off-Broadway horizon as the 1970 contract neared its end. The demands for raises and other benefits struck a familiar note with Off-Broadway producers who claimed Equity was out to cut their throats and rid the world of Off-Broadway once and for all. Why, they queried, make it so difficult to produce Off-Broadway when Broadway itself (then in a terrific slump) was so poorly off? Negotiations proceeded for weeks as extensions beyond the January 6, 1974, contract expiration date were granted. Equity's salary demands were considered extravagant for all but a tiny group of successful shows that were able to pay the wage levels requested. Most shows were rapid flops, unable to sustain decent runs. *Crystal and Fox*, for example, had opened in April 1973 and lost $60,000 on a twenty-four-performance run, earning only $192 in its final week, while *Godspell* drew $18,231 in one week while averaging $14,000 to $15,000 a week the rest of the time.

Ultimately, on January 21, 1974, when negotiations broke down, a strike was called. It was a Monday night and no loss was felt as the strike lasted only one day, with the issues sent to binding arbitration. Aside from the eventual compromise reached in salaries, the most significant outcome of the dispute was Equity's permission for Off-Broadway to produce in theatres of 499 seats or fewer, instead of 299 or fewer, as a way of helping producers increase their grosses and make more money with which to pay actors. Few took advantage of this approval, however, as producers found that the increased costs of running shows in larger Off-Broadway houses were burdensome and that, given the risks involved, they were better off going straight to Broadway.

OFF OFF-BROADWAY

"Good evening, ladies and gentlemen, welcome to La Mama, ETC—Experimental Theatre Club—dedicated to the playwright and all aspects of the theatre." Night after night since 1960 these words, preceded by the tinkling of a small hand bell, were spoken to audiences crowding into the several small theatres known variously as Café La Mama and La Mama, ETC. The speaker was usually the lovely Ellen Stewart, La Mama herself, the *doyenne* of the Off Off movement, of which she was a founder.

Like many others in the widely dispersed loose confederation of low budget theatres called Off Off-Broadway, La Mama originated out of its creator's wish for a place where non-traditional theatrical work could be performed free of the pressures of commercial production. Together with Caffe Cino, Theatre Genesis, Judson Poets' Theatre, and several others, most of them located in the East Village (or Lower East Side) during the early sixties, La Mama offered a home to those many unconventional playwrights, actors, directors, and designers who needed to express themselves without the primary compulsion to succeed or make money. Only rarely was anyone paid for his services. Productions were put on with minuscule budgets and for brief runs, allowing hundreds and hundreds of works to be staged. This activity permitted the development of one of the most fertile seedbeds for the nurture of American theatre talents the nation had ever known.

Free from most union restrictions, Off Off-Broadway continued to mushroom into the 1970s, eventually becoming America's foremost experimental theatre environment. Off Off theatres were established not only in the neighborhood of the originals, but all over Manhattan, and in several of the other boroughs as well. Serious theatre people coming to New York from elsewhere in the country or from abroad often made Off Off theatregoing their principal concern while here, ignoring Broadway and much of Off-Broadway as well.

In the seventies anywhere from 150 to 200 Off Off theatres were presenting their wares, with the avant-garde forming only one part of the total picture. Companies using casts of all Equity actors, part Equity actors, or no Equity actors were putting on a wild assortment of presentations, each company having its own identity. There were the ethnic groups, such as the black, Greek, Yiddish, Hispanic, Irish, Chinese, Italian, and others. Children's theatre, musical theatre, puppet theatre, feminist theatre, political theatre, erotic theatre, gay theatre, and transvestite theatre further demonstrated Off Off's diversity. Some companies did only classics, others only American revivals, others only new American plays, others only works developed by a long, collaborative process, and others only mime. And some companies practiced a studied eclecticism, doing a bit of everything. Visionary artists such as Richard Shechner, Joseph Chaikin, Robert Wilson, Peter Schumann, Lee Breuer, Richard Foreman, André Gregory, Linda Mussman, and Andrei Serban founded their own companies dedicated to each artist's unique conception of the nature of theatre art.

Performances were held in converted churches, garages, lofts, coffee houses, social clubs, catering halls, warehouses, fire houses, and even in apartment kitchens and living rooms. A few groups performed only in the streets. Admission prices were minimal or nonexistent (donations were often accepted), and seating could be in conventional theatre seats, on the hard floor, on pillows, on ladders, or on towering platforms. The average theatre had ninety-nine seats or fewer—an Equity regulation; some had twenty or thirty, others (non-union) over 200. Most theatres put on only one play at a time, but there were those that were multiproduction complexes sometimes giving up to a half-dozen shows in the same building at the same time. Theatre conditions ranged from the slapdash and poverty stricken to the attractive and comfortable. Theatres, especially those in converted premises, had to contend with a myriad of building and fire codes; to conform to most of these would have been beyond the scope of the average budget. Fortunately, no tragic events occurred where violations were in evidence. One theatre, the WPA, was forced to close down in 1975, but it soon opened elsewhere in improved surroundings. For the most part, an annual audience numbering over half a million was able to attend Off Off-Broadway in relative safety, with minimal discomfort.

Throughout its first two decades, Off Off continued to provide many of the American theatre's finest talents in both the administrative and creative fields. Actors who worked for nothing were, before long, commanding six figures or more for movie contracts. Directors and playwrights who began in cellar and loft spaces developed into powerful figures on Broadway and in regional theatres, and on home and theatre screens. And many already established stars of the various media found they could do interesting and exciting work in brief runs on Off Off's tiny stages where the risk of failure bore none of the stigma associated with mainstream production.

Off Off-Broadway theatres are almost all tax-exempt, non-profit, deficit-based operations surviving on grants from all the major funding sources. One estimate placed the total Off Off budget for 1979 at $7 million.[2]

COMMERCIAL TRANSFERS

There was, during the seventies, an accelerating tendency for this beehive of non-profit theatres to develop new plays as tryouts for commercial ventures. Before long, Off Off became a significant source for the Broadway and Off-Broadway playhouses. At one point late in the decade eight current Broadway shows owed their origins to Off Off. As commercial costs soared, producers grew ever wiser to the advisability of keeping their eyes and ears glued to the Off Off scene for potentially hot properties. It was cheaper than a trip to New Haven, let alone London, to drive downtown and catch a promising show. Plays were tried out on Off Off for sums that made even regional and Off-Broadway costs seem excessive. Off Off's character as a place for the unusual and experimental was fast changing to one of a commercial audition center.

Many Off Off companies of the seventies operated on an annual budget of less than $50,000. At the top of the scale (the figures are for 1979) were such theatres as the Ensemble Studio Theatre, with its $200,000 budget, or the New Federal Theatre with its $305,000. Even more impressive was the budget of the Manhattan Theatre Club—$875,000—but it, like the Public Theatre, combined Off-Broadway shows with Off Off. Much lower down came groups such as the WPA with its less than $40,000. Those who ran such low-budget houses often earned no salary. Their actors, throughout the period, earned about $1 a day, barely enough for carfare. Some slightly better off companies paid their actors a bit more when possible. To keep alive, these groups had to hope for a commercial success to shore up their finances. Early in the Off Off to Broadway transfer movement, theatres did not always think ahead to guarantee themselves a cut of the eventual earnings from such moves, but these oversights became rare in later years. An Off Off showcase like the Manhattan Theatre Club's *Ain't Misbehavin'* could bring its theatre as much as 15 percent of its annual operating costs, while a work like *A Chorus Line*, originally an Off Off workshop, helped support the Public Theatre for at least a decade. With the continued shrinking of subsidy sources in the eighties, many Off Off producers have been alert to discover potential hits, thereby abandoning the free-for-all atmosphere that so largely characterized these theatres for so many years.

It does not necessarily follow that an Off Off theatre fortunate enough to have one of its shows moved uptown (or down, as the case may be) automatically profits from the experience. When *Gorey Stories* went from the WPA to Broadway (its $3,000 production costs zooming to $300,000), the WPA was entitled to .5 percent of the gross. But when the show folded on opening night, the company had to reassess its future.

Broadway is not the only fowl that lays golden nest eggs for Off Off-Broadway. Off-Broadway too can support an Off Off company. This happened to notable effect, for example, when *Vanities*, originally produced by Off Off's Lion Theatre Company, achieved long-run status Off-Broadway and contributed a considerable amount to the annual budget of its mother company.

Occasionally, even in the late seventies, a producing theatre did not avail itself of the chance to cash in on a commercial prospect. The experience of *Eubie!*, originally titled *Shuffle Along*, illustrates the point. This show provides a representative example of the process by which an Off Off production transfers to Broadway.

Julianne Boyd, a young director who had worked in New York since the early seventies, principally Off Off, conceived the idea of doing a revue of show tunes by the nonagenarian composer Eubie Blake, whose work was currently enjoying a revival of interest.³ She settled on the old Blake and Noble Sissle musical *Shuffle Along* as the basis of her revue, which would eliminate the book and concentrate on making charming sketches of the songs that remained. She brought the idea to the Manhattan Theatre Club, then involved in developing the show that became the smash hit *Ain't Misbehavin'*. Since *Shuffle Along* was a bit too close to that show in concept, the MTC told Boyd to return with it at a later date. Not to be put off, the director presented the concept to Patricia Peate, artistic director of the Theatre Off Park, located on West Thirty-fifth Street near Park Avenue. Peate was immediately intrigued by the idea, as she was hoping to find a show that would help her theatre celebrate Black History Week.

Shuffle Along, which opened in February 1978, was staged in the tiny basement theatre seating about seventy people. A single piano accompanied four singer-dancers who performed within the three brick walls formed by one end of the narrow room. There was one entrance/exit on the stage. The only decor was a white cartooned musical pattern painted on the black walls. The show lasted about an hour and five minutes. Eubie Blake, celebrating his ninety-fifth birthday, attended the opening, thereby attracting John Wilson of the *Times* to the event. On the Saturday following the opening Wilson printed a rave review, and other positive notices appeared elsewhere. Boyd was immediately besieged by twelve major producers who were interested in considering the show for Broadway (one was after it for a regional company). A special matinee for the producers had to be set up (involving some typical haggling with Equity). Boyd, after discussing the possibility of a Broadway mounting with those who remained interested, chose Ashton Springer, who had a hit with *Bubbling Brown Sugar*, another black revue.

Springer and Boyd agreed to change the title to *Eubie!* and to expand the show by including more Blake music and a larger cast. Only one of the original four performers (Lynnie Godfrey) was retained, the others receiving several weeks of Broadway salary as compensation. With a cast of twelve, and nine musicians, the show was budgeted at $350,000 but overran that projection and came in at around $600,000. Off Off-Broadway it had cost less than $1,000. The Theatre Off Park never asked for a piece of the pie so it did not benefit from the show's earnings.

Eubie! opened in Philadelphia in June, only a bit more than three months after its Off Off opening. It was a hit, and soon New York theatre owners were anxiously offering it available theatres. The Ambassador was chosen. The show opened on September 20 during the 1978 newspaper strike, forcing it to spend a lot of money on TV ads (thus the cost overrun mentioned in Chapter 1); it met with a favorable reception. It had taken Boyd less than a year from her initial conception to a Broadway opening. She had come up with the right property at the right time. Her salary for the Off Off version was nothing. For the Broadway mounting she received a fee of $5,000, a percentage of the gross as director, and another percentage as conceiver. She also was entitled to 50 percent of the subsidiary rights to the show. *Eubie!* ran for 439 performances but did not recoup its investment. According to Boyd, a good deal of money was lost when the show sent out a national company in the dead of winter; severe blizzards kept theatres in which the show was booked empty of audiences.

Boyd was very lucky with *Eubie!* Her next Broadway show, *Onward Victoria!*, was also originally done Off Off-Broadway, by the Joseph Jefferson Theatre Company. She had been working at it on and off for five years before it reached the Main Stem. Once there it closed in a single night.

SHOWCASE CODE

Off Off-Broadway had no long-run hits, but it did have a long-running labor controversy, one that augured ill for its many theatres. During its earliest years Off Off had been free to use whatever actors it chose, without worrying about union policies. Because its essential nature had not yet surfaced, Off Off-Broadway was largely ignored by Equity. As more actors began to spend their time in this environment in the mid-sixties Equity began to sniff around suspiciously. Soon it decided to issue a "Showcase Code" governing actors' participation in these theatres.

Actors came to Off Off-Broadway for a variety of reasons. They wanted a place to do plays and styles of theatre in which the commercial theatre had no interest; they wanted a chance to keep their skills fresh and growing during the frequent and long layoff periods between paying engagements; and they wanted a stage on which to showcase their talents for uptown producers, directors, and casting agents.

Equity, seeing its actors working voluntarily for no salary in Off Off's tiny playhouses—theatres that often lacked heat and proper plumbing—yelled "exploitation!" and tried to prevent its members from appearing there. To the actors, the union was being over-protective; they demanded the right to work when and where they pleased and to determine their own working conditions. Throughout the decade they fought with their union over its constant attempts to tighten the conditions of employment and payment Off Off-Broadway.

Beginning in the mid-sixties with codes promulgated to govern Café La Mama, Equity began to assert its prerogatives regarding the participation of its members in Off Off-Broadway theatre. It prohibited actors from giving more than ten performances in a non-paying showcase (later this was changed to twelve), and would not allow actors to contribute to the show's costs, nor would it permit these shows to advertise or charge admission. Through one subterfuge or another the theatres ignored most of these requirements; if they had not they would have closed down. In the seventies the code was more strictly enforced, although ads and admission charges were permitted to become standard practices.

Off Off-Broadway in the seventies was too successful to be ignored by Equity, which wanted its actors appropriately compensated according to the amount of income received annually by a theatre. Off Off theatres were not, in principle, against paying their players; many had been doing so for years. The problems that arose as Equity tried to create new codes from 1973 to 1980 were related to its demands for a system of payment that most considered exorbitant when viewed in terms of the incomes produced at the theatres concerned. Many feared they would have to fold if forced to pay actors at the rates dictated by the union. Sensing the possible decline and end of Off Off's existence, the actors fought back against their union's regulations. Many fiery meetings were held, votes taken, referendums conducted. Off Off was represented throughout by an umbrella organization, the Off Off-Broadway Alliance (OOBA), founded to promote and support Off Off's activities. Not recognized by Equity as a legal bargaining agent, OOBA found great difficulty in getting the union to "negotiate" terms with it.

After years of wrangling Equity seemed to have gotten the upper hand by the end of the decade. As the finalized codes were about to go into effect in September 1979, the theatres made a last-ditch attempt to circumvent them by employing non-union actors or by suspending their seasons. A few theatres did sign with Equity, though, and these proved the necessary chink in the OOBA defense. By May 1980 the other theatres were all falling into line, like a row of dominoes.

The new codes required each theatre to be placed within one of four tiers according to its gross income. Theatres at the lowest level, Tier 1, fell within the gross income range of $25,000 to $145,000, and had to pay actors 15 percent of that in salaries. Because 15 percent is a very large part of the gross, these theatres were hard put to pay the required amounts. Equity, therefore, came to terms with them on an individual basis and allowed them, for example, to pay only 7.5 percent the first year and 10 percent the next. In another case, it might have permitted a Tier 2 theatre to operate temporarily at Tier 1 levels. The burden of salary payments forced these companies to reduce their seasons and to be more circumspect in the plays they selected for production.

Also at issue—and pointing up the extent to which Off Off had veered from its initial mission as an alternative to theatre-as-money-maker—was the requirement by Equity that the actors in a showcase that went on to be produced commercially must be employed in that commercial production or be handsomely compensated for their contribution to the success of the original. Even more disturbing was Equity's demand that the original actors be paid a percentage of the show's eventual profits. The controversial provision making the ultimate payment the playwright's contractual obligation led to more than 500 playwrights signing a petition declaring that they would not put their names to the showcase code. The issue became news in 1980 when Michael Weller's *Split* was closed by the union after he refused to sign the code. Equity's showcase committee was convinced that the developmental work done on a script by the actors should be rewarded by their being offered their original roles in a later production or being well compensated for their original services. The situation was not resolved until late in 1982, when, following an antitrust suit brought by the dramatists against the union, the former were released from any financial obligation to the actors.[4]

Economics held its sharpened dagger ever more closely to Off Off's jugular vein at the decade's end. Several theatres were unable to go along with the demands of the unions while fighting the attacks of rising costs. A number simply could not hack it any more, and Off Off had to say farewell to, among others, the Impossible Ragtime Theatre, the Direct Theatre, and the Counterpoint Theatre, all of which had been around for several years and were respected institutions.

EXPERIMENTAL THEATRE

Thanks to the emergence of the Off Off-Broadway movement, New York became the home of dozens of experimental theatre groups in the sixties and seventies. New York's experimental ferment soon led to similar activities across the country. Radical ideas in staging, acting, and playwriting gradually emerged from the experimental, non-commercial companies and began to infiltrate the for-profit domains of Broadway and Off-Broadway. In 1970, for instance, a successful Broadway show based on experimental methods, *Paul Sills's Story Theatre*, was developed collaboratively by a company of actors working improvisationally on fairy tales by the Brothers Grimm. The idea of a sort of actors' collective ensemble devising their own script under the guidance of an inspirational director (Paul Sills in this case) was very much a part of the avant-garde theatre in the sixties, though the actors in *Story Theatre* were not part of a true, ongoing company. They did, however, add a new, though unsuccessful, piece to their repertory when *Ovid's Metamorphoses* opened in 1971.

Other theatrical concepts cooked up in the avant-garde cauldron continued to appear in the directorial and writing techniques of mainstream artists. Sometimes this was apparent in the controversial staging of revivals, as when Peter Brook shocked theatregoers with his deromanticized, circus-like version of *A Midsummer Night's Dream*. At other times, original works, such as the enormously popular *Equus*, were able to attribute a large part of their success to the employment of innovative techniques. *Equus* used an onstage audience seated on bleachers, thereby converting the proscenium playhouse into a theatre in the round; it depicted six horses through the use of mime and masks; there was free passage of the action from time past to time present, and the occasional blending of both into a simultaneous past/present; both direct and indirect address were employed; full frontal nudity was incorporated; the setting allowed actors who were not involved in the immediate action to remain onstage seated on benches; and so on.

Such formalistic concepts as these were the essential preoccupation of experimental groups in New York and elsewhere in the seventies. Their greatest thrust was in finding new ways to communicate levels of consciousness; new configurations of space for handling the relationship of actors to audience and actors to setting; and new ways of involving the ensemble in collaborative methods of production development. *What* was being said or shown was frequently of less concern than *how* it was being shown. The emphasis shifted from a sixties absorption in political and social issues to a seventies addiction to visual and aural aesthetics. The exceptional success of the decade's avant-garde designers and directors in conceiving startlingly innovative stage images was directly related to their close association with the most advanced artists in the non-theatrical areas of painting, sculpture, dance, music, video, and film.

The most productive and important avant-garde theatre work of the period grew out of non-profit resident companies led by a directorial or conceptual staging genius. In most cases, the ideas and talents of the company members had significant effect on the final work, but in some groups the guru-leader was a totally autocratic artist who used his acolytes as a sculptor uses clay—molding them entirely to his vision. Because the works produced under these generally collaborative conditions were so closely linked to the performances of the companies that created them, they were almost impossible to understand or appreciate in the form of printed scripts; consequently, they were incapable of revival by others. Their lack of conventional dialogue, characters, plots, recognizable settings, and familiar movements and gestures led the critics to dislike calling them plays, preferring instead such ambivalent terms as "theatre pieces" or "events."

Most of the principal companies failed to last out the decade; they were torn asunder by the usual pressures of financial need and internal dissension. Some of their leading practitioners were eventually drawn away from their mother companies by the lures of commercial opportunities, but most continued to work within the general framework of the non-profit institutions, although on projects of a more traditional nature, such as directing unconventional classical revivals.

The seven leading groups involved in producing experimental, non-traditional, or idiosyncratic theatrical works were, in order of the dates of their founding, the Bread and Puppet Theatre (1962), the Open Theatre (1963), the Ridiculous Theatrical Company (1967), the Performance Group (1967), the Ontological-Hysteric Theatre (1968), the Mabou Mines (1969), and the Byrd Hoffman School of Byrds, (1969). Of these, only the Bread and Puppet Theatre, the Ridiculous Theatrical Company, and the Mabou Mines made it into the eighties. Except for a few productions, the work of these groups was confined to Off Off-Broadway.

The Bread and Puppet Theatre

Peter Schumann, founder of the Bread and Puppet Theatre, the oldest continuing group of non-traditional theatre artists in America, is also its producer, director, designer, writer, composer, mask-and-puppet-maker, and chief performer. The Silesian-born Schumann once expressed his vision of the group's purposes in these words:

We want you to understand that theatre is not yet an established form, not the place of commerce that you think it is, where you pay to get something. Theatre is different. It is more like bread, more like a necessity. Theatre is a form of religion. It is fun. It preaches sermons and it builds up a self-sufficient ritual where the actors try to raise their lives to the purity and ecstasy of the actions in which they participate.[5]

Schumann's thoughts betray the period in which his theatre came to life, the ravaged sixties; they reveal the political fire that burned in the hearts of various groups of that decade, especially with regard to the Vietnam War. Schumann never went so far as to take a specific ideological stance towards the war or other issues, but each of his company's works of the sixties and seventies was clearly on the side of good against evil, of brotherly love, individual freedom, peace, nature, and godliness. These issues were evoked not in overtly political treatments, but through theatricalist means derived from the popular theatre of street shows and circuses that raised them to a universal plane where their effect could be appreciated above and beyond the level of conventional political differences.

New York-based during the sixties, the company moved to Vermont in 1970, making periodic excursions to other places, and appearing in New York with at least a dozen works during the seventies. Several of their seventies productions, however, were never brought to the city. The company, entirely non-commercial, has long subsisted on a near poverty level, because of its members' heartfelt abhorrence of the ways of modern civilization; they prefer simplicity in all their living arrangements, and this has colored their theatrical existence. They rarely advertise and are consequently difficult to document, aside from those instances where their work has been sponsored by such institutions as the Brooklyn Academy of Music or the Public Theatre.

New York presentations during the decade included *The Grey Lady Cantata; Emilia; Coney Island Cycle; That Simple Light May Rise Out of*

Complicated Darkness; Grey Lady Cantata #4; Meadows Green; White Horse Butcher; Masaniello; Ave Maria Stellis; Joan of Arc; Ah! Or the First Washerwoman's Cantata; and *Stations of the Cross.*

As some of these titles suggest, religious images and sources crop up frequently in the Bread and Puppet productions; the effect is often like that of a morality play, in which the message is embedded in a dense theatrical context of a naive and crude, but overwhelmingly persuasive, iconography of masks, puppets, placards, tableaux, and other dramatic concepts. The shows, some of them staged indoors and some outdoors, often succeed in creating a bond of communion between the spectator and performers because of the unpretentious, gentle, folk-art manner of the performers and production style.

During their seventies work, the Bread and Puppet Company normally greeted audiences with a rousing musical prologue performed as a celebration of the communal event by musicians playing an assortment of brass, string, and percussion instruments, some of them children's toys. Soon, chunks of home-baked rye bread were passed among the audience and actors so that all might feel the unity of this rite in which they shared.

The plays themselves incorporated many puppets, both tiny and gigantic, all built by the company itself (as was all the theatrical paraphernalia used in the shows), and a variety of powerfully expressive masks of differing sizes. The puppets were often shells inside of which the actors moved around. They were rarely articulated in the sophisticated manner of more familiar puppets, but were rather roughly made so as to suggest potent archetypal images and not illusionistic human doubles. Everything in the shows, from costumes to props, looked like a found object, which it frequently was. An air of casual craftsmanship disguised the highly polished art that underlay the homemade aspect.

Wry, ironic humor mingled with ineffable pathos in plays that depended more on visual and aural effects than on straightforward dialogue and dramatic action. Where necessary, these pageant-like works were accompanied by Schumann acting as a narrator. Characters represented various levels of reality, abstract and concrete, human and non-human, living and dead, profane and divine. There was usually a simple story line; often a picture-book program filled with artless drawings and phrases was distributed to help the spectators follow the plot on both its actual and symbolic levels. There was also considerable use of banners and cardboard signs to communicate verbal ideas.

Spatial arrangements varied from show to show and were often linked to the nature of the place in which the production was given. Where required a proscenium or end-stage orientation was used, but environmental arrangements, according to which the play determines the space, were common as well.

The Open Theatre

The Open Theatre disbanded in 1973, after an eleven-year period during which it had become America's most noted experimental acting ensemble. Led by director Joseph Chaikin, originally a highly respected actor (he appeared onstage only once during the group's existence), the company pioneered in the evolution of the collaborative company concept, wherein a work would be created over a period of a year or more before being shown to the public. Their creative range extended from essentially non-verbal, highly physicalized works to pieces employing equal amounts of verbal and physical material; however, the words and movements were so closely blended in their imagistic, non-discursive nature that one was, in a sense, the expression of the other. Characters were generally emblematic, not naturalistic, and represented types or concepts, with the actors moving swiftly from role to role according to dramatic need. The open nature of their characterizations allowed women to play male parts, and vice versa, without the effect of campy humor.

To develop the almost choreographic fluidity of their presentational style, the company worked at length on a variety of exercises devised mainly by Chaikin so that they could move with ease from character to character or idea to idea without the intrusion of abrupt transitions. The results of their work brought the Open Theatre recognition as the leading American force in the search for new approaches to the actor's art. Chaikin's actors learned to convey feelings, moods, and ideas in vocal and physical ways the realistic theatre had rarely explored.

Although there was some humor in the Open Theatre's work, the troupe evoked an aura of utmost seriousness. They would select a theme of importance to the entire company, and then examine with close scrutiny each of their responses to the theme as it affected their lives. As Margaret Croyden points out in *Lunatics, Lovers, and Poets*, the group's life grew out of a fundamental dissatisfaction with the social/political environment, but they never became overtly political in the dogmatic sense.[6] Their main concern was to make artistic statements, not to change the world. Playwright Susan Yankowitz, a contributor to their work, has described their method: "In the Open Theatre, the process of finding and realizing the play is an end in itself; the group does not perform in order to please an audience or make money, it works to communicate something that may or may not please. The product is secondary to the process."[7]

As this suggests, the company's focus was actor-centered. Writers participated in the process, but mainly to edit and clarify the dramatic outline. The job was described by Yankowitz as "To observe what was happening in workshops, to distill and focus ideas, and to create original material which would elucidate the themes with which we were working."[8] Other writers associated with the Open Theatre in the seventies were Sam Shepard, Jean-Claude Van Itallie, and Megan Terry.

Most Open Theatre pieces were staged in an end-stage arrangement, the actors on one side, the spectators on the other, because such an arrangement was the easiest to realize in the multifarious environments the group found themselves in when touring. Their style was suggestive of what experimental Polish director Jerzy Grotowski called "poor theatre," with barely any scenery or props, only a few wooden units that were abstract enough to be used for most scenic needs, and costumes that were simple and unadorned. Occasionally, the actors' well-worn street clothing was used for costuming. Stage makeup was rarely worn. Music, generally of a folksy type, was used extensively as background and for sound effects, and no attempt was made to hide the musicians or, for that matter, the actors who were "offstage" waiting to make an entrance. Lighting was usually non-gelled and non-illusionistic.

The three Open Theatre pieces of the decade were *Terminal, The Mutation Show,* and *Nightwalk.* Roberta Sklar, Chaikin's co-director on the first, called it a "confrontation with mortality," since it investigated the company's feelings toward death.[9] *The Mutation Show* took for its subject the processes of human and social change, and was partly inspired by the story of Kaspar Hauser, also dealt with in Peter Handke's *Kaspar.* The state of sleep was explored in the group's final work, *Nightwalk.*

Much speculation has occurred as to why the group split up when they were at a peak of critical acceptance. Chaikin, interviewed shortly after the breakup, said that the company sensed that outside pressures were forcing them to freeze, unable to advance in their tracks.[10] They found themselves being institutionalized, encapsulated, and pigeonholed by audience and media expectations. This outside interest in their work, said Chaikin, was leading to a derailment of their original impulses, thus suggesting the possibility of their moving into areas that would weaken their sense of mission.

Various company members continued to work on projects related to their Open Theatre work, most of these being limited to brief Off Off-Broadway runs. Chaikin himself became recognized as an innovative Off-Broadway director of such plays as *The Dybbuk* and *Endgame* and even returned to acting, though not to the complete satisfaction of either the critics or himself. In the late seventies he started up a new group, the Winter Project, with some former members of the Open Theatre and a few new people, and presented several pieces at La Mama. These works represented no new breakthroughs and even struck some viewers as slightly dated in approach.

The Ridiculous Theatrical Company

Founded in 1967 by actor-director-playwright Charles Ludlam, the Ridiculous Theatrical Company provided a string of campy parody-type comedies throughout the decade. Like many of the other offbeat groups looked at here, the company was formed with non-professional actors, most of whom appeared in all the shows. Leading actors were Ludlam himself, Bill Vehr, Black-Eyed Susan, Lola Pashalinski, and John D. Brockmeyer.

The Ridiculous Theatrical Company, an offshoot of John Vacarro's Playhouse of the Ridiculous, from which Ludlam was fired in 1967, offered New Yorkers well over a dozen broad farces, most of them redolent of gay "in" humor, and based largely on the familiar icons of pop culture, especially the movies. Stefan Brecht calls Ludlam's production style "queer theatre," by which he means

derisive low comedy and burlesque . . . portraying mankind as low (lecherous and depraved), evil (malevolent and vicious) and ridiculous (preposterously pretentious, foolish and devoid of dignity and stature), and love as the supreme lie, but upholding the aesthetic ideal, aspiring to invest itself . . . with beauty, viz; the beauty possible under these conditions, the beauty of the low, the evil and the ridiculous. . . .[11]

Although nudity, sexual reversals, scatological joking, and direct address to the audience were featured in most of the plays, the company's fundamental method, when compared with most of the other avant-garde groups, was a rather traditional, even realistic one, oriented toward the performance of a fully scripted text in which verbal expression played a dominant role. The entire seventies repertoire was written or adapted by Ludlam, who crafted his plays out of the collaborative contributions made in rehearsal improvisations by his actor-buffoons. These densely plotted farces, tightly stuffed with every type of comic wordplay and allusions to the world of classical and modern cultural artifacts, were produced independently and in repertory, depending on the needs of a particular season. As a continuing company, they could revive favorites of the past whenever necessary.

The Ridiculous Theatrical Company played at various theatres during the early seventies but settled in their own playhouse at One Sheridan Square in 1977. The troupe had moved from amateur to professional status during the period, though salaries remained low and they were not members of Actors Equity.

Major productions of the company during the seventies (aside from revivals of earlier work) were *Bluebeard; Eunuchs of the Forbidden City; Corn; Camille; Hot Ice; Stage Blood; Caprice; Der Ring Gott Farblonjett; The Ventriloquist's Wife; The Enchanted Pig;* and *A Christmas Carol.* Reviews were often very favorable, especially for *Camille,* in which Ludlam played the Lady of the Camellias in drag, with little attempt to disguise his hairy chest; for *Hot Ice,* a spoof of crime films inspired by the James Cagney movie *White Heat; Der Ring Gott Farblonjett,* a broad takeoff on Wagnerian opera; and *The Enchanted Pig,* a romp through the comical-erotic underside of a romantic fairy tale.

The Performance Group

During its ten years of existence, the Performance Group did not offer a prolific production schedule, nor were its half-dozen works rapturously received by the public or critics. Its greatest success came in 1968 with its first production, *Dionysus in 69*, following which its work made no great advances. Yet the group's position as a leading force in the experimental theatre movement was widely recognized. The reason for this probably owes more to the man who led the group, Richard Schechner, than to the work itself; Schechner, a professor at New York University, wrote extensively of his ideas in a series of influential books and articles and thereby helped to make his company's activities accessible to a large number of people.

Produced in the Performing Garage, a converted garage on Wooster Street in the Soho district, the company's work became synonymous with the term "environmental theatre," a form that Schechner's studies of anthropology, psychology, and sociology convinced him was the most appropriate for what he saw as the ritualistic basis of the theatrical event. In each of the Group's productions, they attempted to redefine the performance space—30 feet by 55 feet—in terms that best expressed the content of the work. The specific environment was developed by actors, designer, and director during the long collaborative rehearsal procedure that led to the final production. Even after opening to the public, new elements were introduced as the need arose from the performance process.

Audiences and actors were thrown into an assortment of new physical arrangements and performer-spectator relationships, these often requiring audiences to climb ladders to their seats on balconies and platform towers. Schechner himself would frequently prod spectators to move around the acting area during the performance so that they could see from varying vantage points. In a few cases, the garage doors leading to Wooster Street were opened and the action flowed out onto the sidewalk.

Schechner's environmental concept was indistinguishable from audience participation; his productions frequently involved the audience in direct contact with the actors; one work, *Commune*, was so structured that the action could not continue until the audience had come to a specific decision. This allowed the element of chance to enter the performance.

To Schechner, the audience acted as a collaborator in an open-ended production technique, where feedback was not only psychological but physical as well. Audiences were made to feel a part of the event from the start, as when, in *Commune*, they were not permitted to enter the theatre unless their shoes were removed. At intermissions a greater sense of audience-actor intimacy was likely to be encouraged by allowing the performers to socialize with the spectators. The idea was to destroy the sense of the theatre as a place of illusion, to reveal the elements that make it tick, even to the extent of permitting the audience to view the actors engaged in their warmup exercises preparatory to the actual performance.

The company's acting style grew out of numerous intense rehearsals in the use of physical space, and the exploration of vocal and movement possibilities. An important impetus to their progress was the work of Jerzy Grotowski. The company rarely settled for pat answers to any of the production problems they set themselves, but continued to investigate new approaches to their work, even after numerous showings. In this sense they were one of the most purely "experimental" of all seventies groups.

During the decade the Group's work moved from a collage piece, *Commune*, composed collaboratively by the company, to the performance of a new script by David Gaard, *The Marilyn Project*, about a sex-goddess movie star. It was performed simultaneously by a double cast, each occupying one side of the space, thus producing the effect of a mirror image. There were also three well-known plays, Seneca's *Oedipus*, Brecht's *Mother Courage*, and Sam Shepard's *The Tooth of Crime*. The company's core membership of Stephen Borst, Spalding Gray, James Griffiths, Elizabeth LeCompte, Joan MacIntosh, and Timothy Shelton was augmented by others when necessary. Although the name of the troupe remained intact until near the end of the decade, they did no collective work as such following *Mother Courage*.

In 1975 two original members, LeCompte and Gray, began to proceed on an independent track doing their own experimental work based on Gray's autobiographical accounts of his memories. Their first production was called *Three Places in Rhode Island*, and this was followed by several other works which helped these artists gain a position of respect as outstanding conceptualists of the late seventies. Eventually, they took over the company's administration and changed its name to the Wooster Group. Under their management (LeCompte is the artistic director) Schechner returned to direct two plays, Terry Curtis Fox's neo-realistic *Cops* and Jean Genet's *The Balcony*.

The Ontological-Hysteric Theatre

In each of the groups described above, collaboration was a life-giving energy that infused all of their creative work. Each had a leader of original talents and innovative ideas, and each of these leaders had a variety of artistic capabilities. In none, however, was the work of the group so dominated and driven by the total vision and presence of their leader as was the Ontological-Hysteric Theatre by Richard Foreman. Everything seen and heard in this determinedly provocative theatre was the product of director-playwright-designer-performer Foreman's fertile imagination.

During the seventies the Ontological-Hysteric Theatre produced about ten works, all by Foreman, from the simply titled *Total Recall, Evidence,* and *Particle Theory*, to works with formulaic and enigmatic titles such as *HcOhTiEnLa or Hotel China: Part I* and *II; Sophia-(Wisdom) Part III: the Cliffs; Pain(t); Vertical Mobility: Sophia-(Wisdom) Part II; Pandering to the Masses: A Misrepresentation; Rhoda in Potatoland (Her Fall Starts); Book of Splendors (Part II) Book of Levers: Action at a Distance (A Chamber Piece;* and *Blvd. De Paris (I've Got the Shakes)* or *Torture on a Train (Brain-Mechanisms of the Re-Distributed French Virgin)* or *Certainly Not (A Tortuous Train of Thought)*.

Foreman was also prolific of works produced outside the company framework. His other New York work included several musicals co-written with composer Stanley Silverman, *Dr. Selavy's Magic Theatre, Hotel for Criminals*, and *The American Imagination*; some original Off Off-Broadway plays directed either by himself or by others, but with themes and characters related to his Ontological-Hysteric work; and the direction of both the highly praised Lincoln Center revival of *The Threepenny Opera* and the egregious Broadway disaster *Stages*.

Until he opened his tiny loft theatre on downtown Broadway in 1975 (he closed it in 1979) with *Pandering to the Masses*, Foreman's company played at a variety of Off Off houses. The sixty-seat loft allowed him to control all elements of the production to a greater degree than had previously been possible; it was here that his work became known to more than his hardcore followers, though a season rarely played to more than 750 people. The audience sat in an auditorium sixteen feet deep, packed closely together on seven backless tiers, and watched his pieces unfold on a long narrow stage 75 feet deep by 14 feet wide, built on a stage floor divided into three levels with the central section (30 feet deep) raked. The audience-to-performance orientation was end-stage. No attempt was made to disguise or hide the lighting, sound, or other technical appurtenances.

On Foreman's tunnel-like stage strange, unsettling tableaux of actors and scenery came eerily to life, as screens and panels were used to reshape the scenic area into diverse spatial configurations in which tricks of perspective frequently drew the eye toward seemingly distant objects. During the normally intermissionless proceedings, various new visual patterns would emerge to startle and amuse the viewer, the effect frequently suggesting techniques of cubist painting. A few simple colors, blacks and browns being most common; right angles, and parallel placement of props and furniture; non-gelled, unatmospheric lighting; strings drawn tightly across the stage in various arrangements to break up the space in unexpected geometric patterns; and an odd assortment of props ranging in size from miniature to very large—these were the fundamental aspects of the decor. Within this painterly world of imagistic designs the actors moved almost like programmed androids through a complex series of rigidly established, highly formalized movements, gestures, and tableaux composed down to the very direction in which their eyes were staring, with slight shifts in movement often occurring on each new word in the text. Generally, this stare was directed straight at the audience. As the actors and sets moved into ever more eccentric or surprising pictures, the voice of Foreman himself would be heard over the speaker system, reciting the bulk of the script. The actors got to perform lines only sporadically and would frequently begin a speech only to have their words segue into a pre-recorded version on tape. Throughout the piece, Foreman would remain visible to the spectators while seated in a little niche, surrounded by all his technical equipment, running the show as a sort of stage manager-conductor, and constantly interrupting and prodding the actors to make required transitions by using various sound effects, including a buzzer and the spoken word "cue."

Foreman's plotless plays were considered "moment-by-moment" expressions of the artist's shifting states of consciousness and thought processes during their composition and, as "diary plays," were autobiographical. As insights into Foreman's teeming mind, these works afforded no other theatre worker the opportunity for personal expression; of the actors only Foreman's attractive woman-friend, Kate Manheim, who, along with other actresses (and an occasional actor), often appeared nude, was recognized as a compelling onstage presence. Manheim and the other performers, all of them amateurs who willingly became the autocratic director's puppets, were given names that continually reappeared in the plays. Manheim was always Rhoda, while others, some appearing in the same role in several plays, acted characters named Max, Leo, Ben, Eleanor, and Sophia, to mention the most common. They all had symbolic functions related to Foreman's mental attitudes: Max, for example, was seen as a reflection of Foreman himself. In general, though, their actions and meaning were too abstractly presented for most theatregoers to accept on any but the most subliminal of levels.

To many, the overall effect of a Foreman work was surrealistic or dreamlike, but not threatening or nightmarish. There was never a sense of psychological or emotional involvement with the characters or action, for Foreman deliberately embraced a Brechtian array of estrangement devices for cutting the audience off from such absorption. One had to exercise one's brain continuously in adapting to the shifting intellectual nuances served up in the densely allusive, yet monotonously intoned, spoken text. Most chose to simply watch and listen without making an effort to puzzle out the slippery references and thematic purposes. Momentary boredom was a concomitant of viewing an Ontological-Hysteric production, but this feeling lasted only briefly as new and intriguing images appeared to rearouse the lapsed observer.

The Mabou Mines

In 1969, a small group of theatre artists, some of whom had known and worked with each other as early as 1962 in San Francisco, created a company which took its odd name from the Nova Scotia mining town where they were spending the summer. Like all the other groups examined in this section, Mabou Mines had a visionary leader, Lee Breuer, but to an extent perhaps paralleled only by the Open Theatre, the work done by the company emerged from a truly collective spirit and blending of talents.

The initial core of performers in Mabou Mines included Breuer, Ruth Malaczech, Joanne Akalaitis, David Warrilow, and composer Philip Glass, then married to Akalaitis. All of these individuals were eventually recognized as brilliant talents in their own right, exclusive of their attachment to the company *per se*. Several others later worked with the Mabou Mines, most notably Frederick Neumann, William Raymond, and Ellen McElduff.

The group's initial public acclaim derived from a series of Samuel Beckett performances, some of them apparently never intended by the author for the stage. In addition to such specifically stage-oriented works as *Play* and *Waiting for Godot*, the company brought theatrical life to pieces like *Come and Go*, *The Lost Ones*, *Cascando*, and *Mercier and Camier*. There was also Akalaitis' inspired realization of Colette's *Dressed Like an Egg*, Akalaitis' *Southern Exposure*, and Malaczech's *Vanishing Pictures*. Breuer's own creations were of extreme importance; they included his "animations" trilogy of *The Red Horse Animation*, *The B. Beaver Animation*, and *The Shaggy Dog Animation*. Breuer also provided the Mabou Mines with *The Saint and the Football Players* and *A Prelude to Death in Venice*.

In all their work the Mabou Mines combined the striking visuals of conceptually oriented imagist theatre, such as one thinks of in the work of Foreman and Robert Wilson, with a surprisingly deep and psychologically penetrating acting method. This use of internalized acting states makes them differ from the untrained Foreman and Wilson disciples.

Mabou Mines evolved its visual and performance features under the collaborative shelter of the collective ensemble. Many months went into the development of a piece; as the work progressed the group continually edited, discarded, and created. Although a director always was in charge of the total conception, many of the best ideas arose only because of the reliance on ensemble contributions in discussion and rehearsal. Experiment for the group was mainly a matter of what happened in the creation of a piece, rather than in the crucible of actual performance.

The Mabou Mines, based in the Soho area, were in direct contact with the work of the best talents in modernist painting and sculpture. Their sets and costumes represented a superb blending of advances in the visual arts, especially when the conceptualists participated in the actual design process, as in *Dressed Like an Egg*. In some pieces, music, film, sculpture, painting, movement, and sound were merged with excellent effect to produce truly successful works of total theatre art.

Breuer's animation texts are considered representative of the company's original offerings. These works provided material for the evolution of a performance style that moved from the largely physical expression of *The Red Horse Animation* (the text was published as a comic book in Bonnie Marranca's *The Theatre of Images*[12]) to the highly textured verbal character of the later pieces. In the animations the central characters are animals—a horse in the earliest, a beaver in the second, and a dog in the third. Actually, these creatures are metaphorical figures representing the plight of human beings in today's world, and their animal natures are cleverly linked to aspects of human psychology. As is true of much seventies avant-garde work, there is a largely autobiographical streak in Breuer's writing, and the animations trilogy has definite textual resonances that carry themes and characters through from one piece to the next. Breuer has said that he is chiefly interested in exploring narrative modes in the theatre; his texts, alive with literary mannerisms, contain no dialogue but are expressed through a variety of choral techniques. The animations are, in the conventional sense, plotless and conflictless; their literary richness and poetic tone suggest the influence of Beckett, Brecht, and Gertrude Stein. Comic overtones are vivid; occasionally they have the power to evoke bellylaughs.

Of the three "animations," the best received was the last; it was also the longest and most technically sophisticated. Centered on the dog, Rose, it employed amplified speech and music, a complex choral presentation of Rose's words, and, in addition to human actors, sensationally expressive three-quarters-life-size puppets modeled after the methods of Japan's Bunraku theatre, which has had a strong influence on Breuer (similar puppetry appeared in *A Prelude to Death in Venice*). *The Shaggy Dog Animation* is structured like a traditional shaggy-dog story to convey the enactment of a "Dear John" letter written by Rose to her former lover/master from whom she has finally achieved liberation—making the piece a feminist tract of sorts. Set against a potent pop culture symbol—a gigantic radio station-frequency band—the play's performance style varied according to the place on the band the needle happened to land—soap opera, rock and roll, country-western, Latin, jazz, and so on. Music was a vibrant means of expression for this exceptional company, in this and most other works.

Byrd Hoffman Schools of Byrds

Richard Foreman and Robert Wilson are considered the foremost practitioners of what has been called the Theatre of Images or the Theatre of Visions. Both began working in this mode in the late sixties, but each had a unique style and method that led to vastly different results. Wilson, for the first half of the seventies, did shows that grew out of workshops and exercises with a loosely constituted band of disciples that he founded in 1968 as the Byrd Hoffman School of Byrds. He derived the name from a dancer-speech therapist who had cured him of a speech impediment when he was a boy of seventeen. Wilson's disciples in the Soho-based company were privileged to be considered Byrds. Gradually the use of the name dwindled and today Wilson's own name is mostly used in connection with his work.

Wilson himself came to do theatre work as an extension of his interests in painting and therapy. His unforgettable stage sets and costumes, which he either designed himself or had a great influence in designing, reflected his artistic training (he had studied architecture at Pratt), while the subjects and treatments of his shows were deeply enmeshed in his therapeutic concerns. Wilson achieved noted success as a brilliant speech and movement teacher for children with various functional disabilities. Some of his most outstanding theatre work emerged from his relationship with two boys, a deaf-mute named Raymond Andrews, and an autistic child named Christopher Knowles. Rejecting the term therapy as a description of his teaching approach, Wilson asserted that he achieved his remarkable breakthroughs in getting these youths to confront the world by accepting them as unique individuals possessed of special powers of perception unknown to the average person. He believed that Andrews and Knowles were capable of communicating with their environment on levels that did not coincide with the everyday conscious reality of most people. It was his desire to express on stage the world of their special perceptions. Thus, in developing *Deafman Glance*, very little of verbal import was employed, only selected sound effects that were somehow related to the world of the deaf. Andrews appeared as a principal actor in the play. The hearing actors learned in workshops how to communicate in an environment that recreated the inner workings of a deaf person's mind. Similar concepts were at work in the mammoth *The Life and Times of Joseph Stalin*, which introduced young Chris Knowles to the stage doing a piece of verbal music he had composed using two tape recorders.

As these examples suggest, Wilson was not particularly concerned with traditional acting or actors, and favored amateurs who could comfortably be themselves within the abstract scheme of his production design. Many of his Byrds were avant-garde artists and others were simply interested individuals, most of them without any formal theatre training, a situation akin to Foreman's Ontological-Hysteric Theatre. In creating a production he allowed the company to use their own personal qualities; opening up to him their individual natures during workshop sessions, they took a great part in the shaping of the final work. Wilson's visual and auditory effects may have been closely merged with his own private fantasies and dreams, but the expression of these images bore as much relation to the personalities of his performers as it did to himself. Here he differed dramatically from the single-mindedly autobiographical mode pursued by Foreman's theatre.

Stefan Brecht's definition of Wilson's style in his book *The Theatre of Visions: Robert Wilson* states:

Theatre of visions is the staging, with live performers, movements and development in such a fashion as to appear a world or reality or the representation of one by an individual and seeming personally important and significant to him (or her) independently of verbal, intellectual or discursive analysis. . . . The making of such theatre can not be construed as the making of a statement. . . . It is not an imitative or in any way a significative act: there is, for the maker, no question of meaning. The maker's intent is to impart the vision and a sense of its importance. Theatre of visions is a stage designer's theatre. . . .[13]

In Wilson's major New York works of the seventies, *Deafman Glance*, *The Life and Times of Joseph Stalin*, *A Letter for Queen Victoria*, *The $ [Dollar] Value of Man*, *Dia Log*, and *I Was Sitting on My Patio This Guy Appeared I Thought I Was Hallucinating*, the thematic purport was rarely clear to the uninitiated, although the underlying ideas of the later works were somewhat more accessible than those of earlier years. Brecht, in fact, asserts that the Theatre of Visions period was over by 1973 and that the later work represented a diminution of this artist's original impact.

As with almost all the other experimentalists examined here, plot and character do not function in Wilson's work as they do in conventional drama. His seventies productions presented enigmatic, symbolic, archetypal, fantastical, and familiar "characters" in a mysterious blend of theatrical effects designed to be viewed objectively as pictures of suggestive, if elusive, beauty. The material worked on the spectator's unconscious, stimulating him to bring whatever meanings he might wish to the event before him. Often, the pace was astonishingly slow and there were several marathon productions among Wilson's early works. *The Life and Times of Joseph Stalin*, for example, lasted twelve hours, from 7:00 P.M. to 7:00 A.M. As the images moved almost imperceptibly from one to the other, the audience could see elements ordinarily invisible when performed at the normal pace of human movements. A quality of Zen tranquility and stillness pervaded such performances.

Not everything in Wilson's work was thus attenuated, and some works conformed more to traditional time periods and included a considerable degree of conventionally and very fast-paced action. Dance, especially, was frequently seen in Wilson's pieces, in particular a type of whirling, spinning movement at which his dancers (mostly professional) excelled. Choreographers Lucinda Childs and Andrew DeGroat were closely associated with Wilson's pieces. Wilson himself acted and danced in his productions, and his dancing had a highly individualistic, if spastic, manner of its own.

The actors appeared in artfully composed tableaux against a variety of exceptional backgrounds. Some—including members of the Surrealist movement itself—believed Wilson's visions surpassed those of the original surrealists. Wilson's tableaux sometimes employed large groups—over 100 performers were in *Stalin*—but small groups were used effectively as well.

In *I Was Sitting on My Patio* only two performers, Wilson and Childs, appeared.

All activity was definitely set for a production before it opened, but a degree of freedom to improvise was permitted the players during the actual execution, provided the precision of established timing, movements, entrances, and exits was followed. Speech was minimal in the early works, but verbal experiments using non-discursive language played an increasingly vital part following *The $ Value of Man*, because of Wilson's exploration of Knowles' use of language.

Wilson's works were typically staged in proscenium theatres such as those of the Brooklyn Academy of Music and Broadway's ANTA Theatre (where *A Letter for Queen Victoria* was staged). The costs involved were ruinously high, and Wilson found it increasingly difficult to get the funding necessary to stage his often grandiose spectacles. (He was soon welcomed to continental Europe where subsidized theatres allowed him to continue his productions.) Wilson's plays were staged for only a very few performances each, and his one shot at an extended run on Broadway closed in half the period reserved for its month-long limited engagement. Because certain of his productions were scheduled for only a couple of performances, they became major news events, as when his five-hour opera, *Einstein on the Beach*, with score by Philip Glass, filled the Metropolitan Opera House's 5,000 seats on two evenings. Despite the esoteric nature of the proceedings, very few of the spectators present on either night left the theatre before the final curtain fell.

* * *

The importance of the experimental work of the seventies loomed even larger in the early eighties, when only the Ridiculous Theatrical Company and the Mabou Mines remained as active local fixtures. Robert Wilson returned with a revival of his *Einstein on the Beach*, but his other major new work was not seen in New York. Richard Foreman, active primarily as a free-lance director, did one Ontological-Hysteric piece at the Public. The Bread and Puppet Theatre made only rare incursions into the city's environs. On the whole, the excitement of the avant-garde seemed dissipated by mid-1985, at least as far as locally based companies were concerned. Some new ensembles were active, but none seemed capable of generating the kind of sustained creative energy of the previous decade's groups. The seventies, in retrospect, appeared to be a high point in the development of the American experimental theatre.

NOTES

1. David J. Skal, ed., *Theatre Profiles 4* (New York: Theatre Communications Group, 1979), pp. 107, 42.

2. Sy Syna, "The Many Faces of Off Off-Broadway," *New York Theatre Review* 3 (August/September 1979): 5.

3. Much of this information was provided by Mrs. Boyd herself.

4. Although a settlement was announced, the situation continued to create problems into the eighties. (See, for example, "OOB Producers Protest Terms of Equity-authors Settlement," *Variety*, 9 September 1981, p. 79; Samuel G. Freedman, "Playwrights and Actors in Dispute Over Rule," *New York Times*, 12 December 1984, Sec. III, p. 25; and, "Viewpoint," *Equity News* 70 [May 1985]: 1.)

5. Peter Schumann, "Bread and Puppets," *The Drama Review* 14 (No. 3, 1970): 35.

6. Margaret Croyden, *Lunatics, Lovers, and Poets* (New York: McGraw-Hill, 1974), p. 189.

7. In Erika Munk, "Working in a Collective: Interviews with Susan Yankowitz and Roberta Sklar," *Performance* 1 (December 1971): 85.

8. Ibid., p. 82.

9. In Paul Ryder Ryan, *"Terminal*: An Interview with Roberta Sklar," *The Drama Review* 15 (Summer 1971): 154.

10. In Richard Toscan (interviewer), "Closing the Open Theatre," *Theatre Quarterly* 16 (November-January 1975): 37.

11. Stefan Brecht, *Queer Theatre* (Frankfurt am Main: Suhrkamp, 1978), p. 9.

12. Bonnie Marranca, *The Theatre of Images* (New York: Drama Book Specialists, 1977).

13. Stefan Brecht, *The Theatre of Visions: Robert Wilson* (Frankfurt am Main: Suhrkamp, 1978), p. 9.

★ 3 ★
PLAYS
AND
PLAYWRIGHTS

In 1979, Bernard Jacobs, co-chairman of the Shubert Organization, argued with director Gordon Davidson that "There's really a war between the Broadway theatre . . . and the non-profit theatre. Actually, the non-profit theatre is appropriating a lot of our material. Sixty to seventy percent of the plays they're doing originate on Broadway. The rest of what they do is the classics, and maybe ten percent is original work."[1] Surprised, Davidson argued back that Jacobs had the numbers reversed, and that the non-profits are themselves the source for the best new Broadway shows. Whatever the precise figures, there can be no doubt that Davidson was far closer to the mark, and that a revolution had indeed occurred in the New York Theatre.

Once the bulwark of America's theatre, with close to 100 percent of the product seen elsewhere in the country having originated on its stages or, if foreign, having received its American premiere in the city, New York in the sixties began to lose ground as the chief testing place for all important new material; the tempo of change was speeded up rapidly in the seventies as increased private and public subsidy made it possible for theatres to arise all over the country and to serve as viable launching pads for new plays and musicals. Locally, the institutional theatres of Off- and Off Off-Broadway served the same function, thus depriving Broadway of its vaunted status as the great originator. By the mid-seventies it was clear that the New York commercial theatre, meaning primarily Broadway, had become not so much an arena for premieres as a showroom for the best work created elsewhere. The economics of the commercial theatre had simply made it impossible or extremely difficult for a major show to begin from scratch in New

York, when for a reasonable sum or even a relative pittance a work could be initiated and developed either in a regional theatre or in an Off Off show-case theatre. This meant, of course, that Off Off was losing its former posi-tion as an alternative venue and becoming merely a commercial spring-board—which was largely the case by mid-decade—but this was an all-too-natural outcome given the economic facts of the situation.

Whatever its disadvantages, there were many benefits to be reaped from the new arrangement. Because of the existence of outside support, com-panies were able to come into existence not to make a quick killing with a hot new script, but to nurture and foster a playwright's talent through workshops, readings, and other means. Some groups came into existence for the sole purpose of developing, but *not* producing, new playwrights, and most of the established production companies created frameworks within their institutions for new play development. Nor did musical theatre writers and composers lack the same treatment. Furthermore, in another manifestation of subsidy's importance, many playwrights were able to survive financially during the developmental period because of the increas-ing number of grants that were made available to them from the big founda-tions and government agencies.

As we saw in Chapter 2, works developed in shoestring Off Off show-cases could leap within a year to six- or seven-figure Broadway financing and national attention. Or they could be bought for production outside of New York at a regional theatre. Or the regional theatres could themselves develop plays that would be brought to New York for Off- or on-Broadway mounting. Or there might be several other scenarios. However one looked at it, one had to admit the inaccuracy of Jacobs' assessment and acknowl-edge that the function of the New York theatre had undergone considerable revision. This is not, however, to deny that New York remained and would remain the nation's theatrical capital. New York approval of a work continued to be as important as it always had been to most plays' commercial futures, and the financial gain that might accrue from a profitable New York run could not be duplicated elsewhere, but it was now also possible for an American play to be successful without ever even having a major New York production—as happened, for example, with Jerome Lawrence and Robert E. Lee's *The Night Thoreau Spent in Jail* in 1970.

The situation was fraught, of course, with not-so-subtle dangers. For example, Broadway's reluctance to produce serious new plays or revivals of the classics can be understood, if not condoned. But institutional theatres showcasing or premiering new works were also likely to become too con-cerned about the ultimate commercial value of their choices, and thus to overlook challenging or unconventional new works. Since most such theatres operate at a loss no matter how many seats they sell, their need for funds is an ever present imperative; what could be a more appropriate source of support than the profits from a work they helped to create? Playwright Edward Albee saw the dilemma when he said that the success of the regional companies as tryout locales for Broadway derives from "a total misuse of their function."[2] He believed that the managements of these companies were "allowing themselves to be used by the forces of the commercial theatre in [a] shameful . . . way." Critic Martin Gottfried warned of the danger in 1970, when the regional-to-Broadway movement was still in its infancy.[3]

Just how prevalent was the rise in Broadway's dependency on work created elsewhere? Approximately 530 works appeared on Broadway during the decade. Of this number, at least 120 were produced in resident theatres before coming to New York. (Some were staged in England or elsewhere abroad before their resident theatre production.) Broadway's reliance on the Off-Broadway scene is clear from the fact that approximately 45 Off-Broadway shows moved to Broadway auspices in the seventies. (Some were first done in resident theatres and others moved from Off Off to Off before making a second move to Broadway.) And the importance of Off Off-Broadway was underlined when about 25 works originating there moved to the Great White Way (some in a direct leap, others by means of successful Off-Broadway staging). When we add to these an estimated 100 works first staged in foreign countries, we get a total of 290 Broadway shows out of 530—or 55 percent—that began elsewhere than on Broadway. As noted above, Bernard Jacobs' estimate that only 10 percent of the non-profit product was original was egregiously inaccurate. Broadway's status as a "showroom" should no longer be in doubt.

A look at the winners of the various annual awards for best Broadway plays and musicals rams the point home. Of the twenty Broadway musicals and plays winning Tonys, Broadway's best-known award, from 1971 to 1980, four began life in the resident theatres, six started Off-Broadway (one was produced in London before its Off-Broadway version), one came from Off Off-Broadway, six were first done abroad (five in London), and only four were originally produced for Broadway alone.

Besides those in New York, resident companies and institutional theatres providing Broadway with new work are spread all over the nation, though their greatest concentration is in the East, especially Connecticut. They include the theatres under the aegis of the John F. Kennedy Center in Washington, D.C.; the Mark Taper Forum in Los Angeles (part of the Center Theatre Group, which also includes the Ahmanson Theatre); the Long Wharf Theatre in New Haven; and the Arena Stage in Washington, D.C. These were the most prolific in the number of contributions. Also significant were the Actors Theatre of Louisville, Kentucky; the Goodspeed Opera House, East Haddam, Connecticut; the Goodman Theatre Center, Chicago; the Yale Repertory Company, New Haven; the Studio Arena Theatre, Buffalo; the Eugene O'Neill Theatre Center, Waterford, Connecticut; Ford's Theatre, Washington, D.C.; the Ahmanson Theatre, Los Angeles; the Hartford Stage Company, Hartford, Connecticut; the Alley Theatre, Houston; the Hartman Theatre Company, Stamford, Connecticut; the Academy Festival Theatre, Lake Forest, Illinois; the Organic Theatre Company, Chicago; the McCarter Theatre, Princeton, New Jersey; the Guthrie Theatre, Minneapolis; and the Lenox Arts Center, Lenox, Massachusetts.

Off-Broadway, the most active non-profit theatres moving their wares to Broadway's showroom were the New York Shakespeare Festival, the Negro Ensemble Company, the Roundabout Theatre Company, the Chelsea Theatre Company, the Circle Repertory Company, and the Harold Clurman Theatre.

The foreign nations which first produced works eventually seen on Broadway in English or English translation were England, the most fecund, with forty-eight, followed by France (seven), Canada and Ireland (six each), Israel (musical revues only) (four), South Africa (three), Germany and Italy (two each), and one apiece from Sweden, the Soviet Union, and Czechoslovakia. Moreover, a small number of British plays and one from Australia premiered on Broadway before being seen on their native stages.

These figures do not include the frequent revivals of foreign plays in English translation, but it should be observed that many of the offerings on Broadway during the decade (new and revivals) were in the hands of visiting foreign companies. Broadway hosted successful productions by the Young Vic, the Royal Shakespeare Company, the National Theatre of Great Britain, and the National Theatre of Greece.

Off-Broadway was, in its own right, a showroom for work first mounted elsewhere. Of the approximately 875 shows produced Off-Broadway during the decade at least 100 originated in an Off Off playhouse. La Mama, the New Federal, the Judson Poets, the New York Shakespeare Festival, the Circle Rep, the Manhattan Theatre Club, the Quaigh, and Playwrights Horizons were the most significant contributors. Off-Broadway was also in the debt of the resident theatres. These provided close to a hundred works for Off-Broadway, some of them going to Off Off before being picked up for a more complete mounting. (Several of the Off Off companies listed here, of course, were also active in the production of plays under Off-Broadway auspices.[4])

Numerous foreign works came to Off-Broadway, including twenty-nine from England, ten from Canada, six from Ireland, six from Germany and Austria, four from South Africa, three from the West Indies, two from Australia, and one each from Japan, Sweden, Belgium, China, Poland, and India. (In some cases, the figures might vary because of differences of opinion about whether a play was really a new one or should be considered a revival.)

On both Broadway and Off-Broadway a significant number of older foreign plays never professionally produced before received their premieres, thus leading to the problem of classification mentioned in the previous paragraph. Broadway saw four of these while Off-Broadway put fourteen on the boards. At the same time Broadway witnessed three New York world premieres of recent English plays (*Find Your Way Home*, *The Merchant*, and *A Matter of Gravity*), one of an Irish play (*The Faith Healer*), and one of an Australian play (*Players*).

Off-Broadway was more receptive to foreign visitors than Broadway, with companies arriving almost annually from Czechoslovakia, Germany, France, the Soviet Union, Poland, Yugoslavia, Japan, Spain, Hungary, China, Israel, Ireland, and, of course, England, which sent over the Oxford-Cambridge Shakespeare Company, the Royal Shakespeare Company (three times), the Actors Company, the National Youth Theatre of Great Britain, and the Young Vic.

New York was a veritable feast of international theatre throughout the decade. The presence of foreign guests was increased considerably by the frequent visits sponsored by Off Off's busy La Mama, by the Asia Society, and by other institutions.

* * *

The remainder of this chapter is devoted to a bird's-eye view of selected dramas and comedies seen on New York stages in the seventies. The material is divided into relevant sections and subsections based upon the nationality of the authors concerned. Only Off-Broadway and Broadway productions are covered, although those with Off Off origins are appropriately credited. The discussion offers a picture of the general response to the plays mentioned, but is not intended as a work of criticism. The total number of performances is given for plays which had at least 200, and totals for several works with fewer performances are also cited. Years of production may be found next to the respective titles in the index. Because of the occasional disparity among responsible sources as to the dividing line between on- and Off-Broadway, Otis L. Guernsey, Jr.'s *The Best Plays* series, an annual account of New York theatre, has been used as the arbiter in questionable cases.

AMERICAN PLAYWRIGHTS

Throughout the 1970s the American playwright was engaged in a fierce rivalry with his British counterparts, who sent a stream of dramas and comedies to New York in productions often using members of the original casts. Buoyed by the universally praised technical and artistic virtuosity of English acting and directing, these imports often made the homegrown products look depressingly meager by comparison. American dramatists did, however, make some positive contributions to the world's dramatic library.

Established Dramatists

Activity among America's old-line dramatists, those who had gained success in previous decades, was vastly overshadowed by the work of dynamic new writers. It was, on the whole, a disappointing decade for the established authors, barely any of whom had what would be considered an artistic or commercial hit. Only Neil Simon, America's most popular playwright, continued to offer successful plays with regularity, although these often smarted from the stinging acid with which the dramatists' critics habitually filled their pens.

Tennessee Williams and Arthur Miller, America's two most prominent playwrights, were each represented by new works, but the revivals of their major plays of the past made their recent output seem insignificant. One old Williams play, *Summer and Smoke*, appeared in a considerably revised version called *Eccentricities of a Nightingale*, and some hailed it as a great improvement over the original. Williams was more prolific than Miller in the seventies, as he always had been. The longest running of his six new plays was *Small Craft Warnings*, about a group of dismal barflies in a shabby Southern California saloon; its 200 Off-Broadway performances were partly attributable to the late playwright himself taking over the role of "Doc" midway in the run—his professional New York acting debut. Williams even admitted that his performance was a stunt to shore up sagging ticket sales.

Williams' other plays of the decade were *Out Cry, Vieux Carré, A Lovely Sunday for Crève Coeur*, and *Clothes for a Summer Hotel*. *Clothes* was the last new Williams play to be produced locally before the playwright's bizarre death in 1983 from choking on a bottle cap.

Arthur Miller, like Williams, had to depend on excellent revivals of his old plays to help sustain his reputation. His one new play of the decade, which failed after twenty showings, was an ambitious philosophic/comedic treatment of the Book of Genesis, *The Creation of the World and Other Business*. He later made it into a musical play which also did not succeed.

Edward Albee's presence on the New York theatre scene was more frequent, but also fitful. Of his three new Broadway plays, *All Over, Seascape*, and *The Lady from Dubuque*, the second gained the greatest acclaim. Frank Langella and Laura Esterman played man-sized lizards to the human characters of Deborah Kerr and Barry Nelson in a satirical work dealing with problems related to the evolutionary process. It had a mixed critical reception and a poor audience response but nevertheless was awarded the Pulitzer Prize.

Of the other important contemporary serious playwrights of the pre-seventies era, Broadway and Off-Broadway saw the work of several, but their new offerings were not popular. These were William Gibson, Jack Gelber, Frank Gilroy, Robert Anderson, Arthur Laurents, and the team of

Jerome Lawrence and Robert E. Lee. Of these respected dramatists, the latter had in *First Monday in October* the only thing approaching a success. This was about a curmudgeonly old Supreme Court Justice and a woman Justice, the first elected to that august seat. A vehicle for Henry Fonda (Jane Alexander played the part that soon became an historical fact when Sandra O'Connor was chosen to fill a Supreme Court vacancy), some thought it succeeded more because of the star's performance than its innate quality.

Broadway ko'd a number of other well-known playwrights with impressive credentials, among them Norman Krasna, Archibald MacLeish, Samuel Taylor, and Gore Vidal. Each entered one effort in the ring and then threw in the towel.

Of the established playwrights specializing in serious subjects, only Ira Levin and Ronald Ribman produced work that was widely considered acceptable. Levin's two failures during the decade were made up for by the long-run murder mystery *Deathtrap* (1,793 performances). A suspense drama with a prime assortment of nerve-chilling laughs, the work parodied the genre while offering edge-of-the-chair frissons in its own right. It was played in a setting suggesting the weapon-lined country-house study of a famous mystery-writing playwright, and combined the proven stage formulas of theatrical shoptalk, sexual deviancy, and murder most foul. It told of how a fading writer colludes with a younger one to kill the writer's wife and set up house in homosexual bliss. These ingredients turned *Deathtrap* into the longest-running suspense play in Broadway history.

Ronald Ribman's first two plays of the period, one Off-Broadway and one on, did not do well, but he found an appreciative response with *Cold Storage*, first done Off-Broadway. It was a sensitive yet humorous depiction of two men of contrasting personalities and backgrounds in a hospital ward for terminal cancer patients. Following its limited original run, it was revised (for the better, said most critics) and moved to Broadway under a new director.

One of the most poignant and thoughtful treatments of an individual suffering from a disability was Arthur Kopit's *Wings*, originally staged at the Yale Repertory Theatre, then seen briefly Off-Broadway, and finally on Broadway. It featured Constance Cummings in a tour-de-force portrayal of a stroke victim; the play was an imaginative expression of the confusion and struggle for clarity of the stricken woman's mind.

Of previously recognized playwrights working in a comic vein, there were approximately half a dozen important ones active during the decade. Two of them, Herb Gardner and Jean Kerr, had one Broadway production each, and both failed. Henry Denker, best known for his serious plays, tried two light comedies, but both were soon discarded. Bruce Jay Friedman was similarly unlucky. His *Steambath*, starring and directed by Anthony Perkins, was a diverting comedy about the afterlife, in which limbo was a steambath and God (Hector Elizondo) a Pureto Rican attendant; it ran for a couple of months Off-Broadway. Murray Schisgal was the recipient of devastatingly negative reviews for *An American Millionaire* but was better treated for *All Over Town*, a satirical Broadway farce on liberal attitudes toward minorities. Staged by Dustin Hoffman in his professional directing debut, it lasted 233 performances.

Another satirical force was the plays of cartoonist Jules Feiffer. He produced in *Knock Knock* a highly praised picture of two aging New York Jewish intellectuals, one a pessimist and the other a romantic, living in the woods and visited by, of all beings, Joan of Arc. This fantasy, centering on the men's comic philosophical debates about the meaning of faith, was sparklingly staged by Marshall W. Mason for the Circle Repertory Company. It later moved to Broadway with its original cast, but toward the end of its run the cast was entirely replaced by a new one and the direction was redone by José Quintero. The controversy aroused by the switch was exacerbated by the complaints of some critics that the new version was vastly inferior to the first and that artistic slaughter had been committed in the interests of economic gain. Feiffer was also responsible for an Off-Broadway concoction, *Jules Feiffer's Hold Me!*, based on his popular cartoons about urban angst.

More successful and prolific was Terrence McNally, a writer of offbeat comedies, who made seventies audiences laugh with three new plays, the latter two being most effective. *Bad Habits* hopped, skipped, and jumped, in classic seventies style, from Off Off to Off to on Broadway, racking up a total of 369 performances in its commercial incarnations. This was a funny pair of one-acters, both set at mental sanitoriums with their loony nurses, far-out patients, and wacko doctors. McNally's outlandish humor returned to Broadway in *The Ritz* (400 performances), a campy farce set in a gay men's bathhouse where a fat, middle-aged straight, played by Jack Weston, goes to hide out from a gang of mobsters. Rita Moreno was a standout as a singer who entertains at the baths.

The greatest success story from amidst this crew of comic dramatists was America's master of the form, Neil Simon, history's most financially successful writer. A native New Yorker, Simon packed up his bags and left in mid-decade for California's sunshine and freer life style. His decision was partly based on a need he felt to change his environment following the death from cancer of his wife of twenty years, Joan. His remarriage to actress Marsha Mason (from whom he was subsequently divorced), whom he met while she was rehearsing for his *The Good Doctor*, had important reverberations in his work, as Mason appeared in leading roles in several important Simon stage and screen scripts.

Neil Simon's output in the seventies put him at the top of the Broadway ladder once again, his total reaching eight new plays for the decade. Simon's fertile muse inspired several plays that did not fit the mold of formula situation/rapid-fire gag writing for which he previously had gained acclaim. In *The Gingerbread Lady*, he sought to explore the problems of a famous singer whose life has been shattered by alcoholism. Despite Maureen Stapleton's memorable performance, the play disappointed critics and audiences. *The Prisoner of Second Avenue* dealt with a typical Simon subject, the deleterious effects of New York high-rise living. Enhanced by the work of actors Peter Falk, Lee Grant, and Vincent Gardenia, among others, it packed a strong enough laugh-provoking wallop to keep audiences laughing for 780 performances. New York and old-time show business proved an irresistible combination in Simon's next hit, *The Sunshine Boys* (538 performances), about two irascible ex-vaudevillians of the Smith and Dale school, played by Jack Albertson and Sam Levene. Simon's propensity for viewing himself as a sort of latter-day Chekhov was expressed in *The Good Doctor*, an interesting critical and box-office failure that wove a series of Chekhov stories and situations together via Simon's 1970's comic perspective. Chekhov himself, played by Christopher Plummer, was the evening's host. Simon was critically slapped on the wrist for trying to mingle serious dramaturgic aspirations with his unique talent for urban "schtick."

God's Favorite came about as a result of the author's attempt to exorcise his personal anguish following his wife's death. It was a retelling in modern sit-com style of the Job story, with a wealthy Jewish businessman (Vincent Gardenia) as the poor schlemiel whose faith is sorely tested. The critics pounced all over it, and its life was fairly brief. With the 445-performance *California Suite* he was up to his old tricks again, putting four one-acts together against the same hotel room background, only with different characters in each scene. The formula had been a hit with *Plaza Suite* in the sixties, so Simon celebrated his new West Coast surroundings with this amusing comedy. It also began his practice of premiering his plays at Los Angeles' Ahmanson Theatre instead of on Broadway.

The dramatist's personal life again informed his treatment of a play when he composed *Chapter Two*, about a well-known writer's (Judd Hirsch) attempts to get his life back on track following the untimely demise of his spouse. Marsha Mason played the role she had experienced offstage, that of the new love in the writer's life. This mingling of sentiment and chuckles wrung Broadway heartstrings for 857 performances. *Chapter Two*'s hero lived in the Big Apple, but *I Ought to Be in Pictures* (324 performances), also about a writer, was set in Los Angeles. Its struggling screenwriter hero (Ron Leibman) is visited by his teenage daughter (Dinah Manoff) whom he has not seen since leaving her and her mother behind years before.

Simon struck it rich one more time in the seventies, with the book for the 1979 mini-musical, *They're Playing Our Song* (1,082 performances), based on the love affair of songwriters Marvin Hamlisch and Carole Bayer Sager; it made Broadway stars of Lucie Arnaz and Robert Klein.

Transitional Dramatists

If the decade was disappointing for the older dramatists, aside from Simon, it was distinguished by the infusion of vitality and talent from a considerable number of new playwrights. Apart from several who had first appeared on the scene in the late sixties, this was as exciting and promising a group as any decade in the recent past had produced. Using Broadway as a convenient if not always artistically defensible yardstick, the presence may be noted of several new writers who made the bright lights there shine with renewed effulgence. However, some of the best of the lot never did arrive on Broadway and several who did found the waters too rough and chilly for survival. On the whole, Broadway was getting ever more unreceptive to the efforts of creative dramatists writing, however untraditionally, in the traditional modes of comedy and drama. As noted, these playwrights were able to survive—probably even to come into existence—only because of the presence of the non-profit Off- and Off Off-Broadway theatres and their regional counterparts. Their plays were often too linguistically idiosyncratic or too uniquely formalistic in method to be of much interest to a mass audience forced to pay exorbitant sums to see what they hoped would offer "sure-fire entertainment." They wanted tears at their drama, laughs at their comedies, and escape from their problems. Only a few of the playwrights were attempting to write in that commercial mode, so, to fill the vacuum, Broadway succumbed to musical mania, revival rapture, and "Simon Says." Even within this cautionary atmosphere, a few thoughtful American plays captured Broadway and Off-Broadway's plaudits and profits.

Several of the "new" playwrights might, from a chronological point of view, be considered "transitional"; they sprouted buds in the sixties, a few even sending forth a juicy piece or two of fruit, but looked to the seventies as a period of ripening and fulfillment. Most were between thirty and forty years old for the bulk of the decade. Among the less successful of these transitional writers we may count Mart Crowley, Leonard Melfi, and Jean-Claude Van Itallie. More of an impact was made, however, by Tom Eyen, Israel Horovitz, Paul Zindel, John Ford Noonan, John Guare, Lanford Wilson, and Sam Shepard.

Eyen, a popular Off Off denizen in the sixties, became a media celebrity as director and author with his four Off-Broadway productions, beginning with the hit *The Dirtiest Show in Town*. A nudity and sex-oriented anti-Establishment revue, this work used the dangers of air, water, and "mind" pollution as its focus. Like most of Eyen's work, it moved to Off-Broadway from La Mama where Eyen ran a resident group called the Theatre of the Eye Company.

During the rest of the decade audiences were amused by Eyen's campy spoofs, *Why Hanna's Skirt Won't Stay Down*, which received several stagings, *Women Behind Bars*, in which the transvestite Divine made a splash, and *The Neon Woman*, also featuring Divine.

Israel Horovitz had emerged in the previous decade with several interesting works; his seventies output was largely confined to a healthy number of Off Off productions, but Off-Broadway saw his one-acts pair, *Acrobats* and *Line*, and *The Primary English Class*. In the latter, a black comedy, Diane Keaton played an inexperienced young teacher coping with the problems of teaching English to a night-school class of foreigners.

The Effect of Gamma Rays on Man-in-the-Moon Marigolds had been one of the best new Off-Broadway plays of the late sixties, but its author, Paul Zindel, did not follow it with any important work in the seventies. His three Broadway plays, all about the malaise of contemporary women, *And Miss Reardon Drinks a Little*, *The Secret Affairs of Mildred Wild*, and *Ladies at the Alamo*, were failures. The most popular was the first, about three spinster schoolteacher sisters (Estelle Parsons, Julie Harris, and Nancy Marchand) on Staten Island and the efforts of two of them to determine whether they should send the third to a mental home.

A success Off-Broadway in 1969 had been *The Year Boston Won the Pennant*, by young John Ford Noonan. An imaginative playwright with a gift for off-center plots and highly enriched dialogue, Noonan provided New York with three Off-Broadway plays in the decade. The last, *A Coupla White Chicks Sitting Around Talking* (440 performances), was a critical and popular success. This two-character comedy concerned the invasion of a loud and friendly new neighbor (Eileen Brennan) from Texas into the squeaky-clean suburban kitchen of a young married woman (Susan Sarandon) with a compulsive drive for orderliness. The brassy Texan succeeds in cracking the uptight young matron's prim exterior and getting her to let loose.

John Guare had been represented by two plays in the late sixties; in the seventies he had a 342-performance Off-Broadway hit followed by a series of failures, three Off-Broadway and one on. The hit was the surrealistic black farce, *The House of Blue Leaves*, winner of the New York Drama Critics Circle Award and an Obie. Sometimes incoherent, sometimes brilliantly insightful, this loony tunes cartoon about social misfits in a Queens apartment belonging to a zookeeper (Harold Gould) who hopes to become a Hollywood songwriter was forced to close when its playhouse burned down.

It was Lanford Wilson and Sam Shepard who made the transition into the new decade most successfully and emerged as the nation's most widely respected playwrights in the thirty- to forty-year-old age range (Wilson was born in 1937, Shepard in 1943). These men share several similarities: their rural upbringings (Wilson was raised in Lebanon, Missouri; Shepard, born near Chicago, was brought up on a ranch in Duarte, near Los Angeles); their development in the "underground" Off Off world of Caffe Cino and Theatre Genesis in the sixties; their extreme fecundity (by the end of the decade Wilson had written about forty plays, the majority one-acters, while Shepard's agent acknowledged about thirty, though some claimed he had written about one hundred); their each having been awarded the Pulitzer Prize (Wilson in 1980 for *Talley's Folly*, Shepard a year before for *Buried Child*); each is said to be the most frequently produced modern American playwright after Tennessee Williams; each is associated with a specific theatre company and director (Wilson, since 1969, with New York's Circle Rep, which he co-founded, and its director, Marshall W. Mason; Shepard, since 1976 with San Francisco's Magic Theatre and the director Robert Woodruff); and, among other things, a concern in their plays with capturing a vision of America's lost innocence in the face of modern life's brutalities. Each also in his later works has shown a strong attraction for family themes, although Shepard's work tends toward the more negative implications of his themes, while Wilson has been taking an ever more positive, if not romantic, approach to his characters and situations. There is little hope at the end of a Shepard drama; Wilson offers his audience an emotional and moral uplift. Both are also seriously concerned with non-urban backgrounds, with life on farms, in small towns, and wherever the sense of "an America that once was" can somehow be imagined.

Wilson, by the decade's end, was the more commercially acceptable of the two, with three Broadway productions, two of them in the late sixties. He also had written the third longest-running straight play in Off-Broadway history, *The Hot l Baltimore*.

Shepard, by contrast, for all the words spilled about him in the media, many of them related to his newfound success as a screen star, remained a coterie playwright in New York. Wilson, like Shepard, had written many early plays in an opaque experimental style, but Shepard remained immersed in this poetically suggestive, surrealistic vein far longer; consequently, he alienated those who felt his writing was too restricted and ambiguous for broad acceptance and appreciation. The brilliance of his mythic, surrealistic, and poetic conceptualizations was not strong enough to overcome the antipathy of commercial producers toward his work. By 1980, his only play approximating a Broadway presentation had been the poorly received *Operation Sidewinder*, done at the close of the previous decade by the Lincoln Center Repertory Company. His works are staples of the more adventurous Off Off and resident theatres, although he did have a commercial mounting of *Buried Child*. This work, and his one other play of the late seventies, *Curse of the Starving Class*, revealed a shift toward a more accessible, if nevertheless symbolic, even mystical, type of writing; also, the family-oriented themes of these works brought them more closely into the tradition of mainline dramaturgy. Most admirers found these works the apex of Shepard's work thus far, and they helped convince a growing number of critics that Shepard may be the premier contemporary American dramatist. Others, notably Walter Kerr, Shepard's best-known nemesis, remained unimpressed. "With Mr. Shepard," he complained, "I am always at arm's length, elbowed away from the action, refused entry to the people."[5]

Shepard's themes, noted Robert Coe, encompass "the Old West, B pictures, melodramas, rock-and-roll, the occult, science fiction, detective novels, criminology and revolution."[6] His major works of the seventies mirror most of these concerns. These plays were *The Tooth of Crime*, *Killer's Head* and *Action*, *Seduced*, *Tongues* and *Savage/Love*, and the plays already mentioned.

Curse of the Starving Class was the first of Shepard's works written after an extended period spent in England, where it was produced in 1977, a year before New York saw it. Its fuzzy plot tells of a bizarre California farm family—the boozing father, his wife, and their teenage son and daughter—living on an increasingly barren and unproductive farm, proclaiming themselves non-members of the "starving class," while an empty ice box metaphorically contradicts them by suggesting their hunger for happiness and contentment. The staging mingled surface naturalism with non-illusionistic elements, including soliloquies spoken to a solo saxophone jazz accompaniment.

The Pulitzer Prize-winning 152-performance *Buried Child* was so immediate a critical success when it first appeared Off Off that it moved quickly to a commercial version Off-Broadway. There were, however, a hardcore few who refused to acknowledge its values. In *Buried Child* we see another grotesque farm family—the drunken, hate-filled father, his wife, their two demented sons, and a grandson who returns to the decaying Illinois homestead with his girl friend. The grandson sets off by his presence a series of odd, apparently unmotivated actions that reveal the family's rotting innards. Filled with images of incest, barrenness and fertility, murder, and Pinteresque menace, the play closely resembles in style the naturalistic/surrealistic blend of its immediate predecessor.

Shepard did not set foot in New York from 1976 through the end of the decade, refusing to return even for the productions of his plays. Lanford Wilson, however, has become very much a New Yorker, especially because of the symbiotic relationship he shares with the Circle Rep where he can watch his plays take shape under the company's developmental program. He, like about a dozen others, is a resident playwright there, and the company's fame rests largely on his contributions to it. Wilson's plays occur in both rural and urban locales, although the former took precedence in his later work of the decade, plays that reflect his roots in Lebanon, Missouri. Wilson's principal plays of the seventies are *The Hot l Baltimore*, *The Mound Builders*, *Serenading Louie*, the one-act *Brontosaurus*, *Fifth of July*, and *Talley's Folly*. The first and the latter two were the most successful.

The Hot l Baltimore (the "Hot l" is the word "Hotel" with a letter missing, as in a broken electric sign) came after a year and a half during which writer's block prevented the productive dramatist from producing a new play. It catapulted the unknown Circle Rep (then Off Off) to celebrity when its vast success led to a commercial staging (1,166 performances) at the Circle in the Square (downtown). The play is set in a seedy Baltimore hotel, soon to be razed, where a fascinating assortment of semi-derelict characters reside, including several amusing and sentimentally attractive prostitutes. Instead of plot, it concentrates on mood, comic dialogue, character revelation, and poignant longing for an illusory American landscape. The New York Drama Critics Circle Award for best American play of the year was bestowed on it, among other prizes.

Fifth of July (158 performances Off-Broadway; 511 on Broadway) was the first in a trilogy of plays the most recent of which (*A Tale Told*) appeared in 1981. This Chekhovian comedy tells of a family, the Talleys, living in rural Missouri in the late seventies. Winner of the coveted Pulitzer Prize, its successful Off-Broadway production garnered it a Broadway staging that came only in 1980, after the second play in the series already had been produced Off- and then on Broadway. For several months in late 1980, theatregoers could see both *Talley's Folly* and *Fifth of July* at nearby Broadway playhouses. The plays are separated in time by thirty-three years, and only Sally Talley appears in both. In *Fifth of July* she is an elderly lady who has lost her husband, Matt, the Jewish accountant from St. Louis whose wooing of her forms the romantic plot of the charming two-character *Talley's Folly*. She returns from California to the Talley home to bury her late husband's ashes (they are kept in a candy box), and encounters members of her family and their friends from college days as Berkeley radicals. William Hurt first played the role of Kenneth Talley, a Vietnam vet whose wooden legs are replacements for those lost in battle. On Broadway, Christopher Reeve proved less apt at the role than his predecessor. A much noted ingredient in the play is the straightforward and matter-of-fact depiction of the homosexual love relationship of Kenny and Jed Jenkins (Jeff Daniels). Wilson's penchant for realistic and accurately limned dialogue and characters made a great impact on the critics, but there was considerable dissatisfaction with the rambling dramatic structure and lack of focus.

Talley's Folly (44 performances Off-Broadway; 277 on) was the decade's ultimate romance, set on a moonlit summer night at a Lebanon boathouse in 1944. Judd Hirsch was exceptional as the exuberant Matt Friedman pursuing the reluctant spinster of Trish Hawkins.

New Dramatists of the Seventies

There remains a group of American playwrights whose contributions may be thought of as wholly within the seventies, although one or two did produce a promising earlier work. Some of these playwrights were too young to have created more than one or two interesting plays that saw New

York production, others were more prolific. Because it has become customary to consider black playwrights and female playwrights as belonging to distinct categories, they are discussed in subsequent sections.

In terms of total output, consistency of critical acceptance, and representation by at least one Broadway production, the most conspicuous new arrivals were the two Davids, Rabe and Mamet, as well as Mark Medoff, Michael Weller, and Bernard Slade.

Rabe, a native of Dubuque, Iowa, came to prominence in 1971 when Joseph Papp produced his play about a sad-sack dog soldier seeking his identity during the Vietnam War, *The Basic Training of Pavlo Hummel*. It proved a resoundingly successful first play and was even given a major Broadway revival starring Al Pacino later in the decade. Rabe followed it the same year with an even more impressive work, *Sticks and Bones*, about a returning blind Vietnam vet, his Ozzie and Harriet-like family of insensitive cardboard cutouts who are unable to understand the horror of what he's been through, and a ghostly reminder of his Asian experiences who follows him around unseen to all but him. *Sticks and Bones* moved from Off-Broadway's Public Theatre to Broadway and won the Tony for the best new play of 1972.

Rabe met with failure on his next two outings, *The Orphan* and *Boom Boom Room* (later revised and retitled *In the Boom Boom Room*), but his star rose once more with the 1976 Mitzi E. Newhouse Theatre mounting of *Streamers*, a powerful and violent drama about men in a boot camp barracks awaiting assignment to Vietnam. Described as the third in Rabe's trilogy of Vietnam plays, it depicted a group of young soldiers, their boisterous sergeants, and a walking time bomb of a black G.I. (Dorian Harewood) who erupts in a meaningless act of ferocity against another man. *Streamers* won several prizes, including the New York Drama Critics Circle Award. After *Streamers* no new Rabe play was seen locally for the rest of the decade.

David Mamet, a Chicago playwright, scored with a series of plays in which a remarkable facility for expressing the patterns of conversational speech was employed against a number of original backgrounds. Off-Broadway's successful *Sexual Perversity in Chicago* was a serio-comic examination of current male-female mating practices, using heavy doses of profanity and told in a series of blackouts, on a bill shared by the one-act *Duck Variations*. Mamet had another Off-Broadway hit with the two-character *A Life in the Theatre*, a delightful piece that looks at the actor's life onstage and backstage through the experiences and relationship of a mature thespian (Ellis Rabb) and a younger one (Peter Evans). Of the three subsequent Mamet plays, the greatest favor accrued to *American Buffalo*, starring Robert Duvall. During the early eighties Al Pacino found a meal ticket in his several revivals of the play. In it, Mamet assaulted Broadway theatregoers with a barrage of vulgar language so creatively managed that some critics thought they were hearing a new kind of prose-poetry. This three-man play, set in a junk store, revealed a trio of petty hoods plotting a robbery they never do pull off. Dialogue, character, and atmosphere were all.

Mark Medoff had three important works shown in New York. Medoff was chairman of the drama department and resident playwright of New Mexico State University; his local and university experiences colored his writing in such Off-Broadway plays as the Obie-winning, 302-performance *When You Comin' Back, Red Ryder?* and *The Wager.* In the former, a melodramatic situation unfolds in a setting reminiscent of Robert E. Sherwood's *Petrified Forest* as an aggressive, armed, well-educated gun-runner (Kevin Conway) and his girl friend terrorize the customers and staff at a New Mexico roadside diner. Its stinging dialogue and disturbing violence held the audience's attention tightly.

The dramatist scored a coup in 1980 when he came up with *Children of a Lesser God* (887 performances), a Tony winner that originated under Gordon Davidson's direction in Los Angeles. This moving drama was inspired by the playwright's meeting deaf actress Phyllis Frelich in 1978 at the University of Rhode Island. When Frelich informed him that there were no regular plays for deaf actors, he agreed to write one. Frelich and her hearing husband, Robert Steinberg, and their children went out to New Mexico to live with Medoff and his family as he wrote the play, based largely on the emotional experiences, if not the factual ones, of the actress and her scene designer/actor husband.

Children of a Lesser God is a stirring story about the difficulties in the relationship between a hearing teacher of the deaf (John Rubinstein) and an embittered deaf woman (Frelich) who refuses to buy the standards of the "normal" world about what she should accept in life. The unusual sight of actors, several of them truly deaf, signing throughout much of the dialogue, was one of the key constituents in this worthwhile play's production.

Moonchildren was Michael Weller's introduction to the decade, arriving on Broadway in a highly touted version from Washington, D.C.'s Arena Stage. An earlier form of the play called *Cancer* had been produced in London at the Royal Court Theatre. In New York it achieved quite favorable reviews yet somehow failed to attract audiences and had to close after two weeks. It explores the lives of a group of seven eccentric college students sharing a rundown apartment near their university in the late sixties. Sex, war, cancer, and peace marches make up the topics of their conversation. Perhaps it was too late for those in the original, but *Moonchildren* was revived with a new cast Off-Broadway only a little over a year later (1973) and clicked so well (394 performances) under a new director that its believers were vindicated.

Weller was represented by several other works during the seventies— *More Than You Deserve, Fishing,* and *Loose Ends*—but only the latter, staged at the uptown Circle in the Square, appealed to the critics. It had first been seen at the Arena. In this 284-performance play Weller presented the closely observed relationship over nine years of two young lovers—later spouses—and their eventual breakup. It was a noble effort, outstandingly acted by Kevin Kline and Roxanne Hart.

The last of the new playwriting powerhouses was a middle-aged man when he turned to writing for the stage. Bernard Slade, born in Canada, had for years been ensconced as a topflight Hollywood screen and TV writer before he decided to try his hand at commercial dramaturgy. It was not long before he had written three Broadway comedy hits. His work often has been termed slick and superficial; Slade's plays, however, provide not only good escapist entertainment but widely appealing, if simplified, perceptions about contemporary human values.

His first success was *Same Time, Next Year*, a two-character comedy that reached 1,453 performances, making it the longest-running straight play of the decade and the ninth longest-running Broadway hit in history. Charles Grodin and Ellen Burstyn were the first of many stars to play the roles of the married man and woman who meet at a motel in California. They begin an affair that continues one weekend a year for the next twenty-five years. Touched with many felicitous laugh lines and grounded on a bedrock of sentimentalities, the play rarely went for cheap guffaws or insulted the audience's intelligence.

Slade returned, but not as strongly, with the more moderately esteemed *Tribute*, a piece that totaled 212 performances largely on the strength of an excellent job by its popular star, Jack Lemmon, back on Broadway after nearly two decades. Lemmon's presence allowed the show to pay off its backers on opening night. He played a beloved clown of a press agent, Scottie Templeton, who is dying from leukemia but confronts his impending demise with typically self-deprecating humor.

The final Slade play of the seventies, which received mixed reviews, was the hit *Romantic Comedy* (396 performances). The somewhat implausible plot cast Anthony Perkins as a successful playwright and Mia Farrow as his kookie new collaborator. They have a profitable career together, but it takes fourteen years before they start up a romantic relationship.

Other important new dramatists of the decade with two or more major productions include Albert Innaurato, Louis La Russo II, Thomas Babe, Jack Heifner, Milan Stitt, Isaac Bashevis Singer, Martin Sherman, Steve Tesich, Jonathan Reynolds, Dennis Reardon, Christopher Durang, Michael Sawyer, A. R. Gurney, Romulus Linney, Jay Broad, Frank Chin, Patrick Meyers, and John Bishop. Space allows only brief discussion of the first eight.

Albert Innaurato served as a resident playwright at the Circle Rep and the New York Shakespeare Festival. He had the biggest commercial success of the writers named when his *Gemini* struck Broadway paydirt after development in productions on Long Island, Off Off, and Off-Broadway. It ran at the Little Theatre for 1,819 performances, despite middling reviews. *Gemini* is a riotous, exaggerated ethnic comedy in the self-described "bizarre" mode of the author's early work. In it several of his recurring themes are obvious: obesity, sexual ambivalence, the sense of rejection suffered by the lonely, and the conflict between WASP society at large and the insulated subculture of South Philadelphia working-class Italian-Americans. The play offers a cross-section of straight and far-out character types as seen during a birthday party for a twenty-one-year-old Harvard student thrown for him in their tenement backyard by his father (Danny Aiello).

Innaurato also gained attention with his one-act, *The Transfiguration of Benno Blimpie*, and the full-length *Ulysses in Traction*, both Off-Broadway.

Another writer whose milieu is normally that of working-class Italian Americans (usually from Hoboken) is Louis La Russo II, who had more plays on Broadway than any newcomer. These were *Lamppost Reunion*, *Wheelbarrow Closers*, and *Knockout*. Off-Broadway La Russo saw mountings of *Momma's Little Angels* and *Marlon Brando Sat Right Here*. The most successful (154 performances) was *Knockout*, a boxing drama in which a well staged grudge match formed an important part of the action. La Russo's plays are written in a tough-talking, frequently melodramatic and sentimental slice-of-life style that has been likened to that of grade B movies of the forties. Danny Aiello starred in three of them.

A couple of new playwrights were favored by Off-Broadway stagings of a prolific sequence of works, but were not able to interest Broadway producers in their wares. The most critically fortunate of them was Thomas Babe, who had five ambitious and thematically varied dramas mounted, all of them by the Public Theatre, and all in the decade's second half. Babe's materials were eclectic, ranging from the subject of a rock star in *Kid Champion* to the Civil War in *Rebel Women* to the world of contemporary detectives in *A Prayer for My Daughter* to the trial of labor organizer Joe Hill in *Salt Lake City Skyline*. In 1979 he enjoyed a fine achievement with his all-female play *Taken in Marriage*, which employed a stellar cast including Meryl Streep, Colleen Dewhurst, and Elizabeth Wilson, among others. It pictured a bride-to-be, her relatives, and a singer/stripper hired (as a joke) to entertain at the wedding; while waiting for the wedding rehearsal to begin (it never does), the women reveal, under the stripper's prodding, their personal problems.

Jack Heifner hit it big with *Vanities*, a tremendously popular bitchy comedy-drama about three vacuous Texas belles, seen at three stages of their lives: from 1963 high school cheerleaders to 1968 college sorority sisters to 1974 matrons. All three were based on actual girls Heifner had known in his Lone Star State youth. *Vanities* moved from a $200 Off Off production to a showing at Huntington, Long Island's Performing Arts Foundation, to a commercial Off-Broadway version in which, despite mixed reviews, it became the longest-running straight play ever in that venue (1,785 performances). Within that period it gave rise to over 200 productions worldwide and became America's most produced play between 1977 and 1979. Heifner's only other offering was an unsuccessful pair of one-acts, *Porch/Patio*.

Milan Stitt's *The Runner Stumbles*, a play he had worked on for close to a decade, was one of the more vital dramas of the period and ran for 191 performances on Broadway. It was later revived by the Circle Rep. *The Runner Stumbles* is a courtroom drama using flashbacks to investigate the relationship between a priest and a nun living in an isolated Michigan community, and the facts behind the nun's murder. Stitt's *Back in the Race*, however, was an Off-Broadway disappointment.

In the seventies famed Yiddish fiction writer and Nobel Prize winner Isaac Bashevis Singer turned to writing plays. His two offerings were both on Broadway, each done in collaboration with another author. On *Yentl, the Yeshivah Boy*, he worked with Leah Napolin to adapt one of his own short stories. Eve Friedman aided the aged writer with another adaptation, *Teibele and Her Demon*. Both were tales of life and love among the village Jews of old Poland, but only the former excited continued interest.

Yentl first appeared at the Chelsea Theatre and then, in a revised and shortened version, was moved to Broadway for 224 performances. It made a star out of young Tovah Feldshuh who played the part of a girl who circumvents Jewish proscriptions about females becoming scholars by dressing as a boy and entering the Yeshivah in that guise. Soon she is embroiled in a love affair with another student (John Shea) and even gets involved in a marriage to the student's girl friend.

The ignominy of a one-performance flop greeted Martin Sherman's first play, *Cracks*, but his 1979 *Bent*, starring Richard Gere and David Dukes, made an impression following its London success with Ian McKellen. This controversial piece dealt with the historical period of the Holocaust from the unusual perspective of the persecution endured by homosexuals in Nazi Germany. The harrowing plight of one such individual, his refusal to acknowledge his sexual deviancy, his attachment to another homosexual in the confines of a concentration camp, and his ultimate acceptance of his nature were materials provocative enough to help this play achieve 241 performances.

About a dozen new playwrights made a strong impact on the basis of only one play. Most appeared too late in the decade to do more than show promise for future work in the eighties, but Jason Miller, who is also an actor, saw his *That Championship Season* done in 1972 and did not subsequently provide another play. This multi-award-winning drama, which moved to Broadway from the Public, was one of the most outstanding successes among new American plays. It ran for 834 performances and won the New York Drama Critics Circle Award, the Pulitzer, the Tony, and others. The play is a naturalistic, profanity-riddled story about a group of small-town Pennsylvania men who gather for a reunion twenty years after their high school team, using dirty tactics, won a basketball trophy. Miller reveals the cynicism and despair that has pervaded each of their lives as old dreams prove present failures. Director A. J. Antoon carved a gorgeous ensemble performance out of the actors' work in this drama.

Also in 1972 was Bob Randall's *6 Rms Rv VW* (247 performances), a popular Broadway comedy starring Jerry Orbach and Jane Alexander about a pair of New Yorkers who meet while inspecting an apartment for rent. They get locked in together, have a brief fling, but return to their respective spouses at the end. Randall failed to offer another play, but he did write the critically panned book for the successful musical *The Magic Show*.

Famous novelist Kurt Vonnegut, Jr., tried his hand at dramaturgy early in the decade with some success; the play was *Happy Birthday, Wanda June*, which moved from Off-Broadway to on during the 1970 Off-Broadway actors' strike. This comedy was a modern version of the final section of the *Odyssey*, only here we had a Hemingway-like husband (Kevin McCarthy) returning from the wilds of the jungle to the mixed-up wife (Marsha Mason) he left behind.

One of the best-loved comedies was the 1976 *Sly Fox* (495 performances) by TV-writer Larry Gelbart (*M*A*S*H*), whose first New York play this was although he had written the triumphantly funny book for the 1962 musical *A Funny Thing Happened on the Way to the Forum*. In *Sly Fox* he updated Ben Jonson's Jacobean study of venality, *Volpone*, to a late-nineteenth-century San Francisco setting and gave star George C. Scott an opportunity to display rarely seen comic gifts.

Preston Jones promised to be a powerful new force in American theatre, according to the hype about him emanating from Dallas and from Washington, D.C., where his *A Texas Trilogy* was performed to acclaim before coming to New York. This trio of tenuously linked full-length comedy-dramas about life in a small Texas town was performed in repertory on alternate nights, never a very effective idea for Broadway's commercial maelstrom (as Alan Ayckbourn's British trio, *The Norman Conquests*, also learned). The trilogy idea, however, did not damage this promising author's debut as much as did mediocre reviews, although some thought the work outstanding. Unfortunately, Jones died before another test of his skills could be mounted.

Michael Cristofer, a talented young actor, scored highly with *The Shadow Box*, originally titled *News from the City of Hope*. It was one of Broadway's more successful treatments (315 performances) of the subject of mortal illness and death. It came to New York in a splendid Gordon Davidson staging imported from Los Angeles and went on to snare both the Tony and the Pulitzer. As with all serious works that do well on Broadway, it had its outspoken critics, but the play appealed to audiences normally uninterested in such morbid themes. *The Shadow Box* is leavened with a generous amount of laughs, a necessary ingredient in plays of this sort. The title, as the author told an interviewer, comes from the way a shadow box "delineates a tiny scene and throws light on it so you can see it more clearly" and because of its suggestion of "shadow-boxing," i.e. "fighting an unseen enemy."[7]

Cristofer's drama, which took five years to get produced, takes place at a rustic sanitorium for terminally ill cancer patients and shows how three widely varying individuals—a laborer, a homosexual writer, and an old lady—and their loved ones manage to live in the face of impending death.

Robert Patrick is one of New York's most prolific playwrights. His many plays (at least 125 by 1975) were regularly done Off Off, and he was, in a sense, a self-proclaimed mayor of the Off Off scene via his bi-weekly column in the now-defunct theatre newspaper *Other Stages*. *Kennedy's Children*, Patrick's sole mainstream production, however, had to be produced Off Off and in a hit version in London, as well as in several European mountings, before it could earn a showing on Broadway. This play is a barroom saga set in Phebe's, the Off Off mecca on the Bowery and East Fourth Street, where Patrick often hung out. Here, an assortment of five sixties characters drink up and spew forth, in a series of monologues (there is no dialogue per se), their dreams, anguish, and crushed ideals. The local critics were divided and the play folded in two months.

It is not common for a play to be produced on Broadway, end its run, and then come back for another stab a year later, with the same stars, but Ernest Thompson's first play, *On Golden Pond*, had just that experience. It had moved to Broadway from the Off Off-Broadway Hudson Guild and opened in late February 1978 as the first production of the newly renovated New Apollo Theatre, used for years as a movie grind house. The show closed in June and reopened in September 1979, at the smaller Century, under new producers.

One of the decade's considerable number of plays about the elderly, it shows the deep affection of a husband and wife (Tom Aldredge and Frances Sternhagen) whose marriage of forty-eight years will soon end because the eighty-year-old husband is dying, a fact he accepts with a touching mixture of rage and wit. The play achieved 126 performances in its first attempt, and added another 252 in its second.

D. L. Coburn also found a happy reception for his play about the aged, but his characters were not as emotionally heartwarming as were Thompson's. Coburn's two-character, 517-performance, comedy hit, *The Gin Game*, his Pulitzer Prize-winning first play, showed a picture of the growing relationship between two outsiders at a home for the aged, with the woman (Jessica Tandy) continually beating the increasingly grumpy man (Hume Cronyn) at gin rummy.

Another first play, one that startled Broadway by its potent ability to draw audiences despite the somberness of its subject, was Bernard Pomerance's *The Elephant Man* (916 performances). Pomerance is an

American writer who lives in England, where this play was first produced. Before it brought him international recognition he was committed to working with a small, politically oriented, theatre group, the Foco Novo. Set in the fogbound grayness of late nineteenth-century London, *The Elephant Man* relates the true story of one of history's most pitiful freaks, John Merrick (Philip Anglim), a man with a grotesque skin and bone condition that led to his being exhibited in cheap side shows until he was rescued by a sympathetic doctor, Frederick Treves (Kevin Conway). Treves placed Merrick in a London hospital and although unable to cure him, made him relatively comfortable; the doctor's efforts to get the artistically sensitive Merrick to adapt to conventional social patterns were doomed to heart-rending failure. To play him, Anglim dispensed with elaborate makeup by forcing his physique into the unnatural positions Merrick himself assumed against his will. The play garnered the Tony and the New York Drama Critics Circle Award.

An ethnic group which came forward with several exciting new dramatic voices in the seventies was the Hispanic. From this culture emerged the Puerto Rican playwright Miguel Pinero, whose *Short Eyes*, winner of the New York Drama Critics Circle Award, shocked many but held them spellbound with its cuttingly brutal revelation of life in the dayroom of a New York prison. Language as crude as had ever been heard on a stage filled the air in this penetrating look at the way men pass their time in jail. Pinero was himself an ex-con who, even after he gained fame as a playwright, continued to get in trouble with the law.

Like several other works of the last two decades, *Short Eyes* was largely a product of cooperative developmental creation, using a group of actors doing improvisations under a director's supervision with the dramatist shaping the results into a play. The group here was The Family, composed of members of a workshop founded at the Bedford Hills Correctional Facility by professional director Marvin Camillo. *Short Eyes* went from an Off Off to an Off- to a full Broadway mounting when it moved to the pristine surroundings of the Vivian Beaumont.

The only other mainstream Hispanic production was the work of Los Angeles Chicano playwright/director Luis Valdez, who, throughout the sixties and the seventies, was intimately involved in developing agit-prop theatrical works designed for California's migrant farm worker population. His Teatro Campesino company did one of these pieces for the Chelsea in 1974, but Valdez' pre-eminent contribution was the play-with-music *Zoot Suit*, a hit at the Mark Taper, but a Broadway flop. It was based on a real race-prejudice incident among early 1940s Los Angeles Chicanos, and employed a highly theatrical style mixed with documentary techniques.

Other critically lauded one-shot offerings on Broadway were Tom Topor's psychological courtroom drama, *Nuts*; Abe Polsky's *Devour the Snow*, about nineteenth-century pioneers accused of cannibalism; Eric

Bentley's *Are You Now or Have You Ever Been?*, also seen Off-Broadway, about the McCarthy subcommittee hearings of the fifties; and David Berry's *G. R. Point*, first seen Off-Broadway, dealing with the members of a Vietnam Graves Registration Unit. Off-Broadway audiences applauded Ralph Pape's *Say Goodnight, Gracie*, a 417-performance comedy hit about a group of thirty year olds gathered in an East Village apartment before a high school reunion; Peter Parnell's *The Sorrows of Stephen*, a romantic comedy concerning a wistful young New Yorker and his troubles with women; Edward Moore's barroom romance, *The Sea Horse*; Dick Goldberg's *Family Business*, about the difficulties of several brothers in handling the family estate after their father's death; and James Lapine's comic sketches of Jewish family life, *Table Settings*.

Black Playwrights

So far, almost all the playwrights looked at have been white. The contribution of black dramatists, however, was so dynamic, sudden, and significant that it has been thought best to discuss it as a single phenomenon so as to express its total impact more effectively and help to focus on its unique accomplishment.

The intensity of black theatrical activity in the seventies would have seemed exaggerated if described by some crystal gazer two decades earlier. There had been so little black presence in the mainstream theatre until 1957 brought Lorraine Hansberry's *A Raisin in the Sun* to Broadway that her play might, in the long run, have appeared anomalous. But by the 1960s there were definite stirrings as powerful new works by writers such as LeRoi Jones (Imamu Amiri Baraka) and James Baldwin followed Hansberry's lead, and as the explosion of civil rights activity and concerns turned black artists to the theatre in their search for an adequate means to communicate the social and political anguish felt by black Americans.

By the late sixties and early seventies the lid of the pressure cooker on black life had blown sky-high, and black-oriented theatre groups erupted everywhere. These ranged in theatrical approach from the exclusively black to the more integrated, from the polemically minded to the humanistic, from the ritualistic to the realistic, from the dramatic to the musical, from the narrow to the eclectic, from Off Off to Off-Broadway. Amas, the New Federal Theatre, the Negro Ensemble Company, the New Lafayette Theatre, the Billie Holiday Theatre, the National Black Theatre, the Richard Adler Center for Culture and Art, and the Urban Arts Corps were among the more visible and well known.

Black plays, musicals, and revues were, for the first time in history, becoming a prevailing force on and Off-Broadway. Black players acted in integrated productions of the classics, stars such as James Earl Jones and Ruby Dee playing Hamlet's parents (in different productions) with a white actor as their son. Blacks appeared in leading musical roles that might a few years before have gone to whites, such as Judas in *Jesus Christ Superstar*. Black versions of famous white musicals, like *Guys and Dolls* and *Hello, Dolly!* were popular, and one new show, *I Love My Wife*, went so far as to replace its white principals with black ones in the middle of its run. Joseph Papp organized a troupe of minority or "Third World" actors to play the classics. Numerous plays by white authors had important roles for blacks, not the old stereotypes of servants and other menials.

Serious black authors, such as Ed Bullins, Richard Wesley, Gus Edwards, Ntozake Shange, Steve Carter, Paul Carter Harrison, Philip Hayes Dean, Charles Fuller, Samm-Art Williams, Joseph Walker, Leslie E. Lee, Alice Childress, and others made audiences of all races laugh, weep, and think. Unhappily for these writers, however, the commercial theatre was more receptive to the musical than the dramatic skills of black artists, and the number of black plays that made it to Broadway, though greater than in past decades, was still not impressive; much of the best work remained in the non-profit institutional theatres that spawned them. Nine black-authored plays were produced on the Great "White" Way, but of them only *The River Niger, For Colored Girls Who Have Considered Suicide/When the Rainbow Is Enuf*, and *Home* had decent runs.

The rise in black theatre activity on and Off-Broadway led to a vast increase in black attendance. However, many black shows found largely white audiences in their seats. With more well-written plays for blacks to act in, direct, and design, their theatre skills were able to develop to new heights; nevertheless, since nearly all of these new works were produced at non-profit theatres, few actors could earn more than a subsistence level of income.

The voices of several of the major black writers of the sixties were largely stilled as a new generation arose to take their place. Aside from one Broadway revival and several Off Off productions, little was heard of the likes of Baraka, Baldwin, Lonnie Elder III, or Charles Gordone. Broadway did, however, briefly experience the ghostly sensation of seeing a "new" play by the late Lorraine Hansberry, who had died in 1964. This was *Les Blancs*, an unfinished work completed by Hansberry's husband, Robert Nemiroff. Set in an emerging African nation, the play proved still incomplete, but its provocative anti-colonialist foundations stirred considerable debate.

Ed Bullins is a Philadelphia-born playwright who came to public notice on the West Coast in the sixties and whose seventies creations helped to sustain and broaden an already well-established reputation. The new and old plays of this prolific writer seemed to be opening all the time in the early seventies, although he was at first leery of allowing mainline theatres to do his work. He preferred the protected environment of selected Off Off-Broadway theatres. By the decade's close Bullins' prodigious output included fifty-five plays, twenty-seven of them full-length. Five were seen in Off-Broadway mountings between 1971 and 1975.

Bullins was often a controversial figure in theatre and society, partly because of his publicly perceived persona as a Black Nationalist, and partly because of his striking indictment in his plays both of what he conceives to be the black bourgeoisie's complacency and of the insidious racism he discerns in American culture. Considered by many the leading black play-wright in America, he writes in a variety of styles, including naturalism, but often prefers a distanced manner employing direct-address monologues, overtly schematic non-linear plot development, and frequent jazz accompaniment.

Many of Bullins' plays are part of a projected twenty-play cycle in which the same characters appear at different stages of development. One charac-ter, Steve Benson, is believed to be the playwright's alter ego. Some of the new plays in the cycle were seen Off Off-Broadway. Those shown Off-Broadway were *In New England Winter*, *The Duplex*, and the one-act *The Corner*. Other important new Bullins plays were *House Party* and *The Taking of Miss Janie*. The latter was his most successful work. It is set in California and details the lives of a group of young blacks and their white acquaintances. Its story expresses Bullins' perception of white/black relations in the sixties through an allegorical plot in which the main character, the black poet, Monty, waits ten years for the chance to rape his close white friend, Janie. This controversial work earned the Drama Critics Circle Award and an Obie.

Bullins' penchant for controversy was never so visible as during the fiery debate he instigated in 1972 by his conduct during the production of his *Duplex*. Most of the critics enjoyed this work set in Southern California and focusing on the romantic relationship between Steve and Velma, the wife of a gangster. The play had first been done at Harlem's New Lafayette Theatre; it was transferred to the bastion of white theatregoing, Lincoln Center, in the intimate playhouse then known as the Forum. It was to be Bullins' first major exposure to New York audiences. Directing was Gilbert Moses, a distinguished black director who had previously staged other Bullins plays without incident.

Shortly before the play was to open, Bullins began to issue statements to the press protesting that the production was a "coon show" exploitation of his work. He later told an interviewer, "They turned the . . . thing into a burlesque show, complete with a 'Darktown Strutters Ball' kind of musical score and an overall mood that's straight out of 'Amos 'n Andy.' "[8] He was peeved, he said, not so much at the director and cast—"paid mercenaries"—but at Lincoln Center artistic director Jules Irving and his staff who condoned "this theatrical degradation of Black people." Having been to a dress and musical rehearsal he was convinced that Irving was conspiring to "sell to White people a negative image of Blacks as bestial types, fornicating all over the stage, acting like lustful clowns." Other white establishment theatres, he declared, meaning the American Place in particular, had been much more sincere in their treatment of his work.

When the playwright's protests failed to cancel the production, he took radical action. On Saturday night, March 18, 1972, he descended on Lincoln Center with the members of a playwrights' group, the New York Theatre Strategy, to decry the situation. This group avowed that they were seeking to alter the custom by which a dramatist's work becomes the director's property through the latter's interpretive mayhem. They felt the writer should have the last word in the staging of his plays. The group made their own mayhem when they were unable to buy tickets. Security guards and police had to be brought in to keep order as the group accosted the intermission crowds spilling out of a play at the adjacent Vivian Beaumont Theatre. Irving himself soon showed up for a lobby confrontation with the recalcitrant Bullins. The producer agreed to let the author address *The Duplex*'s audience during its intermission, but it seemed that it was now too late for that, as the second act had begun; Irving thereupon stopped the action in mid-performance and gave Bullins ten minutes to make his statement and leave. With the angry cast on stage behind him, Bullins delivered his harangue only to earn, in response, a loud denunciation of him by the spectators and company. When the shouting grew too loud and Bullins refused to depart, Irving ended the show and sent the spectators home.

According to subsequent explanations, Bullins had not come to a rehearsal of the play during its formative period, despite numerous invitations. He came only to have his picture taken at the photo call, shortly before public previews began, remained briefly at the music rehearsal (neglecting to make any comments), and immediately began to issue public pronouncements condemning the show. He also attended one dress rehearsal with his lawyer but left without making any statement. Soon after, at a special Dramatists Guild meeting, Bullins read his demands, his lawyer at his side, and refused to discuss his objections with Gilbert Moses. Irving wrote in the *New York Times*, "It is probably the first time in our knowledge that a producer and a director have sought the good offices of the Dramatists Guild in a fervent attempt to persuade a playwright to come to rehearsals and work on his own play."[9] In fact, wrote the producer, the contract proved that not only had Moses been hired at Bullins' insistence, the playwright also had required that Moses write the music for Bullins' words. As it turned out, the critics did not think the playwright's complaints held water. Ironically, three years later Moses directed Bullins' *The Taking of Miss Janie*.

Another productive black playwright was Chicago-born Philip Hayes Dean, who, with four dramas, was second only to Bullins. Dean received mixed notices but won wide respect and a Drama Desk Award for his *Sty of the Blind Pig*. It featured Moses Gunn as a blind street singer in a domestic drama set in a mid-fifties Chicago ghetto just before the great civil rights movement. This symbolic, enigmatic work was followed by two effective plays, *Freeman* and *Every Night When the Sun Goes Down*, and then the showcase for James Earl Jones' talents, *Paul Robeson*. The solo actor in this piece was supported by an onstage piano accompanist. It aroused considerable debate when a black group (the National Ad Hoc Committee to End the Crimes Against Paul Robeson), who felt the work was a distortion of Robeson's life, attempted to create a boycott of it. Factual accuracy in a play about the controversial left-wing performer-athlete-lawyer was deemed essential by those who wished his true story known. The fifty-six members of the committee included some very distinguished citizens; many of them, it developed, had never even seen the play they were protesting.

The attempted boycott raised cries of censorship, especially from Jones, who spoke to his audience from the stage on closing night. Despite the controversy, the critics held that *Paul Robeson* was a superficial depiction of the great man's story.

One of those who reportedly had a financial interest in *Paul Robeson* was the author of *For Colored Girls . . .* , Ntozake Shange (born Paulette Williams to a wealthy New Jersey surgeon and his wife; her African first name means "she who comes with her own things," and her surname means "one who walks like a lion"). Shange provided the theatre with a refreshing new voice and style in her three ambitious offerings. *For Colored Girls . . .* traveled the well-worn route of Off Off to Off- to Broadway where it became a hit and lasted for a surprising 742 performances in addition to the 120 it had enjoyed at the Public. Surprising, because this was no conventional play, but a "choreopoem," a series of poetic prose and verse monologues spoken and danced on a practically bare stage by a group of seven black actresses clad in simple dance costumes. The subject of the monologues was mainly the harsh treatment of black women by their husbands and lovers. (Shange had been married at nineteen, then divorced, and had attempted suicide four times afterwards.) The author was in the original cast when it debuted Off Off-Broadway and stayed with it until it reached Broadway.

Shange did not have similar luck with her next two outings, *A Photograph* and *Spell #7*, both at the Public; her final gift to the decade was her adaptation of Brecht's *Mother Courage*, transposed to the American Southwest with the characters depicted as pioneer blacks.

Lennox Brown, Steve Carter, Gus Edwards, Charles Fuller, Richard Wesley, and Judi Ann Mason were new black writers represented by two plays each. All showed promise, but Carter, Fuller, and Wesley received the greatest critical support. Carter's *Eden* moved from non-profit auspices to a 181-performance Off-Broadway run. This first play by the then forty-six-year-old writer was set among the members of a 1927 Manhattan family, the proud West Indian father of which must reckon with his children's differing values. Even better liked was his *Nevis Mountain Dew*, about a Queens family of West Indian background in 1954; they are celebrating the fiftieth birthday of the strong-willed father, who is confined to an iron lung with infantile paralysis.

Charles Fuller failed with his *In the Deepest Part of Sleep* but scored strongly with *The Brownsville Raid*, an exceptional drama based on an actual historical event occurring in Brownsville, Texas, in 1906. A black regiment stationed there and resented by the white citizenry was accused of shooting up the town; without a trial and on the flimsiest of evidence its 167 men were ordered by President Theodore Roosevelt to be dishonorably discharged.

Richard Wesley was selected by two separate committees as one of the most promising new playwrights of 1971-72. This was in response to his *The Black Terror*, a gripping and controversial work about the ethical dilemma faced by a black revolutionary who is ordered to slay a moderate black "in the interests of the revolution." Wesley's other work of the period included a one-acter, *Black Visions*, and *The Mighty Gents* (originally *The Last Street Play*). It came to Broadway, where it failed, after developmental work Off Off and in the regional theatre. The play drew heavy fire from some, but others commended it strongly as one of the decade's more powerful plays. *The Mighty Gents* was a loosely constructed play, with real and surreal elements of language, action, and music, about the plight of Frankie, war lord of an aging band of Newark street toughs, who comes to realize that he and his strung-out compatriots are on a one-way street to oblivion.

Black women were making inroads in all phases of theatre in the seventies, including playwriting. Ntozake Shange and Judi Ann Mason already have been mentioned. Several others were among that group of new black writers who had at least one mainstream play reach the boards. These were Alice Childress, J. E. Franklin, Aishah Rahman, Elaine Jackson, and Alexis De Veaux; men in the group were Ray Aranha, Bill Gunn, Paul Carter Harrison, Leslie E. Lee, Ron Milner, and Samm-Art Williams.

Of the women named, Alice Childress and J. E. Franklin provided the best-received new plays. Childress' *Wedding Band* (175 performances) is a touching piece, set in 1917, that tells of a long-term romance between a white baker (James Broderick) and a black woman (Ruby Dee) in a Southern city. The Theatre de Lys was the stage upon which Franklin garnered 234 showings of her *Black Girl*, a naturalistic play concerned with the difficulties faced by a teenage girl, living in a Texas ghetto, as she attempts to transcend her sordid environment.

Of the men listed, only Paul Carter Harrison did not get a Broadway level production, but his musical play, *The Great MacDaddy*, proved a popular Negro Ensemble Company production and merited a revival later in the decade. On Broadway there were Ray Aranha's *My Sister, My Sister*, Bill Gunn's *Black Picture Show*, Leslie E. Lee's *The First Breeze of Summer*, Ron

Milner's *What the Wine Sellers Buy*, and Samm-Art Williams' *Home*. This last named was the most successful (278 performances), moving to Broadway after its inception at the Negro Ensemble. It is a three-character play, highly episodic, in which the story of Cephus Miles (Charles Brown), North Carolina farmer, draft resister, country boy in the city, and finally farmer once more is told in a folksy style with two actresses playing all the other characters.

Women Playwrights

A remarkable feature of the black theatre activity of the seventies was, as reported above, the highly visible presence of women dramatists. These writers were still a minority in terms of their numerical ratio to black male playwrights, but the ratio was a lot healthier than that of white female playwrights to white male writers. The seventies may have been an age of flowering for the women's rights movement, but, despite gains in most other areas of American culture, successful women playwrights remained a distinctly hard-to-find species. Women were making major inroads as producers and designers but could not find the key to getting their plays produced. (Directing was another nut they had a hard time cracking.)

A study of fifty federally funded American theatres revealed that between 1969 and 1976 only 7 percent of the total output was written or directed by women.[10] A look at a typical seventies week in New York theatre, counting Off Off, Off, and Broadway, would have had an even lower percentage of female-authored and directed plays. Female dramatists complained that the work was there, but was simply not being mounted. They blamed the male power structure and a deep-seated fear of women as the principal reasons for their failure.

As the decade neared its close the outlook was thought to be improving. The problem was being addressed by groups of female theatre artists, and there was a growing public awareness of the situation. One reason for this was the creation of special programs, such as the American Place Theatre's Women's Project, headed by Julia Miles, for the development of new writing by women. There had been, as well, several specifically feminist theatre groups active during the decade, but these were mainly Off Off companies doing workshops. They were more developmental than mainstream, though a number of talented artists emerged from them. One of the most notable companies was the Women's Interart Center on the West Side, presided over by Margot Lewitin. Some feminist groups were concerned principally with work that investigated and revealed the dilemma of being a woman in a world run by men; often, they were lesbian oriented or in other ways agit-prop programs for the expression of a feminist political stance. The very topics of women playwrights turned the attention of certain critics—male and female—to the nature of what women were concerned with in their plays. For many, these dramas were too frequently about issues of feminist self-pity and special pleading, and had not yet gone beyond the excessively autobiographical into broader, more universal areas. Such concerns, in fact, were obvious in works like the musical *I'm Getting My Act Together and Taking It on the Road*, by Gretchen Cryer and Nancy Ford, but the straight plays done in mainstream productions were startlingly free of such overt attitudes. As will be seen, these plays normally concentrated on female characters but were rarely occupied with issues that any male dramatist might not have handled. The problems of being a woman in America, indeed, were often the subject of male playwrights.

During the entire period of the seventies only six American female-authored plays (apart from Shange's *For Colored Girls . . .*) were produced on Broadway and all were critical flops. Off-Broadway was a bit more receptive, with almost thirty plays, several of them well reviewed, and one a definite success. Off Off-Broadway was the most receptive, and several of the Off-Broadway playwrights had their plays done there as well. Among the most interesting and productive of the Off Off dramatists who appeared only in these theatres were Ann Commire, Roslyn Drexler, Helen Duberstein, Gloria Gonzales, Roma Greth, Marcia Haufrecht, Elizabeth Le Comte, JoAnne Akalaitis, Susan Miller, Susan Nanus, Elysse Nass, Jeannine O'Reilly, Sally Ordway, Marcia Sheiness, Marion Fredi Towbin, Jane Chambers, and Julie Bovasso.

Broadway offered little but negative responses to Jane Trahey's *Ring Round the Bathtub*, comedienne Joan Rivers' *Fun City*, co-written with her spouse, Edgar Rosenberg, Ann Burr's *Mert and Phil*, Judith Ross' *An Almost Perfect Person*, and Honor Moore's *Mourning Pictures*. The only mildly effective Broadway play by a woman (Shange's work excepted) was *Night Watch*, Lucille Fletcher's 120-performance psychological murder mystery about a neurotic insomniac (Joan Hackett) who may or may not have seen a gruesome corpse in the apartment window across the way from her own.

The Broadway crop of female-authored plays clearly was not going to make Lillian Hellman look to her laurels, nor were most of the dramas and comedies provided by the distaff side for Off-Broadway. Among previously recognized playwrights Maria Irene Fornes, Rochelle Owens, and Megan Terry saw their works done there, but only Fornes' *Fefu and Her Friends*, previously done Off Off, was considered noteworthy. This all-female play, directed by the playwright, placed eight friends in a New England house in 1935 and sought to reveal the personalities and relationships of the characters by the unusual expedient of moving the audience about during the action, taking them from room to room as the scenes proceeded. It succeeded in suggesting the sense of oneness shared by the women, but in the main was a critical failure. Fornes also had a one-acter, *Dr. Kheal*, produced.

Of the newer playwrights only Corinne Jacker and Tina Howe succeeded in getting more than one play produced. Jacker provided *My Life* and *Later*. More acclaim came to Howe for her *Museum* and *The Art of Dining*, both seen at the Public. In the former, a unique and often abstract comedy, forty characters played by eighteen actors visit a museum exhibit on its final day and display a variety of interestingly different responses to it. The latter transpires in a New Jersey gourmet restaurant; the action is the preparation and serving of the dishes ordered by the patrons who show up on a wintry night.

Among the approximately ten remaining female dramatists only two had significant plays to present. These were Wendy Wasserstein's *Uncommon Women and Others* and Marsha Norman's *Getting Out*. *Uncommon Women* depicts in flashback vignette form a group of five articulate and interesting women at a luncheon, remembering their final days at Mount Holyoke College six years earlier. Each character is artfully molded through revelatory language and behavior thereby vividly conveying the author's picture of the problems facing educated young women in the seventies. Structural flaws were apparent but the play gained critical affection.

The single most effective women's play—in fact, one of the strongest plays by any writer of the decade—was Marsha Norman's Obie-winning *Getting Out*. The playwright, a Louisville woman in her thirties, wrote a blistering drama about the life of Arlene, a female convict experiencing her first day out of the penitentiary. After premiering at the Actors Theatre of Louisville, it was staged by the non-profit Phoenix Theatre and then transferred to a commercial run at the Theatre de Lys, where it tallied 259 performances. *Getting Out* was based on Norman's actual experience in working with disturbed youngsters at the Kentucky Central State Hospital. Interviews with fifteen women prisoners helped her develop a realistic background for her characters' lives and motivations.

Getting Out employs two actresses (Pamela Reed and Susan Kingsley) to play the young Arlene and her older counterpart. The men in the play are all unpleasant types, but the playwright denied having an anti-male chip on her shoulder.

BRITISH PLAYWRIGHTS

The seventies was the decade of the so-called "British invasion"; had it not been for the large numbers of excellently performed, attended, and awarded British plays, Broadway would never have had the economic boom it experienced during these years. The trend toward importing the most widely appealing new English plays was part of the general pattern that saw New York producers scrambling for work already proven elsewhere under less crushing conditions. It was certainly good business sense to import ready-made works rather than to take a chance on plays that were unknown entities.

The British seemed to be overrunning the New York theatre, not only with new plays but with brilliantly performed revivals of classics and other old plays, as one British company after another visited our shores. British actors were gaining acclaim for their performances and were seen by Equity as an ever-increasing threat to the local job market; several producers had to fight tooth and nail to get the actors' union to allow British stars to play the leads in British plays. It was rare for a British play produced on Broadway with American actors to carry off the proper accents and manner with aplomb. British Equity, for its part, made it just as tough for Americans to act in the West End.

The five most continuously successful British dramatists of the decade were Alan Ayckbourn, Simon Gray, Harold Pinter, Tom Stoppard, and David Storey. Of them, only Pinter and Stoppard had seen local productions before the seventies.

Harold Pinter's reputation as one of the world's most prominent dramatists has grown steadily since his 1958 *The Birthday Party*. His elliptical, puzzling, yet magnetic style and language have made his plays challenging, yet relatively popular. Off Off-Broadway is especially fond of Pinter, partly because his plays, normally set in a single modern interior with a small cast, are fairly inexpensive to mount, but more because he offers a treasure trove of behavioral and linguistic enigmas to explore.

None of Pinter's seventies works were as verbally and emotionally spare as the two Off-Broadway-produced one-acters, *Landscape* and *Silence*, elusive tone poems in which past and present are enmeshed in the memory-laden fabric of the dialogue. Memory and time were continuing concerns of Pinter's other, more conventional, new plays as well.

In Pinter's first full-length work in six years, Broadway's highly praised *Old Times*, a filmmaker (Robert Shaw) and his wife of twenty years (Rosemary Harris) are visited by the wife's old roommate (Mary Ure); during the evening memories of the past mingle with current happenings in a manner that suggests the unreliability of memory according to the predispositions of the one remembering.

No Man's Land, another springboard for scintillating British acting, starred two of England's greatest players in a battle of wits between an elderly, heavy-drinking, poetically inclined, rich magnate, Hirst (Ralph Richardson), and a run-down, aging poet, Spooner (John Gielgud), who may or may not be Hirst's old friend and who jockeys for a valued position in the magnate's employ. Themes of memory, power plays, and the poignancy of growing old were superbly intertwined in this tour de force of language and intelligence.

Betrayal, which won the Drama Critics Circle Award, was the third of Pinter's full-length seventies plays to reach Broadway. The cast was all-

American—Blythe Danner, Raul Julia, and Roy Scheider—and the acting fell short of what the work required. Pinter continued his absorption in themes of time by the idiosyncratic device of beginning the play in the present and showing each of the two subsequent acts as being progressively further in the past. The subject was the relationships among three friends, a married couple and the man who has had an affair with the wife.

Tom Stoppard is another Briton (born, however, in Czechoslovakia) who upholds that nation's dramatic traditions of verbal ingenuity, intellectual deviltry, and philosophical wittiness. Stoppard's gifts are essentially comic, with strong speculative overtones. He came to prominence locally with his 1968 existential comedy, *Rosencrantz and Guildenstern Are Dead*, and kept up his attack in the seventies with five Broadway plays, one Off-Broadway double bill, and one run somewhere-in-between, at the Metropolitan Opera House. The Off-Broadway came first, with two short plays, *The Real Inspector Hound* and *After Magritte* (465 performances). In the former we view a play-within-a-play as the first- and second-string critics of a newspaper are part of an onstage audience watching a conventional Agatha Christie-type thriller. There is a constant switching back and forth between the play and the critics' reactions, thereby satirizing both. The other piece was a less successful attempt that sought to fuse, farcically, surrealistic principles within the context of a melodrama.

Stoppard's *Jumpers*, a curious comedy replete with metaphysical concepts, fared poorly, but his *Travesties* garnered the Drama Critics Circle Award and the Tony. The dramatist's witty conceit is that a number of celebrated people, James Joyce, Tristan Tzara, and Lenin, who actually happened to be in Zurich in 1917 but who apparently never met, were tied together by a sequence of events now vaguely remembered by a certain British consular official (John Wood) then stationed in Zurich.

Stoppard's next New York play was his *Dirty Linen and New-Found-Land*, a comedy combining a political sex farce with an interpolated sequence concerning the application of an American for British citizenship. The American appears to have been based on expatriate director Ed Berman, head of England's Inter-Action Trust, Ltd., a sort of social action group mixing charity with theatrical activities. Stoppard's relationship with Berman led to the founding of the British American Repertory Company (BARC), made up of equal numbers of British and American actors, which debuted locally with *Dogg's Hamlet, Cahoot's Macbeth*. This consists of two tenuously linked parts, the second of which derives from Stoppard's meeting with Czech dissident playwright Pavel Kohout; it shows a living-room performance of *Macbeth* such as theatre people like Kohout are forced to present in lieu of regular performances.

Stoppard's other New York works of the decade were his unsuccessful *Night and Day* and the limited-run eight-performance "play for actors and orchestra," *Every Good Boy Deserves Favor*, directed by Stoppard, for

which André Previn composed the score. Performed at the Met, it featured
René Auberjonois and Eli Wallach in a political satire set in a madhouse
where one of the inmates fantasizes conducting an eighty-one-piece orchestra.

Alan Ayckbourn is often called the British Neil Simon because of his prolific creation of highly successful comedies about middle-class domestic life.
Among obvious differences between the two is the fact that Ayckbourn's
plays occur in the suburbs, while Simon's are usually placed in the heart of
the city. Also, Simon is the gag writer par excellence; his characters and plots
do not reach the imaginative levels of Ayckbourn's.

Ayckbourn is a master of clever plotting, coming up with a new and
ingenious device for each play. His dialogue is dryly witty and understated.
Of the four plays he presented on Broadway, only *Bedroom Farce* and
Absurd Person Singular did well. *How the Other Half Loves* and *The
Norman Conquests* were disappointments. The latter was an interesting
failure, however, being a trilogy each part of which was given at a separate
performance.

Absurd Person Singular (592 performances) has a central concept which
shows three mismatched couples getting together for three consecutive
Christmas parties (Christmas Past, Christmas Present, Christmas Future),
each at the contrasting home of another couple. The shifting social and
economic status of each couple and their relative place within the group is
examined over the several years that pass.

Bedroom Farce (278 performances) opened with an all-British cast from
the National Theatre and later switched to Americans. A play with a title
more suggestive than its plot, it is set in three simultaneously present bed-
rooms; it is the comic behavior of the occupants of these three rooms on a
single chaotic night that occupies the playwright's eye.

Broadway hosted three productions by serio-comic dramatist Simon
Gray; one of his plays, *Rear Column*, also appeared non-commercially Off-
Broadway. Of the commercial offerings, only *Wise Child* did not do well.
This play had a homosexual theme, as did his *Butley*, a depiction of the
crumbling life of a self-destructive homosexual university professor whose
personal and professional relationships so embitter him that he can do little
but fire back with all wits blazing. The play's popularity was greatly
enhanced by star Alan Bates' dazzling performance. Another English star,
Tom Courtenay, scored a bull's-eye with *Otherwise Engaged*, Gray's most
successful work locally (309 performances). This winner of the Drama
Critics Circle Award is a comedy of manners set in a London publisher's
drawing room and revealing the publisher trying desperately but, unlike
Butley, politely to fend off the interruptions of an assortment of acquaintances so that he can relax and listen to a new recording of *"Parsifal."*

All of the British writers whose work has been surveyed are known
principally for their comedies. David Storey, for all his occasional humor,

is not a particularly comic writer. His singular style made his plays events in the New York theatre. Of his four New York-produced plays only *The Farm*, seen Off-Broadway, failed to make a stir. In *Home*, winner of the New York Drama Critics Circle Award, the Yorkshire playwright provided Sirs Ralph Richardson and John Gielgud the first of their two seventies Broadway triumphs. Pinter's influence could be detected in the elliptical dialogue of this seeming satire on contemporary England, set in a mental institution and concentrating on two dapper old inmates. The exceptional ensemble acting of the five-member cast delighted the critics, but several were less than pleased with the play's too subtle manner.

The critics were more voluble in their praise for the controversial *The Changing Room*, first seen in the United States at New Haven's Long Wharf. The talk about this drama centered first on its style—a naturalistic attempt to demonstrate the activity in a men's locker room before, during, and after a semi-pro match of the violent British football game, Rugby League—and second on its use of total male nudity. The nudity, however, was totally within the dramatic requirements of the play and had no discernible erotic overtones.

Storey's method of taking a simple activity and standing back from it in a seemingly objective attitude, letting his characters pursue their functions in a natural manner, was used in both *The Changing Room* and *The Contractor*, a highly praised Off-Broadway ensemble piece, in which a group of men set up and then take down a tent used for lawn weddings; the workmen's participation in the job is a fulcrum for displaying aspects of their characters and those of the wedding party.

A group of over half a dozen other British playwrights were also represented by two or more plays, but none achieved the widespread critical and popular recognition accorded those just described. The best-known member of this group is Edward Bond, but his American experiences have been largely disappointing and have left many puzzled over his major reputation abroad. Broadway viewed only his political parable set in Japan, *Narrow Road to the Deep North*, at Lincoln Center, where it made little impression; *Bingo*, a play about Shakespeare, received a mediocre staging by the CSC. Of all Bond's output, only *Saved*, seen at Brooklyn's Chelsea, made a mark.

Saved is a gripping drama of working-class lives that so effectively rallied the English theatre's forces after it had been banned by the Lord Chamberlain in 1965 that they were ultimately able to topple England's centuries-old official censorship. Bond's first play to be seen in New York, it had been on the verge of opening in two earlier American versions only to be cancelled before being seen by an audience. It proved to be an episodic, realistic/surrealistic tale of a young couple living together in her parents' home, of the girl's affair with another youth who makes her pregnant, and of the violent stoning to death of the baby in its carriage by the second lover and his friend. The stoning scene was considered one of the most horrific ever seen on a modern stage and was the reason for the play's checkered career. Whereas some critics found the work distasteful, others called it "profound," "riveting," "unusually powerful," and "incandescent."

Other talented British playwrights with more than one play shown in New York included Peter Nichols, Christopher Hampton, John Hopkins, Barrie Keefe, William Douglas Home, E. A. Whitehead, and Stephen Poliacoff. A number of these plays were provocative and bore elements of distinction. All were done Off-Broadway except Nichols' *The National Health*, Hampton's *The Philanthropist*, and Home's two comedies, *The Jockey Club Stakes* and *The Kingfisher*. Perhaps the best liked of the group was *The National Health*, whose American inception was at the Long Wharf. A black comedy, set in a welfare hospital and dealing with suffering and death, it was viewed as a metaphor for the ailing state of British society.

The largest group of British writers represented on the New York scene in the seventies offered only one play apiece, but in some cases these were among the most esteemed works of the decade. Of the established dramatists those responsible for the most memorable and/or popular productions were Peter Shaffer (*Equus*), his twin brother Anthony (*Sleuth*), Terence Rattigan (*In Praise of Love*), and Noël Coward (*Noël Coward in Two Keys*). Somewhat less compelling were octogenarian Enid Bagnold's *A Matter of Gravity*, Robert Bolt's *Vivat! Vivat! Regina*, and Arnold Wesker's *The Merchant*. The plays of Peter Ustinov and John Whiting proved merely exercises in futility.

New English playwrights who stormed Broadway and Off-Broadway were Trevor Griffiths, David Rudkin, Brian Clark, Ray Cooney and John Chapman, Anthony Marriott and Alistair Foot, Charles Laurence, Barry England, Ronald Millar, Royce Ryton, Alan Bennett, Mary O'Malley, Heathcote Williams, Caryl Churchill, Paul Ableman, Tom Mallin, Norman Fenton and Jon Blair, David Edgar, David Hare, and the team of Ron House, John Neville-Andrews, Diz White, Alan Shearman, and Derek Cunningham which collaborated on a detective-film spoof called *Bullshot Crummond*. Space permits only a few words on the plays of the Shaffers, Rattigan, Coward, Griffiths, Rudkin, and Clark, all of which, except for Rudkin's, were seen on Broadway.

The Shaffer twins were both well-known writers before their respective successes of the seventies, but only Peter had been recognized for his plays. Anthony was a fiction writer with a penchant for mysteries. In a sense, Peter's *Equus* is a mystery, but one in which the conventional police inspector digging for clues is replaced by a psychiatrist (Anthony Hopkins). The gory crime involves a teenage stable boy (Peter Firth) who cruelly blinds a half-dozen horses with a hoof-pick. The doctor probing for the causes of the boy's behavior is anguished by the contrast between his own sterile life and what he conceives to be the more admirable passion driving the boy to commit his act of violence.

Equus did better at the box office (1,029 performances) than any other British play of the period except *Sleuth*. John Dexter gave it an exceptional staging, using a variety of striking theatrical devices, including having the horses played by well-built young men wearing simple slacks- and-sweater sets and with inventive wire horse masks and hooves added on. A portion of the audience sat on the stage on semicircular risers, facing the auditorium, and thus made the action seem to be occurring in a bullring or operating theatre. Part of the play's notoriety stemmed from a critical love scene played entirely in the nude before a stable full of horses. The role of the psychiatrist became a plum for a series of leading actors, including Anthony Perkins, Alec McCowen, Richard Burton, and Leonard Nimoy.

Most critics agreed that *Equus* was a major achievement, but there were loud dissenters to what was perceived as Shaffer's point of view, namely, that to cure the boy of his "sickness" is to deprive him of a depth of emotional and spiritual experience that is light years away from the emptiness most of us allegedly possess. Nevertheless, *Equus* was voted the best play of the year by the Drama Critics Circle and won the Tony, among other awards.

Shaffer's brother's hit, *Sleuth*, was a far more conventional mystery play, in the classical tradition that places such works in large manorial homes. The author, though, had a number of his own highly inventive twists to the old tradition, including the fact that, for all the actors and characters listed in the program, only two are actually in the play. To a great degree, this laughter-filled chiller is a spoof of the whodunnit genre, although never a campy one; despite its high spirits, it always takes itself quite seriously.

Sleuth is a play of shifting identities and masterful disguises circling an action-filled plot in which a travel agent (Keith Baxter) engages in a pro- longed battle of wits with a famous mystery writer (Anthony Quayle), a jealous man who is being cuckolded by the other. The play was appreciated as much for its tour-de-force acting, using various disguises, as for its tech- nical cleverness. Some critics would have preferred a meatier drama, and turned their thumbs downward, but most were greatly taken with *Sleuth's* urbanity, invention, literacy, and suspense. It won the Tony and attained 1,222 showings, making it the second-longest-running play of the decade after *Same Time, Next Year*.

Both Terence Rattigan and Noël Coward, upholders of the polished school of playwriting that preceded the angry young men of the fifties, died during the seventies, each having had a mildly successful production in the decade. Rattigan's *In Praise of Love* offered Rex Harrison and Julie Harris in a pathos-laden vehicle in which a husband and wife both know that she is dying but each tries to keep the other from finding it out. *Noël Coward in*

Two Keys was originally written in 1966, but not done locally until a year after the author's death. Coward had written these two one-acters with starring roles for himself. His comedies of manners are set in a Swiss hotel; in one a bluff American businessman (Hume Cronyn) decides to leave his wife (Jessica Tandy) and run off with a Countess (Anne Baxter); in the other a renowned writer (Cronyn) is faced by an old flame (Baxter) who threatens to disclose certain letters proving the writer's homosexuality.

Trevor Griffiths wrote the pointedly funny *Comedians*, about a group of six working-class would-be comics who are taking a night course in how to succeed in show business. The play investigates with ruthless accuracy the nature of comedy and its purposes, while touching succinctly on the author's socialist political concerns. Mike Nichols' direction and Jonathan Pryce's performance were considered masterly. An unusual sidelight concerning the production was that it inspired former stand-up comic Charles Lindner to develop a Comedy Workshop, the first of its kind, at Hunter College's Center for Lifelong Learning. When it opened in June 1978 it had the largest enrollment ever achieved by a Hunter College course.

There were also unusual developments that grew out of Brian Clark's hit comedy-drama, *Whose Life Is It Anyway?* This play, in which Briton Tom Conti shone following a lengthy battle with Equity over his non-American status, was about Ken Harrison, a wickedly witty Scottish sculptor who is confined to a hospital bed following an accident; he is totally paralyzed except for his head, and wants nothing more than to die peacefully. Harrison must be played as completely immobile from the neck down throughout the performance.

Whose Life had run on Broadway for 233 performances when Conti had to leave the show. The producers decided to close it until an equally magnetic star could be selected as a replacement. They came up with a surprise when they cast American TV and film star Mary Tyler Moore, making her local stage debut with the role of Ken adapted for an actress and with other script changes to accommodate the new casting. Another 96 performances were thus achieved.

Ashes by David Rudkin is a clinically precise look at a married couple and what they endure in their attempt to conceive a child. Other issues introduced into the play bear on the political situation in Ireland and the husband's onetime flirtation with homosexuality. *Ashes* was proclaimed a powerful work by some, but others felt the political theme was managed too tenuously and that the play was overly didactic.

PLAYS OF OTHER ENGLISH-SPEAKING NATIONS

In addition to producing plays from England and the United States, New York hosted works written in several other English-speaking lands, e.g., Canada, Ireland, South Africa, and the West Indies.

Canada

Not many Canadian playwrights were represented locally although what did get produced often revealed considerable talent. (The work of Canadian-born Bernard Slade has been covered under the section on American playwrights because of his long residence in this country.) Of Canadians with at least two mainstream showings there were only Joanna McLelland Glass and David French. Glass first came to attention with her Off-Broadway one-acts, *Canadian Gothic/American Modern*. Her *Artichoke* was an entertaining Off-Broadway comedy picturing an adulterous situation within a Saskatchewan farm family.

David French's two plays were Off-Broadway's *One Crack Out* and Broadway's *Of the Fields, Lately*, a memory play telling in flashback the story of a father and son's strained relations. It was conceived as part of a trilogy, the first part, *Leaving Home*, having been done Off Off earlier in the decade.

Only two other Canadian plays reached Broadway. One was Michael Tremblay's *Hosanna*, which dealt with the problem of Quebec separatism in the guise of a story about a Montreal drag queen's love life. Another was *Billy Bishop Goes to War*, an essentially one-man play with a piano and vocal accompaniment, about the feats of a famous Canadian World War I flying ace. Its authors, John Gray and Eric Peterson, were also its performers. The play was said to be the first play ever to transfer its run from Broadway to Off-Broadway, rather than the other way around; few remembered, however, that John Howard Lawson's *Roger Bloomer* had accomplished the feat in 1923.

The remaining Canadian plays, by David E. Freeman, Michael Ondaatje, and David Lan, were all seen Off-Broadway. Most unusual was Freeman's *Creeps*, which depicts with wit and compassion the lives of a group of spastics at a home for cerebral palsy victims. (This author is not to be confused with David Freeman, American author of *Jesse and the Bandit Queen*.)

Ireland

For centuries, Ireland has provided the world with one major dramatist after another. Sheridan, Goldsmith, Farquhar, Boucicault, Shaw, Wilde, Yeats, Synge, O'Casey, Behan, and Beckett represent a dramaturgical pantheon of born-and-bred Irishmen. In the seventies, Ireland's crop of dramatic exports consisted chiefly of plays by Hugh Leonard, Brian Friel, Stewart Parker, Conor Cruse O'Brien, Samuel Beckett, Ron Hutchinson, and Bill Morrison.

Leonard and Friel fortified their positions as major Irish dramatists via their several major New York mountings. Leonard (the pen name of John Keyes Byrne) witnessed *The Au Pair Man* and *"Da"* in Broadway productions. His flair for colorful and witty dialogue was evident in both;

each also demonstrated one of the two primary concerns of contemporary Irish dramatists, politics and family life. *"Da,"* the more successful, revealed its author's compassionate, original voice in a tragi-comic autobiographical account of a writer (Brian Murray) returning to his parental home on the occasion of his father's (Barnard Hughes) death. *"Da"* is a memory play in which the writer must confront the ghost of his father and come to terms with what their relationship has meant in his own life, and what it will continue to mean. The most vivid element is the churlish presence of the late "da" who refuses to stay buried and whose specter remains at his son's side. It began locally Off-Broadway and then moved uptown where it won the Tony and the Drama Critics Circle Award. *"Da"'s* 697 performances made it the longest-running Irish play in Broadway history.

"Da" surpassed the previous record holder, Brian Friel's *Philadelphia, Here I Come* (326 showings). Friel was represented by three New York productions in the decade, all of them failures, two on Broadway and one Off. The last was *The Faith Healer*, which brought James Mason back to Broadway in a structurally idiosyncratic piece using four monologues to express the story of a traveling alcoholic faith healer.

Ireland's most respected living playwright, Samuel Beckett, had several of his non-dramatic pieces turned into theatre pieces by the experimental Mabou Mines group, but Beckett's only new play to be produced was his short existential minimalist exercise, *Not I*, in which only a woman's mouth (Jessica Tandy's) and a silent, shadow-shrouded figure appear.

Beckett's play was given an Off-Broadway production, as were all the remaining Irish plays, apart from Stewart Parker's *Spokesong*, seen at the Circle in the Square, and Conor Cruse O'Brien's *Murderous Angels*. Politics played a central role in all these pieces, none of which, however, made much of a dent on New Yorkers.

South Africa

South Africa gave New York several musical shows, but its dramatic contribution came principally from one man, Athol Fugard. This politically dissident white dramatist devoted most of his writing to uncovering the festering results of his nation's appalling racial policies. He was well represented on the seventies' New York stage, with five productions.

Fugard was often in trouble with his government, especially when he wished to leave the country to participate in a foreign production of his work. He ran into difficulty, for instance, when *Boesman and Lena* opened at the Circle in the Square (downtown). The refusal of South Africa to let him travel to this country set off a furor in the American press, particularly when it became apparent that *Boesman and Lena* was more a play of universal themes than of narrowly South African ones. This powerful realistic drama is set in a bleak South African wasteland; in it a colored husband (James Earl Jones) and wife (Ruby Dee)—"colored" meaning they are of mixed blood, being neither black nor white, and thus outcasts from either society—are doomed to wander perpetually, their home on their backs.

Fugard took his critical lumps with *People Are Living There*, a play not concerned with racial issues, but he came back strong with *The Island* and *Sizwe Banzi Is Dead*, both of which he "co-devised" with actors John Kani and Winston Ntshona, who performed them under Fugard's direction. These extraordinary players were members of the Serpent Players, a Port Elizabeth troupe from which the South African government bars white audiences. The plays they brought, which were played on Broadway in repertory, were considered trenchant observations on the inhumanity of apartheid.

The Island depicted the fate of two black political prisoners filling their time at a maximum-security prison by preparing a makeshift version of *Antigone* for a prison show. The play-within-the-play is intended as a burning statement of the black man's determination to fight for his release from the shackles of white oppression. Equally, if not more, harrowing was *Sizwe Banzi Is Dead*, another vitriolic swat at racism, in which a black man comes to the city to find work but is ordered to return to his homeland. The opportunity for him to survive and remain in the city is provided when he steals a corpse's passport and assumes the dead man's identity.

The Manhattan Theatre Club produced Fugard's two anti-apartheid one-acters, *Statements After an Arrest Under the Immorality Act* and *Scenes from Soweto*, both of them using documentary devices.

Survival, a collaborative theatre piece by and with Fana David Kekan, Selaelo Dan Maredi, Themba Ntinga, and Seth Sibanda, was the only other South African drama to come to New York. It was about the prison-like existence of blacks who often prefer the "liberty" of incarceration to the "shackles" of life on the outside.

Scotland and Australia

The nations in this subgrouping gave New York only four plays, one being a Broadway world premiere. This was Australia's *Players* by David Williamson, a cynical look at the world of Australian football. Australia was also the source of two Off-Broadway one-man transvestite plays, *Housewife! Superstar!* and *The Elocution of Benjamin*.

From the land of kilts and tartans came the Off-Broadway showing of Robert David MacDonald's imaginative but unsuccessful biographical account of homosexual ballet impresario Sergei Diaghilev, *Chinchilla*.

The West Indies

Apart from several black plays by writers of West Indian descent living in America, the only plays derived directly from the islands were by Derek Walcott and Mustapha Matura, both of them Trinidadians. All of these works were shown Off-Broadway. The first of Walcott's two works was *Dream on Monkey Mountain*, a poetic/political allegory about a jailed black visionary who seeks to lead the blacks home to Africa. *Ti-Jean and His Brothers* is another allegory dealing with racial feelings. Mustapha Matura's *Rum an' Coca-Cola* was an enjoyable piece about a down-and-out old calypso singer and a younger one who collaborate on creating a new number for a competition; their efforts end in violence.

PLAYS OF NON–ENGLISH-SPEAKING NATIONS

France

The large number of new English and American plays on the New York stage in the seventies greatly eclipsed the production of works from the world's non-English-speaking nations. France, for example, once a principal source for worthwhile new drama, gave to the decade not one commercially viable work and barely any that received critical acclamation. No new French playwright of stature appeared on or Off-Broadway, and the only regularly seen Gallic dramas were revivals.

Surveying the French contribution to Broadway we see the following charmless scene: two limited-run mountings of literary plays by Marguerite Duras, *A Place Without Doors* and *Days in the Trees*, both with Mildred Dunnock; Jean-Claude Carrière's *The Little Black Book*, which made it through a single performance; *Zalmen, or the Madness of God* by Elie Wiesel and *Dreyfus in Rehearsal* by Jean-Claude Grumberg, two flops on the subject of anti-Semitism; and an Argentine company's production of Genevieve Serreau and James Lord's adaptation of a Balzac fantasy, *Heartaches of a Pussycat*. The total number of performances given of all these works combined was 130, of which 92 belonged to the Duras dramas.

Off-Broadway saw only 1971's highly extolled Chelsea production of Jean Genet's five-hour drama of Algeria's anti-colonial strife, *The Screens*, acted in New York ten years after its premiere presentation. Fernando Arrabal's gruesome and controversial picture of life in a Spanish prison for political dissidents, *And They Put Handcuffs on the Flowers*, also stirred much talk. Less interest was paid to Romain Weingarten's *L'Eté* and Yves Jamiaque's *Monsieur Amilcar*.

Germany/Austria/Switzerland

The German-speaking nations were not as well represented as in earlier decades either. Only two plays originally written in German opened on Broadway and both were egregious failures. They were Erich Maria Remarque's *Full Circle* and Peter Hack's *Charlotte*.

The more interesting Germanic pieces were shown Off-Broadway, including three by Austrian avant-gardist Peter Handke. Audiences and critics were exasperated by what Ronald Hayman in *Theatre and Anti-Theatre* calls Handke's anti-theatrical style, in which the dramatist seeks to remove all of an audience's preconceptions about the nature of a theatrical experience.[11] *The Ride Across Lake Constance*, seen at the Forum, was so unconventional in its plotlessness and Dadaist mannerisms that preview audiences were in an uproar and producer Jules Irving had to appear and debate with them. Few critics understood what they were watching, although several ventured their cautious opinions.

Kaspar, given, like *Lake Constance*, a fine production by Carl Weber, was somewhat less baffling. Based on the famous nineteenth-century event in which a sixteen-year-old boy was found on a Nuremberg street after having been isolated from the world since birth, *Kaspar* is about the contradiction between language and experience and the inability of the former to fully register and express a person's reality. Some, like John Simon, were unswayed; he said that no matter what others claimed was Handke's importance, "I say his plays are spinach and the hell with them."[12]

Handke's other work, *A Sorrow Beyond Dreams*, was actually a one-man dramatic adaptation of a book by the playwright in which he fills in a picture of his mother, who committed suicide.

Translations of five other new German-language plays appeared during the period. *On Mount Chimborazo* and *Ice Age* were both by West German Tankred Dorst. Botho Strauss, another German, had his *Big and Little* produced. None of these plays provoked more than mild interest.

The sixties and seventies saw the work of several playwrights who, ignored or not sufficiently recognized in their own day, were thereby reinstated in the pantheon of respected dramatists. One such was Odon von Horvath, an Austro-German born in Hungary who died at thirty-seven in 1938. In 1979 one of his lesser-known plays, *Don Juan Comes Back from the War*, written a year before his death, was staged. It was about a comi-tragic Don Juan figure (Peter Evans) who returns after the first World War, determined to abandon his woman-chasing ways, only to be besieged by females from every side seeking to be the one he will truly love. It was believed a better play than its mounting might have suggested.

Swiss drama in German was provided by two famed writers. Friedrich Dürrenmatt's *Play Strindberg* was a parody of Strindberg's *Dance of Death*. Max Frisch's *Biography: A Game* was an intellectual comedy about a professor who is offered the opportunity to relive his life only to discover that, in doing so, he makes the same mistakes he did before.

Other Nations

Italy, the Soviet Union, Poland, Hungary, Czechoslovakia, Holland, Sweden, and Norway were the other European nations sending us new plays or plays never seen locally before. There was also a Cuban play and one each from China and India. Few made more than a passing impression and only a sampling are mentioned here.

One of the two Soviet offerings was the award-winning *Strider*, staged by Robert Kalfin Off-Broadway and then transferred to Broadway. Adapted from a Leo Tolstoy story by Mark Rozofsky, *Strider* (189 performances Off-Broadway; 214 on) was a play with so much music that its producers resorted to advertising it as a musical when the box office started to slip. It told the story of Strider (Gerald Hiken), a horse, of his good and bad fortune, his love life, and his death from maltreatment. It was seen as an allegory of Russian peasant life and gave its large cast plenty of opportunity for equine mimicry.

Poland, noted internationally for its avant-garde theatre, provided one new play and two old ones never shown here before. The new play, seen Off-Broadway, was *Emigrés* by the well-reputed Slawomir Mrozek, himself a political emigré. It was a work of provocative political import, about two emigrés, called only XX and AA, who spend their days unhappily in a strange nation to which they have fled. The older plays were from the thirties; both were by Stanislaw Ignacy Witkiewicz, and both were at the Chelsea. Witkiewicz, who killed himself in 1939 when Poland fell to Hitler, was a multitalented artist and aesthetician; his plays were written in a style of grotesque expressionism which made them excellent examples of the experimental drama of their day. Their themes and styles were later seen to have many affinities with the postwar methods of the absurdists, and Witkiewicz's works came in for frequent revivals. The plays seen in New York were 1922's *The Water Hen* and 1923's *The Crazy Locomotive*. The latter occurs aboard a madman-driven train racing full speed toward ultimate destruction. The train is a metaphor for a world headed for catastrophe under the pressure of militarism combined with industrialism.

Ivan Orkeny's *Catsplay* was the single new Hungarian play of the decade. Hungary once had been a principal purveyor of comedy and drama for New York's theatres. *Catsplay* arrived in New York only after a number of other American productions. An unexceptional, but popular, bittersweet romantic comedy, it was about a plump, middle-aged Budapest widow (Helen Burns), her lover, and a female friend who starts up an affair with the man. After a start at the Manhattan Theatre Club, the play moved to an Off-Broadway commercial showing.

Looking back over the various plays originating in foreign languages, it is not hard to see that aside from several plays written a decade or more before their New York productions, and apart from a couple of controversial works like those of Handke, not one truly distinguished, widely accepted European or Asian drama was produced in the city from 1970 to 1980. Some will blame the fact on the inadequacy of the productions given those works that were staged. Others will say that there simply were no worthwhile plays being written abroad (other than in England). Yet others will attribute the situation to the fear of New York producers of taking a chance on translations of plays that might not offer them a return on their investments. In fact, without the adventurous programs of less than a handful of Off-Broadway subsidized theatres, like the Chelsea, the Manhattan Theatre Club, and the Public, New York might have seen hardly any foreign plays during the decade. Whatever the cause, the fact has been recorded. One hopes that the future will see an improvement in this necessary cultural link between the nations of the world.

NOTES

1. "The Talk of the Town: Conference in Shubert Alley," *New Yorker*, 19 February 1979, p. 30.

2. Edward Albee, "Edward Albee Talks About the State of the American Theatre," *New York Theatre Review* 2 (October 1978): 9.

3. Martin Gottfried, "What Shall It Profit a Theater If . . . ?" *New York Times*, 23 August 1970, Sec. II, p. 1.

4. In many cases the only way to tell whether a production was Broadway, Off-Broadway, or Off Off-Broadway during the seventies is by reference to the production contract with Equity (a variety of different contract types exist). Plays and personnel moved from one to the other, and a single company could produce plays on each level.

5. Walter Kerr, "Sam Shepard—What's the Message?" *New York Times*, 10 December 1978, Sec. II, p. 3.

6. Robert Coe, "The Saga of Sam Shepard," *New York Times Magazine*, 23 November 1980, p. 58.

7. Joan Alleman Rubin, "The Wonder of Michael Cristofer," *Playbill*, July 1977, n.p.

8. Quoted in Clayton Riley, "Bullins: It's Not the Play I Wrote," *New York Times*, 19 March 1972, Sec. II, p. 1.

9. Jules Irving, "Two Answers to Ed Bullins," *New York Times*, 26 March 1972, Sec. II, p. 11.

10. Peggy Lark, "Seven Percent Solution," *Other Stages*, 29 January 1981, p. 2, citing a statistic revealed at the March 1980 Congressional Hearing for the National Endowment for the Arts.

11. Ronald Hayman, *Theatre and Anti-Theatre* (London: Secker and Warburg, 1979), pp. 95-123.

12. John Simon, "Ethnic But Ethical?" *New York Magazine*, 5 March 1973, p. 66.

★ 4 ★
MUSICALS
AND
REVUES

During the first seventy years of this century the Broadway musical became America's most popular and original contribution to world theatre. The names of, let us say, George Gershwin, Jerome Kern, Cole Porter, Leonard Bernstein, Irving Berlin, Richard Rodgers, Lorenz Hart, Oscar Hammerstein II, Alan Jay Lerner, and Fritz Loewe, alone or in combination with one or more partners, were known wherever American music was heard. Prolific and brilliantly inventive, these composers, lyricists, and librettists produced one outstanding success after another, all the while perfecting and polishing the medium of the musical play until it became a unique art form in which the elements of music, lyrics, and book were seamlessly integrated into a unified whole.

A few members of the old guard were still active in the seventies, but their powers, for the most part, had faded, and were not replaced by any of comparable achievement. The decade produced its mega-hits, of course, and such melodic blockbusters as *Annie*, *A Chorus Line*, *Pippin*, and *Grease*, as well as *Jesus Christ Superstar*, *Evita*, *The Wiz*, *Godspell*, and *Chicago* kept ticket windows busy for years. However, the only American musical theatre artist of note to climb anywhere near the ranks of the Berlins, Gershwins, and Porters was composer/lyricist Stephen Sondheim, and that genius's rather cerebral output was decidedly caviar to the masses. In fact, the most consistently popular artists in the field were the young Englishmen Tim Rice and Andrew Lloyd Webber, whose rock-influenced musicals dispensed entirely with a conventional libretto and had the entire story sung, as in opera.

The true stars of the decade's musicals, for all the gems produced by writers and composers, were the new breed of directors and director-choreographers. This was a period notable for "concept" musicals, shows that were often light on book, and heavy on production elements tied to an unusual theme or approach. Talents like Bob Fosse, Tom O'Horgan, Gower Champion, Harold Prince, and Michael Bennett found success such as had rarely crowned the work of their gifted but less theatrically dominating predecessors. With the emphasis shifting ever more toward the tour-de-force staging of such masterminds, the musical underwent a period of wrenching dislocation; book and lyric writers floundered or even disappeared as the audience's attention was distracted by awesome feats of choreography, spectacular scenic investiture, and clever directorial gimmickry. In many shows the devices used to produce a show took precedence over the characters, ideas, and story content, and this may have been responsible for the dearth of important new lyricists and librettists.

The "non-book" musical—wherein a director or "conceiver" (a credit that became more and more common during the decade) pasted a number of musical pieces together around a central theme with dialogue reduced to the barest minimum—was a significant sign of the times. Similarly, the continuing production of "revues" and anthologies of popular music of the golden past was a seventies characteristic that further made the absence of conventional musicals manifest. Hungry for shows with characters and plot, audiences turned out in force for a number of well-produced musical revivals that were rushed in to fill the vacuum left by the missing new works.

Naturally, the traditional musical was not completely moribund; in addition to Sondheim, other respected artists continued to keep its heart pumping, if only feebly much of the time. Among them were such tune- and wordsmiths as Martin Charnin, Fred Ebb, Micki Grant, Sheldon Harnick, Will Holt, Jerry Herman, Alan Jay Lerner, Stephen Schwartz, Michael Stewart, Peter Udell, Melvin Van Peebles, Cy Coleman, Gary Geld, Galt McDermott, Peter Link, Mitch Leigh, Charles Strouse, Richard Rodgers, and John Kander. Most were unable to muster up more than one hit, despite a modest amount of activity.

* * *

The musicals and revues of the seventies are surveyed in this chapter under several content-related rubrics: Ethnic Musicals, "Hippie" Rock Musicals, Book Musicals, and Revues.

ETHNIC MUSICALS

Jewish Musicals

None of the decade's musicals with Jewish themes came near the tremendous success enjoyed in the sixties by the Joseph Stein, Jerry Bock, and Sheldon Harnick blockbuster, *Fiddler on the Roof*. An obvious source for such shows was the beleaguered nation of Israel, which had close ties with New York's population through the many Jews residing in the city and its environs. Seven Israel-related shows were produced, but nearly all of them were imports first produced in Israel itself. The only American-made show of the lot was the lugubrious *Ari*, an adaptation of Leon Uris' novel, *Exodus*. The other shows were all cast in the revue form, being thematically related sequences of Israeli songs, dances, and sketches.

The principal "Jewish" musicals—all of them failures—on Broadway were, in addition to *Ari*, *The Rothschilds*, *Two by Two*, *Molly*, and *King of Schnorrers*. There were also a pair of Yiddish/English musicals. *The Rothschilds* (507 performances) was based on Frederick Morton's best seller about the founders of the famed nineteenth-century banking family. Despite a score by the same composer/lyricist team that had created *Fiddler*, it suffered a heavy financial loss. An even more distinguished composer/lyricist, the late Richard Rodgers, came up empty with a musical in this category when, in his seventies, he offered a lackluster score for *Two by Two*, based on Clifford Odets' 1953 play about Noah and the Ark, *The Flowering Peach*. Its chief draw was Danny Kaye, making his return to a Broadway musical after three decades. The star's presence helped the show limp along to 351 performances, even when he himself had to limp because of an onstage accident that forced him out of the show for two weeks; he came back in a cast and wheelchair but, despite his popularity, unnerved Rodgers and his fellow actors by his unbridled ad-libbing.

Off-Broadway hosted Elizabeth Swados' ambitious *The Haggadah*, an imaginatively ritualized presentation using magical sets, costumes, puppets, and masks. Elie Wiesel's *Moses: Portrait of a Leader* inspired the narrative portions along with the Passover ritual prayer after which the show was named.

Black Musicals

No decade since the 1920s saw so remarkable a profusion of black-related musical shows as did the seventies. Many of the great shows of this genre over the years had been white, or largely white, creations; one that was running when the decade opened, *Purlie*, is an example. But, for the most part, black was beautiful on Broadway in the seventies, and black song and book writers were better represented than ever before.

There were seventeen predominantly black musical shows on Broadway and seven Off. There were also three Broadway revivals of white shows with black casts. One new show, *I Love My Wife*, opened with a white cast, but switched to black actors in mid-run. Of the sixteen new Broadway shows with a black cast or theme thirteen were the products of black artists. Two others were at least partly attributable to black ideas and/or specific contributions. *Comin' Uptown* (a retelling of Dickens' *A Christmas Carol*) was the only specifically black show written by whites; *Raisin* came from a black source, but was adapted by whites, and *Doctor Jazz* was written largely by whites but employed a mixed black and white cast. Off-Broadway, all the black shows were all-black shows.

Black shows cast in the revue format are covered in the Revue section of this chapter. There were five on Broadway and four Off. The remaining shows are by no means all conventional book shows. Many might be reasonably called revues because of their loosely knit formats, lack of dialogue, and plotlessness. The black musical, like the white one, did not often offer librettists golden opportunities. The decade's first example was Joseph Walker's *Ododo* (the Yoruba word for "truth"), with music by Dorothy Dinroe, an Off-Broadway work that offered an episodic recreation of black history from Africa to Harlem. Then came two Broadway shows by actor-composer-writer-producer Melvin Van Peebles, who was almost single-handedly responsible for two shows during the same season, *Ain't Supposed to Die a Natural Death* and *Don't Play Us Cheap!*. The first (375 performances) employed a largely recitative jazz style, with little melodic line, to present a plotless image of life in the Harlem ghetto. The second, which ran less than half as long, was also set in the ghetto but had more of a story line, and used energetic gospel and rhythm and blues. Despite some good reviews, both shows had many detractors and it was even rumored that Van Peebles had pressured the Shuberts to keep them open or risk being branded racists. Van Peebles returned after an eight-year absence as one of the many writers of the indigestible Rastafarian musical, *Reggae*.

Among the noteworthy black musicals that deserve mention are *The Great MacDaddy*, *Treemonisha*, *Your Arms Too Short to Box With God*, *Raisin*, and *The Wiz*. The first, an Off-Broadway work by Paul Carter Harrison and Coleridge Taylor-Perkinson, was on the border line between musical play and musical. It used folk-tale devices to dramatize events in the black American past and was effective enough to earn a revival within the decade. *Treemonisha* was a 1907 folk opera by composer and ragtime songwriter Scott Joplin, brought to New York in an exceptional Houston Grand Opera staging for a limited run. Joplin died in 1917 having failed to get it produced or published. Set in Texarkana just after the Civil War, and concerned with the story of a black girl who leads the plantation folk of her environment out of ignorance toward knowledge and salvation, *Treemonisha* proved antiquated but entertaining.

Vinette Carroll, the most successful black female director of the decade, conceived many shows with her Off Off company, the Urban Arts Corps. Her most successful (429 performances) was *Your Arms Too Short to Box With God*, a rousing gospel retelling of the Book of Matthew, with music and lyrics by Alex Bradford, and additional songs by frequent Carroll contributor, Micki Grant. The show arrived on Broadway after being produced at the 1975 Spoleto, Italy, festival. More conventional was the book musical *Raisin*, adapted from Lorraine Hansberry's play, *A Raisin in the Sun,* about the aspirations for self-improvement of a poor black Chicago family. Only mild approval greeted the show, but good word-of-mouth assisted it a total of 847 performances.

The Wiz, of course, with its 1,672 showings, became the most popular black show in history. This musicalization of L. Frank Baum's *The Wizard of Oz* won Tonys for Geoffrey Holder's excellently realized directorial and design concepts, and for Charley Smalls' robust rock, gospel, and blues score, but the jivey book was not appreciated.

"HIPPIE"/ROCK MUSICALS

The driving rhythms, blaring amplification, and electronic instrumentation of much rock music offered an elusive vision to many producers. The rich melodic quality of the great old musicals was fine for their now aging audiences, it was reasoned, but if some means of translating rock to the stage could be found, a whole new audience could be lured to the theatre and vast riches could be tapped. Galt McDermott's 1968 score for *Hair* had touched a greedy nerve; before long a string of shows with obvious ties to *Hair* was being created, usually with characters and themes emblematic of the then-prevalent world of hippiedom. Communal living, eccentric clothing, long hair, drugs, nudity, free love, and left wing, anti-war, and conservationist politics were among the laid-back components of the hippie-rock syndrome. Theatrically, these shows often used audience participation, environmental staging, onstage bands with picturesque group names, amateur actors, nonverbal techniques, a celebratory spirit, bookless formats, and racially mixed companies.

Rock was used in some musicals that did not fit this pattern, including a couple of black musicals and works about Vietnam. But the shows that combined flower-child life styles and attitudes with variations on rock musicality were common enough to form their own grouping. Several were huge hits, but most were dispensable ephemera.

The more notable shows of this type included two from Off-Broadway, *The James Joyce Liquid Memorial Theatre* and *The Golden Bat. James Joyce* was brought to the unusual locale of the Guggenheim Museum by a California company; it fused theatre games, dancing, set revue pieces, and rock music in a kind of company/audience party; the show capitalized on the seventies fad for encounter and sensitivity group experience. *The Golden Bat* also used considerable audience participation; it was a Japanese/English concoction, given by a group of Nipponese actors called the Tokyo Kid Brothers. Their free-form evening mingled rock, dance, nudity, and humor in an often touching work about youth's rituals and triumphs.

A number of works tried to rock-musicalize the classics. Shakespeare was fair game for such ventures, but the rock versions of *Romeo and Juliet* (*Sensations*) and *Hamlet* (*Rockabye Hamlet*) were doomed. However, one smash hit (627 performances) did emerge from this path: *Two Gentlemen of Verona*, as adapted by John Guare and director Mel Shapiro, with music by Galt McDermott. First done in Central Park, it eventually moved to Broadway with most of its original cast. The show was transposed to a New York ghetto and its principal roles were taken by such Hispanic and black players as Raul Julia, Clifton Davis, and Jonelle Allen. In the memorable grand finale, all twenty-seven members of the company appeared singing loudly, tossing Frisbees across the proscenium arch, yanking yo-yos, blowing bubbles, paddling rubber balls, riding bikes, and roller skating.

Other rock musicals based on classic literature were *Aesop's Fables*, *Blood*, based on the Orestes legend, and the double bill of *Iphigenia in Concert* and *The Wedding of Iphigenia*. The Bible, of course, may also be considered as classical literature; it spawned three hit shows, *Your Arms Too Short to Box With God*, noted above, *Godspell*, and *Jesus Christ Superstar*.

Godspell, based on the book of St. Matthew by John-Michael Tebelak, with music by Stephen Schwartz, began life as a graduate project at Carnegie Tech, came to Off-Broadway for an extensive run, and, after 2,124 performances, switched to Broadway for another 527. Its original reviews were not much more than tepid, but it struck a popular nerve with its depiction of ten hippie-like youngsters getting together in a city schoolyard for a "love-in" during which the Passion of Jesus is performed. The actors could not resist going into the aisles to share their joy and good spirits with the audience.

One of the most controversial shows of the seventies was *Jesus Christ Superstar*, with lyrics by England's Tim Rice and music by Andrew Lloyd Webber, which continued on Broadway for a solid 720 performances and warranted a concert revival later in the decade. Billed as a "rock opera" because it had no dialogue, it had begun as a phenomenally successful record album; soon, authorized and unauthorized concert versions were springing up everywhere. The first of these to tour America grossed $1.2 million in its first five weeks. In director Tom O'Horgan's hands, the Broadway version swelled into a mammoth, and often tackily tasteless, spectacle of sound and scenery. Images of sexual inversion were prevalent; some saw a touch of queerness in Christ himself. Critics labelled the display trashy, vulgar, and crude. Many clergymen were offended because the show was thought to be damaging to Jewish-Christian relations. Some claimed that it was anti-Semitic. Others decried it as a disgrace to the original story. At the same time, many Christian groups were using the album as a study aid for explaining the story to children. The producer, composer, and lyricist scoffed at the hubbub, claiming that the show's chief target was not religion but the Establishment, and that they never intended the show as a statement.

British music was also responsible for two other rock musicals, *Sergeant Pepper's Lonely Hearts Club Band on the Road*, an attempt to theatricalize a popular Beatles album, and *The Rocky Horror Show*, which caught on here only as a cult film, *The Rocky Horror Picture Show*, but which was hastily removed from the stage.

BOOK MUSICALS

As we have seen, the seventies may have been especially propitious for "bookless" musicals, but shows with traditional librettos did not entirely disappear. In fact, the bulk of the musicals produced had librettos of a more or less conventional nature. Before turning to another form of bookless show, the revue, it would be appropriate to skim the principal book shows not covered by the discussions of ethnic and rock musicals.

For many years, the best musicals have been adaptations of already familiar materials. Straight plays also have a long tradition of borrowing from earlier sources for their plots and characters, and it is entirely possible to discuss plays according to their literary origins. Nevertheless, the majority of musicals done in the seventies derive from someone else's ideas as expressed in a previously published or performed work; this cannot be said for the period's straight dramas, which tended, more often than not, to be original conceptions. Partly because of the great expense involved, many producers feel somewhat more inclined to do shows that are associated with an already well-known source.

To put these many shows into a clearer perspective, they have been arranged for discussion according to their sources; these are classical or pre-modern literature, modern literature, films and TV, and original ideas.

Pre-Modern Sources

One group of the decade's musicals was drawn entirely from pre-twentieth-century dramatic and prose literature, much of it recognizably classic in stature. The Greeks, for example, were represented by several works mentioned in the previous section. Joined to these failures were Broadway's *Home Sweet Homer*, a one-performance flop version of the *Odyssey* starring Yul Brynner, and *Lysistrata*, a musical version of Aristophanes' sex-versus-war comedy with Greek star Melina Mercouri.

England's Shakespeare gave us—in addition to *Two Gentlemen of Verona*, *Rockabye Hamlet*, *Sensations*, and *Pop* (based on *King Lear*)—*Music Is*, a sorry reading of *Twelfth Night* that paled in comparison with a sixties musical adaptation of the comedy, *Your Own Thing*. There were also shows based on Victorian fiction by Dickens, Mary Elizabeth Braddon, and George Dibdin-Pitt, whose grisly 1847 melodrama, usually known as *A String of Pearls*, became *Sweeney Todd, the Demon Barber of Fleet Street*, one of the most significant shows of the era. The decade also saw musicals based on the Italian Renaissance's Boccaccio, the post-Renaissance's Molière, the mid-eighteenth century's Voltaire (*Candide*), and the late nineteenth century's Rostand. In addition, three old American plays were chosen for Off-Broadway musicalization: Royal Tyler's *The Contrast*, Anna Cora Mowatt's *Fashion*, and Mordecai Noah's *She Would Be a Soldier* (retitled *Castaways*).

Both *Sweeney Todd* and *Candide* were directed by Hal Prince, enjoyed long runs, and were financial calamities. *Candide* was one of several shows that gave interested observers the problem of deciding whether it was a new work or a revival. It had the same Leonard Bernstein score as its original incarnation in 1956, and a good many of the original lyrics were intact, but the old Lillian Hellman book was scrapped and a new one by Hugh Wheeler substituted. In these pages, *Candide* is considered a new show.

Candide opened at Brooklyn's Chelsea, a small playhouse which had been turned by Eugene Lee into a completely environmental setting in which actors and audience shared much of the same space. When it moved to the Broadway Theatre, that theatre's interior had to be redone entirely, including the removal of the orchestra seats, to allow an enlarged version of the Chelsea set to be installed. *Candide*, as brilliantly staged by Harold Prince, proceeded to win the Drama Critics Circle Award and a special Tony.

For *Sweeney Todd* Lee designed an overwhelming set reconstructed from an old iron foundry, Wheeler did the libretto, and Stephen Sondheim, who had added new lyrics to *Candide*, wrote the score's words and music. Len Cariou and Angela Lansbury were outstanding in this tale of a murderous, vengeance-seeking London barber and his bawdy neighbor who develops a prosperous business making meat pies out of the tonsorial killer's victims. Sondheim's complex, sardonic, and ironic lyrics were perfectly matched to his intense, sometimes frightening, sometimes lyrical score. About 80 percent of the almost operatic show was sung. It won many awards, including eight Tonys, although it did not win all the critics' hearts.

Modern Literary Sources

Modern literature, from the turn of the century to the seventies themselves, was considerably productive of source materials for new musicals. Shows that derived from novels and non-fiction, however, almost all fared poorly. Five twentieth-century novels or novellas and three plays which were themselves based on modern novels were made into musicals. The only one of note was *The Robber Bridegroom* (145 performances), adapted by Alfred Uhry and Robert Waldman from a novella by Eudora Welty. It began in a musical laboratory, was produced by the Acting Company at the

Harkness, and returned to Broadway a year later in a revised version with a new company but with the same director, Gerald Freedman.

The Robber Bridegroom was one of very few musicals with a country music score and a rural American setting. It took place in backwoods Mississippi during the nineteenth century and was a combination folk and fairy tale about a handsome highwayman (Barry Bostwick), in love with a young woman he has raped in the woods but engaged to marry the homely daughter of a rich plantation owner. The two girls turn out to be the same and all ends happily, amidst square dancing and boisterous high jinks.

Non-fiction was tapped for two Broadway shows, *The Selling of the President*, from Joe McGinness' book, and *Working*, from Studs Terkel's best-seller, but the latter was more like a theme revue than a book show. A non-fiction article by Larry L. King in *Playboy*, however, sparked the blockbuster hit *The Best Little Whorehouse in Texas*, about a "respectable" Texas brothel that was fated to be closed down because of the pressures exerted on the governor by a "watchdog" committee of righteous citizens. The show forged from this story mingled the sounds of Carol Hall's ersatz country music and lyrics with political satire, mildly risqué sexuality, and eye-catching Tommy Tune choreography to create a musical so successful on Broadway (following a workshop at the Actors Studio) that it rolled on for well over 1,300 performances.

Another form of modern literature, the comic strip, had proved a valuable source for several popular musicals of the century, but in the seventies only the tremendously profitable *Annie* stemmed from such beginnings. A gift volume of Harold Gray's *Little Orphan Annie* strip, purchased for a friend, so inspired lyricist/director Martin Charnin that he in turn fired librettist Thomas Meehan and composer Charles Strouse with the idea for a show based on the material. After a five-year period of gestation, the musical went from a troubled opening at the Goodspeed in Connecticut to a run that totalled 2,377 performances. With young discovery Andrea McArdle as Annie supported by veterans Dorothy Loudon and Reid Shelton, and a dog rescued from the pound as Sandy, *Annie*, whose spirit of undaunted optimism matched that of the post-Nixon era, became one of the best-loved shows of the era.

From modern play to musical is a more natural progression than from novel, comic strip, or non-fiction writing; thus, at least sixteen shows chose this route. Source plays that failed to make the transition successfully included works by Synge, Ionesco, Philip Barry, Werfel, McCullers, Capote, Odets, and Patrick. More notable as source plays were William Gibson's *Two for the Seesaw*, Maureen Watkins' *Chicago*, an unproduced John Weidman script, Ben Hecht and Charles MacArthur's *Twentieth Century*, an unproduced James Goldman play, and a French play by Luis Rego, *Viens Chez Moi, J'Habite Chez une Copine*.

Two for the Seesaw, a two-character play, did not seem to be a promising basis for a musical, but it became surprisingly so in librettist/director/choreographer Michael Bennett's smart production, aided by assistants Tommy Tune, Bob Avian, and Grover Dale. *Seesaw* (296 performances) evoked the pulsating energy and rhythm of New York with Michelle Lee and Ken Howard excellent in the love story of a Jewish would-be dancer from the Bronx and a married WASP lawyer from Nebraska. In a supporting role six-foot, six-inch dancer/choreographer Tune nearly stole the show, which also benefitted from a score by Cy Coleman and Dorothy Fields.

Much more successful was *Chicago*, the brainchild of director/choreographer Bob Fosse, whose ex-wife, dancer Gwen Verdon, helped spur the show to SRO profits. It suffered somewhat from comparisons to *A Chorus Line*, which had opened only a week earlier, but Fosse's showmanship was gratefully acknowledged. He took Maurine Watkins' 1926 story of Roxie Hart, the flapper imprisoned for murder who enlists the aid of a shrewd and greedy lawyer (Jerry Orbach) to get herself acquitted, and told it in a metaphorical style that made show-biz entertainers out of all the characters. The music and lyrics of Fred Ebb and John Kander underscored Fosse's pyrotechnics and captured the glitz of the Jazz Age for 898 performances.

Pacific Overtures (193 performances) was not a hit, but it was an unusual and memorable show that represented Harold Prince and Stephen Sondheim's continuing ambition to extend the range of the Broadway musical. The script examined the historical events surrounding the opening of Japan to the West in 1853 by the black ships of Commodore Perry. The story was told from the Japanese point of view and employed various devices adapted from the Kabuki theatre, including a runway through the auditorium for entrances and exits. An all-Asian cast was employed and men played female roles as well as male. Sondheim's score suggested Japanese musical values but was difficult for Broadwayites to appreciate.

The amusing antics of flamboyant Broadway producer Oscar Jaffe (John Cullum) in trying to get temperamental star Lily Garland (Madeleine Kahn) to sign a contract as they hurtle through the night aboard the train from Chicago to New York forms the essence of the story in *On the Twentieth Century* (453 performances), derived from the popular thirties farce. Prince directed this show, too, with a score by Betty Comden, Adolph Green, and Cy Coleman. A brilliant Art Deco conception of the train by Robin Wagner, costing close to $200,000, made the show one of the most visually dazzling of the era. Imogene Coca and Kevin Kline were very important in supporting roles in this Tony-winning production.

Finally, *I Love My Wife* (872 performances) was a mini-musical set in the home of a young New Jersey couple of which the husband is intent on "swinging" with the wife of his best friend. The sexually titillating but all-in-good-clean-fun musical opted for a nice middle-class ending with nothing untoward actually occurring. Michael Stewart and Cy Coleman teamed up to do the amusing score, which was played by a small onstage combo that acted as a chorus to the actors throughout the action. During the run, the white cast was replaced by a black one.

Film and TV Sources

Hollywood has long been known for its reliance on New York stage shows for its production mill, but recent years have seen the trend become a two-way street, with films selected as an important source of stage musicals. Several of these shows were originally novels, but are considered here as adaptations of the filmed word, not the written one.

There were nowhere near as many movie-to-musical adaptations as there were from the standard literary sources, but the number that was produced is significant. These shows sometimes used the titles of the original films, and sometimes devised new ones. The list of flops in this category includes *Gigi*, with the familiar Lerner and Loewe film score, and with Alfred Drake and Agnes Moorehead leading the cast; *Carmelina*, with a score by Burton Lane and Alan Jay Lerner, based on *Buona Sera, Mrs. Campbell*; and *King of Hearts*, based on the famed Philippe de Broca film, its score by Peter Link and Jacob Brackman. Also unsuccessful was *Sarava*, from the film (and novel) *Dona Flor and Her Two Husbands*, which lasted longer than the above-mentioned by the simple ploy of failing to announce an official opening and stretching out its preview period. Movie-to-musical hits counted among their number *The Wiz*, *Shenandoah* (from the film of that title), *Sugar* (from *Some Like It Hot*), and *A Little Night Music*, inspired by the Ingmar Bergman Swedish film classic, *Smiles of a Summer Night*.

Some felt that the book for *A Little Night Music* (600 performances) fell far short of its inspiration, but most found this award-winning show exquisite, replete with emotional mystery, sweet sadness, and heartfelt romance. Its operetta-like fragility was unlike anything seen on Broadway in years. Director Hal Prince and composer/lyricist Stephen Sondheim added the show to their growing list of brilliant contributions, and Sondheim provided for the waltz-dominated score his only song ever to become a popular hit, "Send in the Clowns." The show's plot tells of love affairs, illicit and otherwise, on a summer weekend spent by several upper-class individuals at a manor house.

Off-Broadway was the home of two unusual silver-screen offshoots, *The Umbrellas of Cherbourg*, with its Michel Legrand score, given a lovely Andrei Serban staging, and *Hotel for Criminals*, scored by Stanley Silverman, which was conceived by avant-gardist Richard Foreman from a silent-movie vampire series made by Louis Feuillade.

Television drama was the source of one major musical, *Ballroom*, a $2 million dollar flop based on a show called *Queen of the Stardust Ballroom*.

Original Ideas

The thirty-odd musicals of the seventies based on original ideas fall into several loose categories. One might be the show-business musicals, several of which form a subgrouping because of their nostalgia-based themes, and another would be shows based on historical subjects. A final catchall grouping would have to cover those few shows that fall into no discernible category.

One of the most apparent trends in musical production was the frequency of shows with their feet planted firmly in nostalgia. Such shows featured either pastiches of music from the Good Old Days, or the original tunes themselves. Many revues were likewise beholden to this nostalgia craze. Audiences seemed hungry for the false assurances provided by music and themes created at a time when, in retrospect, life seemed to have been so much simpler and more secure and values absolute. Nostalgia became a preoccupation of many shows, including some of those discussed above. In the examples mentioned here, nostalgia is invariably coupled with show-business stories, for the world of entertainment has always conveyed a special rapture to those who seek escape, not only into the past, but into the realms of glamor and mystique.

Of the seven failures in this vein, the one with the strongest support was *Mack and Mabel*, brilliantly staged by Gower Champion, and starring Bernadette Peters and Robert Preston as silent-screen star Mabel Normand and director Mack Sennett. Jerry Herman's score has become a cult favorite with musical theatre buffs. The seven big guns among the original-conception show-biz musicals were *Follies*, *The Magic Show*, *Over Here!*, *A Chorus Line*, *The Act*, *They're Playing Our Song*, and *Barnum*. Nostalgia was especially rampant in *Follies* and *Over Here!*.

Hal Prince was the director (with Michael Bennett as co-director) of the beautifully conceived *Follies* (521 performances), scored by Stephen Sondheim, which was said to have been inspired by a *Life* magazine photo of screen star Gloria Swanson standing amidst the ruins of the demolished Roxy Theatre. Considered a revolutionary show, *Follies* brought together a group of former showgirls at a party celebrating the imminent destruction of the theatre (wonderfully designed by Boris Aronson) in which they once had shone, and allowed the now middle-aged women to play out their current love lives amidst a bittersweet ambience highlighted by the ghostly presence of their former selves, performed by younger chorus girls. A coup was achieved by casting well-known middle-aged actresses such as Alexis Smith, Dorothy Collins, and Yvonne De Carlo in the leads. There were even some faded *Ziegfeld Follies* beauties in the cast.

Over Here! became a modest hit (348 performances) not because of its words or music but because it starred the remaining two members of the popular forties singing group, the Andrews Sisters, who were given a

chance to resurrect the look and sound (with all new songs) of the Fabulous
Forties during wartime on the homefront.

Of the other show-business shows, in which nostalgia was not so clearly
underlined, *The Magic Show* (1,920 performances), had a mediocre score
by Stephen Schwartz and a very weak book by Bob Randall. Its success lay
in the wonders of prestidigitation created by wizard Doug Henning around
whose illusions the show revolved.

The Act owed its 240 performances to star Liza Minnelli, whose illness at
one point caused the show to close until she recovered. The fragile plot was
all Minnelli needed to display her powers in that it was a thin book wrapped
around a Las Vegas-type nightclub act. Fred Ebb and John Kander provided
the songs.

British actor Jim Dale's versatility was fully utilized in the popular circus
musical, *Barnum* (854 performances), about the great impresario and
master of humbug. In spite of its paper-thin book, *Barnum* was a theatrical
fireball that enjoyed a Cy Coleman score, excellent staging and decor, and a
star performance that had Jim Dale singing, dancing, walking a tightrope,
and performing various odd tricks.

Nostalgia was not the lifeblood of the decade's greatest hit, *A Chorus
Line*, but show business definitely was. In September 1982 it became the
longest-running show in Broadway history, and by mid-August 1985 had
totalled 4,168 performances without showing any sign of letting up. The
show had been conceived by Michael Bennett as a work of homage to the
invincible, yet unsung, heroes of hundreds of Broadway musicals, the
chorus dancers, known as "gypsies." Bennett was himself a former member
of their ranks and well understood the anguish and joy that went with the
territory. To develop his idea he worked for nine months in a workshop
environment with his dancers and collaborators, composer Marvin Hamlisch, librettists James Kirkwood and Nicholas Dante, lyricist Edward
Kleban, and co-choreographer Bob Avian. The Public Theatre subsidized
the work and was repaid many times over by the eventual profits reaped.

During the workshop period Bennett tape-recorded discussions with
twenty-four gypsies, and these were then expanded and polished into what
became the show's book. The nightmares, pressures, and thrills of being a
dancer, as expressed in this material, became a series of monologues, songs,
and dances performed as though within the context of a Broadway audition.

The show opened on April 15, 1975, at the Public and soon moved to
Broadway's Shubert where it was still playing as of this writing. The
marvelous ensemble work of the cast was lauded, with special bravos for
Donna McKechnie, Priscilla Lopez, Sammy Williams, and Carole (later
Kelly) Bishop. Nine Tonys were among *A Chorus Line*'s numerous awards.

Turning back to nostalgia for a moment, we must mention two great hits
which were not specifically show-business in orientation but did thrive
because of their look backward at supposedly more innocent times. These

were *Grease* and *Dance With Me*. The former, by Jim Jacobs and Warren Casey, recreated the world of high-school teenagers of the fifties, with a conventional plot about a love affair between a "greasy" boy and the nice new girl in town, supported by a clever pastiche score that sounded just like real fifties rock and roll. Its gigantic success made it the longest-running Broadway show until *A Chorus Line* surpassed it. *Dance With Me* was another fifties-oriented musical, originally done Off Off-Broadway, later produced at the Public as *Dance Wi' Me*, and finally incarnated on Broadway (after a gap of three years) with the former title. It seemed best in its Public Theatre phase, but ran at a small Broadway house for 396 performances. It thrived on nostalgia as its hero, a guy in his thirties, fantasized about the fifties while waiting for a subway train.

Historical subject matter formed the backbone of a small group of shows. Among the four set in the Middle Ages (three of them about Joan of Arc), *Pippin* (1,194 performances), a Bob Fosse triumph which brought dancer Ann Reinking to prominence, stood out. Its score was by Stephen Schwartz, one of three during the decade that made him a wealthy man. Its action occurred in the eighth century and revolved around the stock plot of a youth searching for his place in life; the youth was Pippin (or Pepin; John Rubinstein), son and heir to the ruler of the Holy Roman Empire. Fosse turned a bland book into an evening of razzledazzle that did not completely cover up the flaws in the writing. Fosse's conception, as in his *Chicago*, looked at the world as a theatrical extravaganza, relating the story of Pippin's adventures through the eyes of a *commedia dell'arte* pack of players led by Ben Vereen as a song-and-dance emcee in modern clothes.

Lastly, there was one show that derived from a modern historical figure, Eva Perón, who died of cancer in 1952, aged thirty-three. The musical, originating in London, was *Evita* (1,568 performances), the brainchild of Andrew Lloyd Webber and Tim Rice. It was a bookless excursion into the life and politics of the wife of Argentina's late dictator, who slept her way from the ranks of B-movie players to the position of a national legend. It was directed by the ubiquitous Hal Prince, and starred then-unknowns Patti LuPone as the eponymous heroine, Mandy Patinkin as Ché Guevara, and Bob Gunton as Juan Perón.

Choreographic movement, action-filled stage pictures, and thrilling use of crowds, projections, and film sequences were used to narrate the cautionary tale of the glamorous Evita, who electrified the oppressed and downtrodden *descamisados* or "shirtless ones" to whom she made promises she only sometimes kept. As produced in New York, certain romantic elements of the material were removed so as not to overglamorize the central figure. Many thought the excisions were too few, because Eva Perón was deemed by them as a depraved, fascistic person, but Webber and Rice insisted that the show was anti-Evita. Like *Jesus Christ Superstar*, by the same team, the show had been born as a best-selling album and had developed a tremendous following for the number, "Don't Cry for Me, Argentina," even before the show had been produced.

REVUES

Rock musicals, we have seen, were one answer to the decade's search for new and innovative ways of making the musical theatre an attractive entertainment for youthful audiences. Their frequent emphasis on hard, driving rhythms, ear-splitting sound, and simple and repetitious lyrics, however, were incapable of serving the traditional needs of the musical form as it had evolved on Broadway. Before long, the book became a barely visible adjunct to the visually flashy staging techniques employed to keep these shows from standing still. The rock concept did produce several hits, but the demands of the musical stage soon made it apparent that rock was no panacea for Broadway's ills. Rock did far better on records and in concerts than when forced to deal with even the slightest pretext for a story and characters.

Musicals with solid librettos may have been considered old-fashioned, but the records show that they were still in demand. The problem was that their numbers were dwindling from year to year. Nevertheless, a look at the long-running shows of the decade reveals that of the twenty-four musicals achieving at least 500 performances, seventeen had conventional books and seven were what might loosely be termed the non-book variety.

The dearth of exciting new librettos and scores, combined with the dizzying climb in production costs, led many producers to substitute other forms of musical entertainment. Their efforts gave rise to an exceptionally large number of shows that can, with some liberty, be called "revues." These shows generally compiled a group of musical numbers, sung and/or danced around one of the following concepts: (1) a famous star's performance; (2) a small group of performers doing the work of a major composer or lyricist; (3) an eclectic assortment of musical materials relating to a literary, historical, or topical theme. A final type of revue might be one in which the music is secondary to the comedy elements, although it is often difficult to separate one ingredient from the other.

Star Revues

The stars who had their own Broadway shows were generally those with multiple talents—singing, dancing, and comedic. In almost all cases they worked with an onstage orchestra and with either a backup group or other acts that appeared while they rested. Frequently, the shows were similar to the kind available in nightclubs; several were actually seen in Las Vegas. The shows were generally offered for limited runs of a week or two, only a few running longer.

Male stars with their own shows included Sammy Davis, Jr., Harry Chapin, Bruce Forsythe, Peter Allen, and, Off-Broadway, Joe Masiell. Female stars were Liza Minnelli, Bette Midler, Diana Ross, Shirley MacLaine, Josephine Baker, and, Off-Broadway, Geraldine Fitzgerald.

An idea of what these shows were like can be gleaned from a brief look at Shirley MacLaine's (*Shirley MacLaine at the Palace*). Her show capitalized on her dancing talents, which were set off by a five-member backup group. She sang some songs, did some acting (including a monologue from one of her films), and chatted casually with the audience. Her glamour was enhanced by frequent costume changes. The much-liked show (except for a tasteless wisecrack in which MacLaine likened New York to a comatose New Jersey girl currently in the news, by calling it "the Karen Quinlan of American cities") gained her a return engagement several months later.

Composer Revues

Revues arranged around the output of a famous songwriter are sometimes called anthologies; they consist of a selection of well-known or, sometimes, unknown songs performed in one of several formats. The material can be staged in the abstract—that is, with one or more singers presenting the words and music straightforwardly with minimal movement; the movement may be formal but not mimetic; or the movement may be mimetic, with the thematic content acted out in situations devised by the director and/or choreographer. Most shows use an assortment of such techniques but lean heavily on one or another. In several instances, the composers themselves appeared, to sing or introduce their songs.

Composers and lyricists represented by their own shows were Kurt Weill (two shows), Jacques Brel, Howard Dietz and Arthur Schwartz, Sammy Cahn, Richard Rodgers and Lorenz Hart, Harry Chapin, Stephen Sondheim, Betty Comden and Adolph Green, the Beatles, Fats Waller, Eubie Blake, all on Broadway, and—Off-Broadway—Noël Coward, George Gershwin, Leonard Cohen, Kurt Tucholsky, Cole Porter, Leonard Bernstein, John Kander and Fred Ebb, David Shire and Richard Maltby, Jr., Charles Strouse, and Fred Silver.

Three of these, the Sondheim, Beatles, and Waller shows were big hits. Their formats are representative.

Side by Side by Sondheim (384 performances) was a sophisticated minirevue originated in London, featuring three singers, a narrator, and two piano players. A well-balanced selection of the composer's Broadway tunes was proferred in a simple, elegant staging, using no fancy pyrotechnics. The players wore fashionable contemporary clothes and used a few selective props, such as top hats, walking-sticks, and feather boas.

Beatlemania (920-plus performances; precise figures are not available as no opening night was ever announced), on the other hand, was in the vein earlier termed "hippie/rock" and was a multimedia presentation; it used the British foursome's music to counterpoint a slide-and-film show devised to reveal the historical events providing the background from which the music evolved. Thirty-six writers, designers, editors, and photographers were employed to create the background images. Look-alikes of John Lennon, Ringo Starr, George Harrison, and Paul McCartney performed the music.

Ain't Misbehavin' (1,604 performances) was born Off Off-Broadway; it was a revue confected primarily to show off Fats Waller's songs, but it also included music of his contemporaries. It succeeded as much because of its songs as because of Richard Maltby's excellent staging, Arthur Faria's choreography, and the versatile five-member black company. Unlike the Sondheim retrospective, the show exploded with movement, humor, sensuality, and earthiness. Each song was staged to bring out its story line, and the performers developed specific characters to which they kept throughout.

Music and Theme Revues

The work of great songwriters was a natural revue subject. Some producers also thought that non-musical writers could, if their writings were set to music, make for effective entertainment, so the poems of Ogden Nash, Walt Whitman, and William Shakespeare were transmogrified for melodic interpretation. Some shows sought to musicalize a group of writers; *Nightclub Cantata* used the words of several modern authors as did *Paris Lights*, based on the words of expatriate Americans in 1920s Paris.

More popular for revue subject matter was a body of music that could somehow be tied with a neat thematic bow. In these works the number of composers represented varied widely; the criterion for selection was the aptness of the music in terms of the theme. Such shows were fairly common, there being eleven of them. Of the several black shows in the genre, *Bubbling Brown Sugar* and *One Mo' Time* were hits. The former, conceived by Rosetta LeNoire, pretended to be a book show, but actually constituted a parade of songs and dances dating from the twenties and thirties. Off-Broadway's *One Mo' Time* (1,372 performances), conceived and directed by Vernel Bagneris, was a resurrection of twenties Dixieland music and humor set within a 1926 New Orleans vaudeville theatre.

The long-running *A Day in Hollywood/A Night in the Ukraine* (588 performances) is difficult to classify because it was really two shows in one. The first half was a well-choreographed (by Tommy Tune) paean to popular Hollywood songs, with several new ones included, sung and danced by the supposed ushers of Grauman's Chinese Theatre. Part Two was a version of a Chekhov play as it might have been staged by and with the Marx Brothers. At least a half-dozen other revues were built on Hollywood nostalgia, but with new tunes.

Another six revues had non–movie-related show-business themes, two of them having a burlesque framework. One of the latter two, *Sugar Babies* (1,208 performances), was a major hit starring Mickey Rooney, in his Broadway debut at fifty-nine, and veteran tap-dancer Ann Miller. The show was put together by drama professor Ralph G. Allen with material gleaned from classical burlesque bits of the golden past.

The model show-biz revue was the Off-Broadway hit *Scrambled Feet* (831 performances) by John Driver and Jeffrey Haddow. This Chicago-created show was a well-balanced, witty melange of comic and musical scenes showing the triumphs and troubles of actors, agents, producers, critics, and audiences as presented by a company of three men, one woman, and a duck on the postage-stamp stage of the Village Gate.

Two final "theatre" revues were concerned with dancing, *The American Dance Machine* and *Dancin'*. The more successful was the latter (1,774 performances), a Bob Fosse inspiration, featuring Ann Reinking, which had no words but concentrated entirely on the delights of terpsichorean art. Fosse devised a series of varying dance routines based on a spectrum of Broadway styles, but the fact that the same man created them all took away some of their potential diversity. One reason for *Dancin'*s longevity was that it could be appreciated by foreign tourists who didn't understand English.

The remaining eighteen or so musical revues were a mixed Off-Broadway batch ranging from *The Club*, with its small cast of women playing turn-of-the-century clubmen and satirizing male chauvinist attitudes, to two often hilarious shows produced under the banner of the *National Lampoon* and bringing young unknowns John Belushi, Harold Ramis, Chevy Chase, Bill Murray, and Gilda Radner to New York's attention. A couple, such as *The Red, White and Black*, had political motives, while several others touched on conservation, ecology, and sex.

Let My People Come (1,167 performances Off-Broadway; 106 on), an Off-Broadway show by Earl Wilson, Jr., had produced a successful album, sent out touring companies, and converted to Equity status, but chose not to invite the critics. Mel Gussow of the *New York Times* decided on his own to see it, despite the producer's objections. He panned it, but its success continued unabated. It was largely preoccupied with sexual experiences (song titles included such ditties as "Fellatio 101" and "Come in my Mouth"), and its cast was nude throughout much of it. At the end, they stood naked at the exits, shaking hands with the departing spectators. Ultimately, the show moved to Broadway.

A small number of the revues about life in modern America were erected on a flimsily plotted scaffolding, so that the audience could identify with characters and situations. Essentially, these were non-book musicals, but can be classed as revues because of their continuing sequence of songs, unabetted by any but a suggestion of a libretto. A good example of the type was Liz Swados' *Runaways* (76 performances Off-Broadway; 267 on), devoted to the problems of runaway kids. With the aid of various youth agencies Swados came in contact with some 2,000 youngsters, some of them runaways themselves, and selected 19 for her show. Doing theatre games and exercises with them in workshops, she gathered the material that she forged into *Runaways*, an often touching show about the harrowing experiences faced by young people when faced by brutality in and outside the home. Related to *Runaways* was the less effective *Working*, based on Studs Terkel's "oral history" of the experiences of working folk.

Black thematic revues moved from the evocation of black musical history to black topical concerns. There was also *Inner City*, based on Eve Merriam's *Inner City Mother Goose*, a white-created but largely black-performed ghetto revue, which cast a jaundiced eye on New York slum life. Micki Grant's *Don't Bother Me, I Can't Cope* was a rock gospel revue about black life that played 1,065 times.

Tuscaloosa's Calling Me, But I'm Not Going (429 performances) celebrated the joys, not the sorrows, of New York life, and did so with widespread critical approval. Some of the less pleasant aspects of the city were the core of another revue, *Potholes*, by former Commissioner of Consumer Affairs Elinor Guggenheimer.

Famous entertainers of the past provided grist for the revue mill in such works as *Dear Piaf* and *Piaf . . . a Remembrance*, about the late chanteuse, and *The Magic of Jolson*.

Four imports were cast in the revue mold (in addition to the Israeli shows mentioned earlier). The Soviet Union gave us *Estrada*; Maori culture inspired *Pacific Paradise*; Irish folk culture sparked *Siamsa*; and South African blacks were behind *Ipi-Tombi*, which caused a stir among those who picketed it for being pro-apartheid, even though only by indirection.

Comedy Revues

Comedy or satirical revues which depended more on their sketches than on their songs were an important presence during the seventies. Several shows mentioned in the previous section might conceivably belong to this genre. Nevertheless, an attempt has been made to separate the primarily comedy-oriented shows into a separate section, even when their stars, such as Victor Borge, were accomplished musicians who used music as significant ingredients in their work.

Several variations of the comedy revue might be considered. There were the one-person revues, the two-person revues, the improvisational revues, the scattershot revues on diverse subjects, and, lastly, the thematic revues in which the subjects might be varied but are within the same general firing range. Naturally, there is some overlapping, but these loose borderlines should help in viewing the terrain.

The one-person revue was represented by *Lily Tomlin in "Appearing Nightly,"* *A Man and His Women*, and *Housewife! Superstar!* The latter two were Off-Broadway drag shows, the former a successful enterprise showing the gifted comedienne's versatility at characterization. *Gilda Radner, Live from New York* centered on the zany comedienne, but she was musically and comedically supported by a crew of other players.

Bob and Ray, the Two and Only; Good Evening; Monteith and Rand; and *Comedy with Music* (with Victor Borge and singer Marilyn Mulvey)— these were the decade's two-person revues. The smash hit of the genre was the second, starring Dudley Moore and Peter Cook, two Britons who had once formed half of the hit comedy revue of the sixties, *Beyond the Fringe.* Part of the show included Moore's virtuoso piano playing.

One of the duos mentioned, Monteith and Rand, used improvisation as part of their routine. Two Off-Broadway revues of the period were almost entirely devoted to comedy created from spontaneous suggestions, although in some cases the bits were preestablished with set speeches and business. These shows were *The Proposition* and *Cooler Near the Lake*, the first of which was a 1,109-performance hit that did well enough to earn a return engagement later in the decade with a new cast.

A few poorly received Off-Broadway topical shows with carefully rehearsed comedy material on a variety of subjects came and went rapidly; the only fully scripted sequence of comedy sketches to score well was Jules Feiffer's drawings of modern urban problems come to life, *Hold Me!*.

* * *

The musical and satirical stage in New York saw a vast degree of diversity in the forms of expression taken by the modes examined in this chapter. The strictly comic revue was becoming an endangered species, as was the conventional book musical, but musical revues, comedy-with-music revues, and bookless musicals were fast rising to take their place. Many viewers were disturbed by these developments, especially those who wanted stories and characters with their songs and dances. Even in those shows that succeeded with conventional books, the book was invariably found by critics to be the weakest link in the chain. Whether this meant that the book musical would eventually become an archaeological artifact, like the operetta, or would be replaced by scripts developed in workshops, like *A Chorus Line*, would become clear only after the passing of another decade or two.

★ 5 ★
PATTERNS

One of the advantages of a decade's-eye view of theatrical activity is that the viewer begins to see various patterns that, from a closer perspective, such as an annual one, are less easy to discern. Within the comfortable yet representative confines of a ten-year stretch, certain persistent subjects and treatments tend to crop up in plays. By identifying these the observer can concentrate on just those areas that seem to dominate creative and audience interests during a specific point in history. The theatre returns over and over to particular topics and issues; the degree of such repetition, if recognized, surely provides a valid image of general social concerns and attitudes during the time in question.

It would require a book of its own just to survey all the patterns and trends that are discoverable in the New York theatre of the seventies. The subjects treated by playwrights can be categorized, subcategorized, and sub-subcategorized until a total picture emerges of just how many plays dealt with each broad subject, character grouping, locale, dramatic genre, and so on. In this chapter only representative subjects and approaches are covered.

Subject matter is examined in terms of characters, the "worlds" they inhabit, and the issues that concern them. Under their own headings are sections dealing with plays about the elderly, women, homosexuals, and blacks. There is also a section that looks at the wealth of biographical plays. Following these are sections that treat of plays about show business, politics, war, religion, and the physical and mental ills of central characters.

Clearly, a degree of arbitrariness is involved in selecting topics; however, the discussion, while necessarily brief, should offer an adequate picture of the areas selected to make clear the preoccupations of the decade's dramatists. Several musicals are included in the coverage, although the musical theatre as a whole is treated in the preceding chapter.[1]

CHARACTERS

The Elderly

The seventies was a period of many social "power" movements, not least of which was that of "gray power." Senior citizens were becoming increasingly vocal in their fight for recognition of the special needs faced by the elderly in a youth-oriented culture. Judging by the number of plays that dealt with the aging, dramatists were beginning to acknowledge the validity of their refusal to be treated as "second-class" citizens.

In some works the idea was to show how peppy and full of youthful life the septuagenarians, octogenarians, and nonagenarians were. Two musicals, 70, Girls, 70 and My Old Friends, and the revue Antiques took this tack. Several pictured the geriatric years as sexually and/or romantically active ones. In this group were Harold and Maude; Something Old, Something New; The Kingfisher; Last Licks; Catsplay; and Do You Turn Somersaults? Others sought to concentrate on the central figure (or two) of an eccentric, and perhaps cantankerous, personality: The Gin Game, A Matter of Gravity, The Elephant in the House, Seduced, Home, "Da," The Sunshine Boys, No Man's Land, and The Oldest Living Graduate fit the picture. Some sought to evoke sympathy for the problems of adjustment faced when growing old (Ice Age, Older People, Days in the Trees, Touching Bottom, and Just the Immediate Family), while a number dealt with the confrontation of the elderly with death (The Shadow Box, "Da," On Golden Pond, Bosoms and Neglect, Twigs, The National Health, and Checking Out).

Women

Actresses have always complained that, compared to actors, there are very few good parts for them. During the seventies many playwrights sought to rectify that situation by producing a stream of works focusing on women and their problems. One sign of the impact of Women's Liberation was the number of plays in which there were no male characters at all. Table 5.1—which excludes one-woman pieces—covers more than twenty plays.

Many of these works were not specifically feminist, nor were the majority written by women. What their number reveals is that women, their interests, and their status in society were becoming topics of sufficient

Table 5.1
Plays with All-Women Casts

A Coupla White Chicks . . .

The Club (revue)

Daughters of the Mock

Fefu and Her Friends

Les Femmes Noires

For Colored Girls . . .

Ladies at the Alamo

Ladyhouse Blues

Later

A Lovely Sunday for Crève Coeur

Parto

Patio/Porch

A Quarter for the Ladies Room (revue)

Slag

Taken in Marriage

These Men

Uncommon Women and Others

Vanities

Wine Untouched

Women Behind Bars

political interest and audience appeal to cause numerous playwrights to focus on them. It should also be remembered that many plays which were not entirely devoted to feminist concerns nevertheless made meaningful reference to them. The works discussed here are a representative selection chosen because of the intensity of their concern for women and their problems. (One-character works are not included here.)

While there were a number of musicals that spotlighted women as their central characters (*Chicago* is the best known), most were fairly conventional in their view of women's social roles. There were about a half-dozen, however, that came into existence specifically to express a political attitude about women. The best example was Gretchen Cryer and Nancy Ford's *I'm Getting My Act Together and Taking It on the Road*, an Off-Broadway hit based on Cryer's own life, in which she starred as a thirty-nine-year-old singer who decides to develop a fresh act, one in which her material bears directly on her experience as a modern woman. Another successful pro-female statement-making musical show was *The Club*.

Apart from overtly lesbian plays, like Off-Broadway's *The Divorce of Judy and Jane*, there were about seven straight dramas that honed in on the myriad anxieties endured by contemporary women. Almost all were Off-Broadway. *A Coupla White Chicks . . .* , *Vanities*, and British playwright David Hare's *Slag*—about three women schoolteachers at a declining girls' high school—were among them.

Several plays by black women bemoaned the state of black females who are abused by their men. *For Colored Girls . . .* was the best known of the group.

Among the five or six other plays dominated by female characters, but not grounded in feminist or anti-male rhetoric, were several that pictured family relations, typically between mothers and daughters. In one of them, *Twigs*, George Furth provided a tour-de-force opportunity for Sada Thompson, who portrayed, in four scenes, three sisters and their dying mother. There was no chance, however, for interplay between the mother and daughters.

The idea of women becoming major figures in American society was fast gaining ground and the decade's political campaigns saw more female candidates plugging for office than ever before. Women became mayors of major cities, presidents of city councils, governors, senators, and so on. Such situations had been exploited in several earlier plays when the idea of women in very high places was relatively anomalous; for some reason, however, plays on this theme were rare in the seventies, being confined to *An Almost Perfect Person*, about the defeat of a female candidate for the Senate, and *First Monday in October*, which anticipated by three years the appointment of the first woman to the United States Supreme Court.

Biographical Plays

One sign of the interest taken in women during the decade was the great number of biographical dramas dealing with famous members of that sex. Biography has been shown to be one of the most profitable of non-fiction genres in publishing, so there is little reason to suspect that its dramatic counterpart would not prove equally popular. It is true, however, that although there were between seventy-five and eighty plays dealing with the lives of distinguished (or notorious) individuals, only a handful may be counted as economic or artistic successes. Not all plays that included historical personages were necessarily biographical; actual figures from the past were occasionally employed because they were helpful for purposes of satire or fantasy, as in Jules Feiffer's use of Joan of Arc in *Knock Knock*.[2]

Tables 5.2 through 5.5 present the historical figures who were treated in the biographical dramas; the tables are broken down according to the following categories: plays about historical persons (with sub-categories for black history and American presidents), literary figures, performing artists,

Table 5.2
Biographical Plays

Plays about Historical Figures
Abelard and Héloise
Albert Einstein, the Practical Bohemian
*Billy Bishop Goes to War**
Clarence Darrow
Crown Matrimonial (Edward VII)
Elizabeth I
Evita (Eva Perón)
Gandhi
Golda (Golda Meir)
Goodtime Charley (Charles VII and Joan of Arc)
Herzl
Joan of Arc
The Karl Marx Play
The Last of Mrs. Lincoln
The Lincoln Mask (Mary Todd Lincoln)
Look Away (Mary Todd Lincoln)
Masquerade (Elizabeth I)
Murderous Angels (Patrice Lumumba and Dag Hammarskjold)
Pippin (son of Charlemagne)
Rex (Henry VIII)
The Survival of Saint Joan
Vivat! Vivat! Regina (Elizabeth I and Mary, Queen of Scots)

Plays about American Presidents
*Bully** (Theodore Roosevelt)
*JFK** (John F. Kennedy)
Jimmy and Billy (Jimmy Carter)
Lincoln (see above for plays about Lincoln's wife)
1600 Pennsylvania Avenue (panorama of American presidency)

Plays about Famous Black Americans
Frederick Douglass . . . Through His Own Words
El Hajj Malik (Malcolm X)
I Have a Dream (Martin Luther King, Jr.)
*Paul Robeson**

visual artists, and outlaws and dissidents. When the title itself does not make it clear, the names of the individuals about whom the plays were written are indicated in parentheses. Asterisks (*) in the tables indicate monodramas.

According to the listing in Table 5.2, the figures who stimulated the greatest amount of interest among dramatists were Mary Todd Lincoln, Joan of Arc, and Queen Elizabeth I.

Table 5.3
Plays about Literary Figures

---

*The Belle of Amherst** (Emily Dickinson)

Bingo (William Shakespeare)

*Blasts and Bravos; an Evening with H. L. Mencken**

*Charlotte** (Goethe's mistress)

Clothes for a Summer Hotel (F. Scott and Zelda Fitzgerald)

*Conversations with an Irish Rascal** (Brendan Behan)

Dear Oscar (Oscar Wilde)

*Diversions and Delights** (Oscar Wilde)

*Dylan Thomas Growing Up**

The Frankenstein Affair (Mary Shelley)

*Gertrude Stein, Gertrude Stein**

Gorky

I Love Thee Freely (Elizabeth Barrett Browning)

It's Wilde! (Oscar Wilde)

James Joyce's Dubliners

Letters Home (Sylvia Plath)

*My Astonishing Self** (George Bernard Shaw)

Night of the Tribades (August Strindberg)

*Opium** (Jean Cocteau)

*Shay Duffin as Brendan Behan**

Strangers (Dorothy Parker and Sinclair Lewis)

Sylvia Plath

Total Eclipse (Arthur Rimbaud and Paul Verlaine)

The one-person plays, or monodramas, among these works used a considerable amount of material written by the figures represented. Such pieces were generally more successful than the conventional dramas listed, not one of which found an audience. The most popular biographical figure in the listing was Oscar Wilde, subject of three works, musical and non-musical;

Table 5.4
Plays about Performing Artists

Barnum

Chinchilla (Sergei Diaghilev and Nijinsky)

An Evening with W. S. Gilbert

Isadora Duncan Sleeps with the Russian Navy

Lady Day; a Musical Tragedy (Billie Holiday)

Lenny

Mack and Mabel (Mabel Normand and Mack Sennett)

Manny (Edward G. Robinson)

Me and Bessie (Bessie Smith)

Piaf . . . A Remembrance

Richard Farina, Long Time Coming, Long Time Gone

Will Rogers USA *

Woody Guthrie *

The World of Lenny Bruce *

Table 5.5
Plays about Outlaws, Outcasts, and Dissidents

The Biko Inquest (Steve Biko)

The Collected Works of Billy the Kid

Diamond Studs (Jesse James)

Ice Age (Knut Hamsun)

The Jail Diary of Albie Sachs

Jesse and the Bandit Queen (Jesse James and Belle Star)

Salt Lake City Skyline (Joe Hill)

perhaps the permissiveness towards homosexuality prevalent in the decade made Wilde ripe for theatrical impersonation. Table 5.3 is notable for its abundance of female authors; Sylvia Plath, the late poet, was an icon of the era, as seen by two works devoted to her.

Artists, performing and visual, have long provided interesting subject matter for the theatre. Only two shows of the period, *Modigliani* and the musical *Not Tonight, Benvenuto* (about Benvenuto Cellini), dealt with visual artists, but plays about dancers, singers, comics, actors, and the like were quite common. Of them, only controversial comedian Lenny Bruce had more than one work devoted to him; this was ironic, as only a few years earlier Bruce's raunchy material would have been thought unfit for a Broadway audience's ears.

In Table 5.5 there are the plays about legendary but actual outlaws and those about contemporary social misfits and political dissidents.

Homosexuals

Plays with homosexual characters go back to the ancient Greeks, and examples can be found throughout the history of drama. Homosexual relations generally have been treated by society as aberrations; when serious attempts to probe the phenomenon appeared in modern theatre, the subject had to be tiptoed around so as not to offend the sensitivities of audiences. As recently as the 1920s Broadway actors were arrested for appearing in such plays as *Pleasure Man* and *The Captive*. In the years following, works such as *The Green Bay Tree, The Children's Hour, Trio*, and *Tea and Sympathy* were considered salacious and sensational, no matter how sympathetically or delicately they depicted the subject.

As the century progressed, society's moral attitudes, for many reasons, underwent violent wrenchings. What would once have landed a person in jail became a badge that was worn proudly. Activist groups fighting for the acceptance of gay men and women as normal, productive members of society were founded beginning in the late sixties, and Gay Lib joined Black Power, Fem Lib, and Gray Power as one of the oft-heard slogans of the age. The theatre, always quick to spot a shift in social attitudes, responded appropriately; the number of plays reflecting homosexual problems, experiences, and tastes rose dramatically.

Donald Loeffler concluded in *The Homosexual Character in Drama* that between 1950 and 1960 twenty-two plays with homosexual characters opened in New York; for 1960-70 his total was eighty-five.[3] His list for 1970-75 contains, apart from several Off Off plays, forty-one titles. In some, however, the homosexuality is merely implied. Also, the identified homosexuals are occasionally minor ones, not central to the action. In a few cases, they are offstage and never appear, only their presence being felt. Still, the great number of homosexual characters and themes in sixties and seventies plays and musicals argued for the growing respectability of gay life and surely was a factor in the movement that led so many gays to come out of the closet and accept themselves on their own terms.

Despite the prevalence of homosexual characters in sixties plays, the subject was normally handled evasively until the late-sixties productions of Lanford Wilson's *Madness of Lady Bright*, Charles Dyer's *Staircase*, John Herbert's *Fortune and Men's Eyes*, and, most especially, Mart Crowley's *The Boys in the Band* put overt homosexuals on the stage and dramatized with honesty their lives and loves. These plays may seem dated now because of their innate pessimism, but they led directly to the full-scale exploration of the homosexual subculture in close to one hundred main-stream works, and countless Off Off works, of the seventies.

The decade saw an explosion of gay theatre activity, particularly Off Off-Broadway where gay companies, such as TOSOS and the Glines, actively sought out new gay plays and artists. Gay-play directories, anthologies and festivals were offered and there was even a National Gay Playwriting Contest. Several gay playwrights of note, most prominently Noël Coward and Tennessee Williams, no longer hid their homosexuality, but some continued to reject the chance to admit their sexual tastes. A controversy arose early in the decade when the pseudonymous Lee Barton, author of Off-Broadway's *Nightride*, refused to reveal his real name for fear of reprisals in the industry that provided his living. Critics were always trying to unearth the alleged homosexual substrata in the work of certain writers, especially Edward Albee.

It is important to keep in mind when considering gay theatre that, in addition to plays attempting psychological, social, or political portraits of the gay character and milieu, a large body of gay work is homosexual not so much in theme or content as in style or manner. The so-called "homosexual sensibility" is best represented by the term "camp"; works that appeal to a largely gay audience because of their humorous in-group associations, especially when dealing with nostalgic aspects of the world of entertainment, are not directly examined in the following.

The new frankness with which writers now were willing and able to handle homosexuality was responsible for an assortment of Off-Broadway shows that might be taken as celebrations of the gay life-style. These included such musicals and revues as *The Faggot, Lovers, In Gay Company*, and *The Bar That Never Closes*. Pain as well as laughter was mingled in some of these works, as in the nine-man *Crimes Against Nature*. The show that some consider the best gay "celebration" was *Fourtune*, a musical about a singing group of two men and two women in which bisexuality was proferred as a highly desirable choice.

It was rare that homosexuals were presented as cringing creatures, frightened to admit their preferences. The problem of coming out of the closet was crucial in only four plays, *Family Business, Nightride, Noël Coward in Two Keys*, and *Bent*.

With all the plays being written about homosexuals, it is surprising that so few were successful depictions of meaningful romantic relationships between gay partners. Love affairs figured in or were tangential to several plays, but few of them were of more than passing interest to most audiences and critics. The most successful in this group of nine plays were the musical *Boy Meets Boy*, Harvey Fierstein's *International Stud* and *Fugue in a Nursery*, and Wilson's *The Fifth of July. Boy Meets Boy* was a spoof of thirties musicals and was about a love affair between a journalist and an English aristocrat who has run off or his wedding day because he did not love the man he was to marry. Fierstein's two plays, about the travails of a drag queen, played by the author, were part of his *Torch Song Trilogy*, which blossomed into a major hit of the next decade.

These shows were about bachelors; plays about gay women were barely visible in comparison. One that had to do with lesbian relationships was Arthur Whitney's *The Divorce of Judy and Jane*. *Yentl* had overtones of lesbianism in its depiction of what its title character refers to as "the divine androgyny of the soul,"[4] but critics insisted that Yentl is heterosexual throughout. In *Best Friend* by Michael Sawyer there were further lesbian implications.

Dramatizations of the dilemmas of divorced or married gays were common. *Night of the Tribades* and *Losing Time* had married lesbians in the cast list. Robert M. Lane's *Foreplay* and Martin Fox's *The Office Murders* as well as *Butley, Ashes, Total Eclipse, Deathtrap, Mecca, The Shadow Box, California Suite*, and, of course, the three pieces about Oscar Wilde presented married men who prefer members of their own sex.

The homosexual world was sometimes depicted as a tragic, frightening one for its inhabitants. Jack Marshall's *The Olathe Response*, Frederick Combs' *The Children's Mass*, Lindsay Kemp's mime-drama *Flowers*, Patrick Meyers' *Feedlot*, George Birimisa's *Georgie Porgie*, the Australian *Elocution of Benjamin*, Sawyer's *Naomi Court*, Pinero's *Short Eyes*, and Eyen's *Women Behind Bars* depicted masochism, sadism, murder, vampirism, drug addiction, rape, voyeurism, bondage, and transvestitism as concomitants of the gay life style. In the most successful of this group, James Kirkwood's *P.S. Your Cat Is Dead*, a young actor apprehends a burglar and ties him over the kitchen sink, face down and bent over. Most of the action concerns the robber's attempt to talk the presumably hetero actor into having sex with him.

A couple of shows used the potential humor of homosexuality and transvestitism for purposes of comedy and farce. *Sugar*, based on the film classic *Some Like It Hot*, was a hit Broadway musical about a pair of heterosexual musicians who must hide from pursuing mobsters by dressing as women and joining an all-girl band; other shows trading on similar confusion were *Wise Child* and *The Ritz*.

Transvestitism, indeed, as can be seen from many of the above examples, was rampant on New York stages. Audiences have been laughing at men dressed as women as far back as Euripides' *The Bacchae*. To get an idea of the prevalence of the practice in the seventies, one need only glance at the following table which lists shows that employed it to one degree or another.

Some of these shows were not specifically gay in theme so much as they were gay-inclined in manner. The list does not include the various revivals of old plays done with all-male casts (or *Fashion*, which was revived with a nearly all-woman company), or with men playing roles that would ordinarily go to women. Dennis Reardon's *Siamese Connections*, for example, used

Table 5.6
Plays Employing Transvestitism

A Man and His Women

Bad Habits

The Bar That Never Closes

Bent

Bluebeard

Caprice

The Children's Mass

The Club

Cracks

The Elocution of Benjamin

Flowers

Hosanna

Housewife! Superstar!

International Stud

Little Black Sheep

Marco Polo Sings a Solo

The Neon Woman

The Nuns

Der Ring Gott Farblonjett

The Rocky Horror Show

Sugar

The Utter Glory of Morrissey Hall

Women Behind Bars

Yentl

---

a man to play a female role, although without a clear reason, and apparently without any attempt to be funny. There were, as well, a number of well-publicized Off Off shows that revelled in their campy transvestitism, including *Tinsel Tarts in a Hot Coma*, *Vain Victory*, and *Heaven Grand in Amber Orbit*.

In addition, there were plays that, while not dealing with clear-cut cases of homosexuality, nevertheless hovered about the topic. In Daniel Hollywood and Richard T. Johnson's *All the Girls Came Out to Play*, for example, a young stud gains easy access to the beds of the local femmes when they suspect him of being queer.

Several plays considered cases of incipient deviance, in each case a youth whose preference leaned towards bisexuality or homosexuality. This psychological state was projected in *A Breeze From the Gulf*, *The Transfiguration of Benno Blimpie*, and *Gemini*. Then there were at least eighteen plays that featured important gay characters in supporting roles, as in *My Fat Friend*, *The Gingerbread Lady*, *A Chorus Line*, *Streamers*, *Kennedy's Children*, *The Kingfisher*, and *Steambath*.

ETHNIC BACKGROUNDS

In the seventies the melting pot of the New York stage was particularly favorable to several distinct ethnic groups. It was not an especially productive period for plays about Native Americans or Hispanics, however, as only a very few works dealt with the lives of these people. Oriental characters were more in evidence, although, apart from a few exceptions (a notable one was the musical *Pacific Overtures*), they were normally played by Caucasians (or even blacks). Plays about Jews were continually in evidence, as they had been for many years, and a wide assortment of Jewish themes, domestic, historical, and legendary was available.

It was blacks, however, about whom the most plays of an ethnic character were written. In Chapter 3 a survey of black playwriting during the period is presented. A rapid overview of the full-length black plays of the decade should make clear their principal concerns. (Musical shows are considered in Chapter 4.)

The sixties had seen several virulently militant anti-white dramas produced, but the tone of most seventies black plays was more subdued, more involved with investigating the day-to-day existence of the average black person and discovering what it means to be black in America. Racism is an invisible thread that pierces nearly every one of these works, but the characters generally are too preoccupied with living their lives and handling their personal relationships to spout rhetorical slogans and attempt to discomfit or rally audiences.

The most overtly political plays were *The Black Terror*, *The Taking of Miss Janie*, *Every Night When the Sun Goes Down*, and *The Twilight Dinner*, but even in these the messages were directed more at the lives of the characters depicted than at combatting anti-black prejudice. Several critics accused the historical-musical cavalcade *Ododo* by Joseph Walker of being stridently anti-white, but others disagreed. By the late seventies the "Get Whitey" play seemed to be a historical artifact. The inward-turning eye of black writers examined such subjects as the role of the black bourgeois and/or intellectual vis-à-vis political outrage; the relations between black women and their husbands/lovers; the debilitating effects of ghetto life; the difficulty of being a black female; and a variety of family and domestic situations.

There were several pieces that tried to use a revue or sketch-like format to draw a cross-section of black character types. Black history, aside from the few biographical plays mentioned earlier, was looked at in only two works, *The Brownsville Raid* and *Ododo*.

Just as black playwrights often included white characters in their plays, white playwrights often wrote about blacks. Of the half-dozen examples of such plays with blacks as central characters, perhaps the most outstanding examples are *Streamers* and Tom Coles' *Medal of Honor Rag*. These two were the only ones that were not accused of conventional middle-class white liberal distortions of their black characters. Coles' play is about the examination by a white Army psychiatrist of a black Medal of Honor winner who is arrested for a violent crime.

DRAMATIC WORLDS

The topics looked at in the last four sections dealt with specific types of individuals, i.e. the elderly, women, homosexuals, and ethnic groups. What follows is concerned with selected subject areas, or dramatic worlds, in which such individuals were likely to exist.

Naturally, there are countless possibilities from which dramatists can choose in providing backgrounds for the behavior of their characters, and there are numerous social issues and behavioral patterns that crop up repeatedly in the plays of any period. In the 1920s, for example, crime and business were exceptionally popular subjects for plays. The world of sports has often inspired plays, as have those of art, journalism, music, education, prostitution, science, law, and literature.

Social problems such as drugs, alcohol, adultery, and obesity make interesting areas for theatrical exploration. Similarly, aging, feminism, homosexuality, and racism are serious issues—although plays on these subjects have been treated above under character concerns. In addition, plays may be viewed in terms of specific stylistic frameworks, such as fantasy, mystery, and science fiction, any one of which may be thought of as a type of dramatic "world."

Each of these subjects, issues, and styles was employed in the seventies, most of them repeatedly; however, the sections that ensue survey only five areas which were, judging by the frequency of their appearance, of particular interest to playwrights of the decade, namely, the worlds of show business, politics, religion, war, and illness, both physical and mental.

Show Business

People who go to the theatre are usually interested in people who make theatre. Few subjects have had as much general interest for theatregoers as the lives, frustrations, successes, downfalls, and glamour of show folk.

Plays with theatre backgrounds go back, as do so many other dramatic subjects, to the ancient Greeks. Aristophanes, it will be recalled, actually wrote a comedy about a contest to decide who was the better playwright, Euripides or Aeschylus.

Audience interest in the back-, off-, and onstage lives of members of the entertainment world must have been quite sharp in the seventies, as such a background was found in over one hundred works. In fact, the longest-running hit in Broadway history, *A Chorus Line*, may be considered the quintessential show-biz musical.

The entertainment world offers many facets for dramatists to explore. One of the most popular is the life and working methods of actors. The seventies offered a healthy share of plays about performers who hope to be the new discoveries of their age. There were also one or two comeback plays about down-and-out actors, while about six plays dealt with acting companies and their travails. Several of these offered a glimpse of actors in rehearsal, a subject that formed a major part of at least seven dramas, including two specifically titled *Dreyfus in Rehearsal* and *Jack Gelber's New Play: In Rehearsal*. And, of course, actors as characters in plays not particularly focused on their work were relatively common.

Playwrights also were frequently seen as characters, as witness the nutty one in *Rich and Famous*, the murderous one in *Deathtrap*, the witty one in *Romantic Comedy*, the dejected one in *After the Rise*, the mysogynistic one in *Night of the Tribades*, the worried one in *Musical Chairs*, and the devious one in *Break a Leg*. Songwriters got their due in *The House of Blue Leaves* and *They're Playing Our Song*.

Dancers were recognized most effectively in *A Chorus Line*, but also in *Chinchilla* and *Jockeys*, which featured ballet dancers, *Isadora Duncan Sleeps with the Russian Navy*, about a founder of modern dance, *People in Show Business Make Long Goodbyes*, about nightclub dancers, *In the Boom Boom Room*, centering on a go-go dancer, and *Got Tu Go Disco*, which gave disco dancing a bad name.

The world of vaudeville was conjured up in *One Mo' Time*, *Variety Obit*, and *The Sunshine Boys*; burlesque came back in *Big Bad Burlesque* and *Sugar Babies*, and the old time revues came to ghostly life in *Follies*.

The tribulations of pop singers were essential to *The Gingerbread Lady* and one or two others, while revelations about nightclub stars were made in *The Act*, *I'm Getting My Act Together . . .* , and several less notable works. Sleazy nightclubs and their wares were hilariously exploded in *El Grande de Coca-Cola*.

Singing groups were prominent in the Andrews Sisters' *Over Here!*, and in *Fourtune*, a paean to bisexuality. Life on rock music's fast track was the basis for five plays and musicals, including *Kid Champion* and *Platinum*, and jazz musicians were conspicuous in *Sugar* and *Doctor Jazz*.

Prestidigitation supplied the background of *The Magic Show* and *Grand*

Magic. Barnum put the audience through musical hoops in its depiction of circus showmanship.

Stand-up comics were handled in two shows about Lenny Bruce, one about Will Rogers, and three others, including the fine British play *Comedians*.

Show biz itself was spoofed in a number of these works, most effectively in the revue *Scrambled Feet*.

Hollywood and its products had been popular dramatic fodder for over fifty years. The seventeen seventies shows with a film background included examples about black screenwriters, down-and-out screenwriters, silent-screen personalities, and filmmakers of the future. Affectionate revues and campy pastiches of cinema glamour were rather common, ranging from *A Day in Hollywood/A Night in the Ukraine* to Christopher Durang's *A History of the American Film*. The passions of campy film buffs were the subject of *The Secret Affairs of Mildred Wild* and *Movie Buff*. Great film stars inspired a small number of plays, including two thinly disguised and rapidly rejected treatments of Marilyn Monroe. If most of these shows dramatized, musicalized, or fantasized about the old Hollywood, a new breed of movie makers were thought a fit subject for two shows about performers in pornographic films.

Another form of the mass media was represented in such radio-related plays as *The Shortchanged Review* and *City Sugar*, both about disc jockeys, and *The Water Engine* and *The 1940s Radio Hour*, each a recreation of a forties-style radio program. Television was not overlooked: *Telecast*, *The Selling of the President*, and *Shelter* all owed their existence to the small screen.

So pervasive was show business in the decade's offerings that several shows not specifically about the entertainment world were presented within a decidedly show-biz format; in *Smith*, for instance, a scientist realizes he is living his life as a musical comedy, and both *Pippin* and *Chicago* told their tales through self-consciously theatrical imagery, albeit one was about a medieval ruler and the other about a Jazz Age murderess.

Politics

Because politics is so important in our lives and is so infrequently a source of satisfaction to the average man, it is customary in free societies to laugh at those officials and policies with which we disagree. Once more, recall the Greeks. Nevertheless, political satire was not especially noticeable on New York's stages in the seventies, despite many issues that cried out for laugh-provoking criticism and comment. Various reasons for this have been advanced: the disturbing polarization of the nation in the wake of Vietnam; the possibility that the radical movements of the sixties and early seventies made political comedy redundant; the painfulness of the issues involved; a growing feeling of apathy and helplessness, and so on. Whatever the cause, political satire was not a fruitful theatrical mode for most of the decade.

The single most potent image for satirists was that of former President Richard M. Nixon, who resigned from office in 1973. Of the seven or eight works that might be termed political satires, four were aimed at him, although the protagonist's name was usually disguised. These were Gore Vidal's *An Evening with Richard Nixon and . . .* , the musical *The Selling of the President*, Peter Ustinov's *Who's Who in Hell*, and *Pop*, a musical farce using *King Lear* as its premise.

Other political satires were *Rubbers* and *Dirty Linen*, the first being a deflation of the New York State Assembly, the second of Britain's Parliament. Political revues included Eric Bentley's *The Red, White and Black* and *What's a Nice Country Like You Doing in a State Like This?*.

Political concerns were present in many plays, but few were directly addressed to the immediate interests of the American people. Most were about foreign situations; the subject matter was usually of universal rather than topical significance. Of the few plays that did look at American issues, two dealt with the era of McCarthyism. One was Bentley's docudrama, *Are You Now or Have You Ever Been?* based on the hearings in the forties and fifties by a subcommittee of the House Un-American Activities Committee (HUAC) inquiring into the political beliefs of major show business figures. An interesting feature of the piece was the use of a series of star actresses to read a famous letter written by Lillian Hellman to the members of the subcommittee. HUAC was also treated in Gerhard Borris' *After the Rise* with its obvious debt to Arthur Miller's *After the Fall*.

Probably the most controversial of the topical political plays was *The Trial of the Catonsville Nine*, a docudrama by Father Daniel Berrigan, S.J., one of the participants in the action. (Saul Levitt adapted the piece for the stage.) It is about the trial of Jesuit priests Daniel and Philip Berrigan and a group of other activists for having used napalm to destroy draft files at Catonsville, Maryland, in 1968. It came to New York from Los Angeles' Mark Taper, opened Off-Broadway, and then moved to Broadway with a largely new cast. The play was viewed as a plea for the necessity of civil disobedience as an act of Christian faith. Many legal and social issues were raised by its attack on contemporary American values and governmental policies, while it also managed to jab sharply at the Catholic Church. It was the author's contention that drama's purpose is to have a moral impact in the light of world problems. He condemned theatre that exists only to pass the time and make money.

The author was a fugitive from the law during the period when the play was making headlines locally. He had been on the verge of being arrested at Cornell University when he enlisted the aid of the Bread and Puppet Theatre who were appearing there. Hiding himself in the framework of one of their huge puppets, he managed to escape in a van, but later served his time in jail.

Plays about political problems pertinent to blacks and women have been discussed in earlier sections. We have seen that politics was not a major enticement for playwrights dealing with these groups. Other political topics touched on by American playwrights were the problems of labor leaders, campaigning for office, the foibles and achievements of past residents of the White House, political skulduggery in a governor's office, upper-class Cuban attitudes toward Castro, and Japanese-American relations in the nineteenth century.

Many of the decade's foreign political plays have been previously described. They include plays about South African racism, a plot to kill Congolese leader Patrice Lumumba, colonialism in Africa, the Irish troubles, fascism, terrorism, and East European dissidents.

Religion

A substantial group of plays during the decade were concerned with religion and the men and women whose lives are devoted to the cloth. Some of these works were religious in the sense that they aimed to reaffirm, strengthen, and support the audience's faith not only in religious principles but in the clerics who give their lives to upholding and communicating the meaning of God. Other works were downright irreligious, mocking priests and nuns, and attacking various church practices at their cores. In such plays, the theatre was being used as a means of flogging the clergy for the disillusionment that disturbed the (usually Catholic) author's peace of mind. The battle was not necessarily being waged, however, by those without faith against a spiritual enigma; the sense that emerges from these plays is that the playwright is a believer who is exasperated and angry at the all-too-secular failings of those who profess to be spiritual leaders.

The three most virulently anticlerical plays—John Grismer's *The Candyapple*, Anthony Scully's *The Little Black Sheep*, and Mary O'Malley's *Once a Catholic*—were all instant flops; they each struck feeble blows at the clergy, charging them, on the one hand, with sexual promiscuity, on the other with sexual repression, foul mouths, insensitivity, and homosexuality.

Questions of faith were aired in several plays, including *The Runner Stumbles*, about a priest accused of murdering a nun, and *Mass Appeal*, the decade's most popular straight play on a religious theme. This play deals with the conflict between a middle-aged priest and a radical young seminarian about the modern role of the church.

God Himself made frequent appearances in plays of the period, His presence made manifest in such unusual guises as a flickering light bulb, a Puerto Rican steambath attendant, projections of famous paintings, a kvetchy Jewish father-figure, a flim-flam man, a modish rock trio called the Unholy Three, and so on. In *God's Favorite*, He sent His messenger, a flamboyant gay from Jackson Heights named Sidney.

Religious values were used to varying effect in close to a half-dozen other seventies plays, such as Tom Le Bar's *Whitsuntide*, in which a congregation takes to speaking in tongues, but most of them acquired few converts.

There were also over a dozen works inspired by the Bible, including the popular musicals *Godspell*, *Your Arms Too Short to Box With God*, and *Jesus Christ Superstar*.

War

Few subjects have the built-in drama and excitement of war. In war plays there are situations involving individuals in dangerous conflict, with opportunities to display thrilling heroism or abject cowardice. The pressure cooker of battle allows playwrights to explore man's psychological, moral, political, and philosophical beliefs and habits. War plays, often great ones, have existed in every age, and have usually been produced with notable frequency during or just after active participation in hostilities. Nevertheless, the outpouring of Vietnam plays that might have been anticipated following the foreign combat in which America was engaged at the onset of the decade did not come to pass, at least not to any noteworthy extent.

About a score of plays can be identified as being related to our nationally divisive conflict, but precious few were actually about the war itself and its specific meaning for history and our society. Most Vietnam plays were more concerned with the men who fought or were on their way to battle; as dramatized, their experiences were not radically different from those of men in earlier wars. It is true that in the late seventies there was a sudden rash of films, TV programs, plays, and musicals about the war, but, as Hans Kooning pointed out in the *New York Times*, the typical treatment looked not at the Viet Cong or the Vietnamese, or at the moral and political implications raised by the fighting, but at such problems as those of the returning veteran and at the recurring deaths of Americans by their own "friendly fire."

In each case we are shown a Vietnam which is nothing more than a handy background for what is otherwise violent American drama. Action gains starkness and contrast there; Vietnam is seen as the testing ground for relations between American young men. It is a convenient place for them to face the basic questions of life, courage, death . . . .Whether, why, or how the Vietnam War was different from any other war is simply not touched upon.[5]

The major implication that can be drawn from these works, writes Kooning, is that "it was all a mess," a soft response to a hard issue. The questions of America's reason for being involved, of the Vietnamese position, of the political context, is completely avoided. Kooning's thesis can be demonstrated by a survey of the pertinent plays.

Rainbow was a rock musical about a casualty who goes to a radio station heaven; Stephen White's *Brothers* was about two brothers, one of whom lives through the war while the other dies in a peace protest; Reardon's *Siamese Connections* was another study of the war's effect on the lives of two brothers. Nick Bellito's *Soldier*, Dan Lauria's *Game Plan*, William Dorn Moody's *The Shortchanged Review*, Lanford Wilson's *Fifth of July*, Robert Patrick's *Kennedy's Children*, and Tom Coles' *Medal of Honor Rag* all were about the problems of social readjustment faced by returning vets. The pain of Vietnam was likened to that of the protagonist in the Orestes legend in Doug Dyer's rock musical *Blood* and in David Rabe's *The Orphan*. Rabe's celebrated "Vietnam trilogy," *Sticks and Bones*, *The Basic Training of Pavlo Hummel*, and *Streamers* were all concerned with issues raised by, but tangential to, the war itself. The playwright even denied being an anti-war writer, claiming that his plays were not designed to get the country out of the war. "All I'm trying to do is define the event for myself and for other people," he said. "I'm saying, in effect, this is what goes on; and that's all."[6]

One of Rabe's concerns had been the brutalization of American men by the mammoth insensitivity of the military machine. George Tabori's *Pinkville* examined the same premise in depicting how a young Marine becomes a robot-like killer. Similarly anti-military, rather than specifically anti-Vietnam, was Romulus Linney's *The Love Suicide at Schofield Barracks*. The My Lai massacre of innocents by American soldiers was suggested by the former work, as well as in the musicals *The Lieutenant* and *More Than You Deserve*.

Towards the decade's end came *G. R. Point*, which Erika Munk declared in the *Village Voice* was, with one or two minor exceptions, "the first American play . . . to deal with the fighting in Vietnam."[7] However, as Kooning noted, its protagonist, while participating in and commenting on the fighting, sheds no light on anything other than war in general. Like *More Than You Deserve*, the play suggests the aroused state of sexuality war confers on its participants, a sex/killing duality also present in the rock musical *Dispatches*, based on a correspondent's book about the war.

As this overview suggests, Kooning's thesis was not farfetched. Perhaps the daily exposure to the war on TV and the other media made theatrical commentary on it unnecessary. At any rate, Kooning's point can probably be extended to all the great war plays of the past as well. From *The Trojan Women* to *Henry V* to *What Price Glory?* and *Journey's End*, the infamy and glory of war have been exploited, not as the premise for a topical investigation, but as the microcosm in which man's behavior under pressure can best be measured in universal terms.

The period was not lacking in war plays about other eras, although these too looked at the universals in each situation. The small number of such war plays covered the Revolutionary War, the Civil War, World War I, and World War II. The most widely appreciated was the long-running musical

Shenandoah (1,050 performances), based on a James Stewart movie, and starring John Cullum as a widowed Virginia farmer who, with his family, is swept against his will into the thick of the Civil War.

Death and Illness

Death, handicaps, illness, and insanity—these are subjects that recur over and over in plays of the decade. The topics were not new, but the absorption of the age in them was. The reasons for such engrossment are difficult to tell. They may in part be owing to the contemporary concern with death as reflected in well-publicized legal cases about the right to die or to perform euthanasia; this was a period when judges gradually assumed the power to allow doctors to withdraw support systems from people with terminal diseases or in incurably comatose states. The era also witnessed a widespread growth of talk about death; books were authored, lectures given, and courses taught on how to face one's own end or that of another. During the decade the media made death and related topics suitable for breakfast conversation. Funeral parlors advertised over the airwaves. Newspapers and TV shows described new methods of treatment for serious diseases, and operations were broadcast in all their surgical detail; there were inspirational stories about real people who had learned to cope with severe disabilities; exposés about the conditions of many hospitals and mental institutions were constantly being written and produced; the principles of psychotherapy were practiced in ever-increasing instances and in numerous new forms because of the strains of modern living; handicapped people became a political force, gaining special legislation to ease the traditional onus on them in the marketplace and to provide access for them to public facilities; the perseverance of the disabled was celebrated in special sporting events, and so on.

In the plays dealing with ill, handicapped, or dying people, the central characters often handle their problems with fortitude and good humor, even with wit; thus, these characters often have seemed the heroes of the age, people who teach us how to live our own crippled lives in a time of war, crime, terrorism, poverty, racial conflict, drug abuse, and political corruption.

How to deal with the dying or with one's own imminent passing formed the nucleus of about ten plays both serious and comic, with cancer being the most widespread cause of distress. *Cold Storage, The Shadow Box, Tribute, All Over,* and *The National Health* were good examples of the genre.

Suicide was fundamental to four plays, including two, *Whose Life Is It Anyway?* and *Nevis Mountain Dew,* in which characters incapacitated from the neck down are determined to have their life support systems unplugged.

A group of plays dealing with what Mel Gussow called "the wounded hero" came to prominence in the seventies.[8] Through these characters, as through those in the plays just cited, was revealed a concern "with an incapacitated hero, someone who is wounded by accident, illness or birth defect." For some, suicide is the only way to face their crisis; others seek to relate to the world, but on their own demanding terms. They often betray pronounced intellectual superiority, a deeper, more enlightened morality, and a greater sense of self-reliance than those in the unmaimed world. The best of such works included *Creeps*, *Children of a Lesser God*, *The Elephant Man*, *Wings*, and *Fifth of July*. The people in such plays, wrote Gussow, "can be used as conduits to our consciousness. The characters may seem remote from us, but we find that we can relate to them—and relating leads to understanding."

Many of the plays mentioned took place in hospitals; approximately thirteen others were at least partially set in asylums where people with psychological problems were depicted. Prominent examples are *Equus*, *Medal of Honor Rag*, *Nuts*, and the one-act farces, *Bad Habits*. Allan Ginsburg's *Kaddish* was not set in an institution, but it was a forceful treatment of the author's mother's bouts with mental illness.

OTHER PATTERNS

There are several other patterns in writing and production that might be mentioned; these are not specifically aligned with the subjects discussed above, but are more related to dramatic form and treatment. Certain settings, for example, recurred with sufficient frequency to draw attention. Thus, as we have just seen, the hospital/asylum play might be considered a pattern. The barroom or saloon play, long a staple of modern dramaturgy because of the ease with which it can gather together a diverse sprinkling of character types, with alcohol a convenient lubricant for opening minds and mouths, enjoyed a vigorous life, with about twenty plays set in such locales. Hotels and resorts are other popular backgrounds for assembling eclectic character lists; about fifteen plays used this ploy.

Prison dramas were well represented with at least twenty examples, including a couple written by ex-convicts. Schools and educational institutions were brought to life in nearly another score of shows, including eight set in British classrooms; school was not a pleasant place to be, according to these works.

Three perennial genres, the thriller or mystery play (and its subcategory, the comedy-thriller), the sex farce, and the courtroom or trial drama continued to be popular. Fifteen-or-so productions fit the serious thriller category, and about a dozen more were of the comedic type. Most were flops, but *Sleuth* and *Deathtrap* were enormous hits. The sex farce provided about thirty examples, some coarse, some delicate, and one a comfortable hit musical, *I Love My Wife*. And of the fifteen courtroom dramas of the period, most of them preoccupied with murders and political crimes, *Nuts* was one of the best-liked and longest-running.

One-Act Plays

For years critics have bemoaned the diminishing number of one-acts being produced. The one-act is a valuable form on which young and inexperienced, as well as mature, playwrights can sharpen their writing nibs. In the seventies one-acts played an increasingly important part, and by the end of the decade several companies were staging festivals and even marathons in which new one-acts were shown to the public. Among the many one-acts performed during the decade, a number were part of full-length works by a single dramatist who chose to tell his story in terms of from two to four related playlets; often, these were set in the same locale. Examples of the type are given in Table 5.7, which is restricted to Broadway, where most of them were produced.

Table 5.7
Broadway Plays Written in One-Act Components

Bad Habits

California Suite

A Day in Hollywood/A Night in the Ukraine

Dogg's Hamlet/Cahoot's Macbeth

Four on a Garden

The Incomparable Max

Noël Coward in Two Keys

Taxi Tales

Twigs

Unlikely Heroes

The Water Engine/Mr. Happiness

Some might argue that several other works in an episodic mode, such as *The Shadow Box* and *Absurd Person Singular*, are also based on the one-act form.

On the Off-Broadway scene, one-acts were also popular, but in that venue evenings of one-acts were normally made up of an assortment by different writers.

One-Person Productions

A singular phenomenon of the seventies theatre was the increasingly popular presentation of one-person shows, a concept that owes its recent revival to the extraordinarily successful Mark Twain impersonations of Hal Holbrook dating from 1954. Holbrook has been returning to his *Mark Twain Tonight!* show periodically and brought it to New York once more in the seventies.

There are several variations on the one-person play, or monodrama. One is the work that shows the actor impersonating a famous figure, historical, theatrical, or literary. Another allows the actor to perform the works of a famous author, but in character terms relevant to the specific selections rather than in the guise of the author himself. In the former, part of the fun comes from seeing how closely the actor's makeup and mannerisms follow the original. In addition, there is the one-person musical revue (surveyed in the chapter on musicals and revues), the one-person drama about a fictional character, and the one-person literary evening featuring an eclectic selection of authors.

A successful monodrama allows an actor to tour with it for years and to revive it with a minimum of fuss whenever circumstances are ripe. It is relatively cheap to produce, although some such shows, like Roy Dotrice's *Brief Lives*, which was revived during the decade, use sets as elaborate as those for conventional plays. Actors find these works appealing, as they do not have to compete for attention with other performers and can revel in the words of great writers or personalities to their hearts' content. Often they adapt the programs themselves. Two monodrama performers of the decade even won acting Tonys for their work (Henry Fonda and Julie Harris). And James Whitmore practically made a career out of his monodrama performances as Teddy Roosevelt, Will Rogers, and Harry Truman.

Other figures who were impersonated in seventies monodramas (including those with a piano accompanist) include Clarence Darrow, Emily Dickinson, Paul Robeson, John F. Kennedy, H. L. Mencken, Oscar Wilde, Gertrude Stein, George Bernard Shaw, Charles Dickens, Brendan Behan, and Dylan Thomas. Works in which the actor did not play the historical author but enacted an assortment of materials from his or her work included *B. B.*, based on Bertolt Brecht's writings, *Jack Macgowran in the Works of Beckett*, and Alec McCowen reading *St. Mark's Gospel* with remarkable effect.

One-person evenings devoted to multiple authors were less frequent, though some were highly praised. They included *Here Are Ladies* with Siobhan McKenna, a potpourri of Irish writing; *I Am a Woman* with Viveca Lindfors presenting feminist literature; *Nicol Williamson's Late Show*; *The Indian Experience*, a collection of Indian writings; *The Square Root of Soul*, black writing starring Adolph Caesar; and the Irish country tales in *In My Father's Time* with Eamon Kelly.

In another category were one-person plays about fictional or semi-fictional personages: *Miss Margarida's Way*, *The Second Greatest Entertainer in the Whole Wide World*, and *The Elocution of Benjamin* were the examples offered.

Several works were autobiographical, featuring the life of the person performing them. *Jane White, Who?* focused on actress White's own experiences; *My Mother Was a Fortune Teller* and *The Madwoman of Central
Park West* both were loosely based on the life of Phyllis Newman; and *An
Evening with Quentin Crisp* was exactly what its witty, avowedly homosexual author/performer suggested by its title.

* * *

One further pattern of significance was everywhere apparent in the New
York theatre of the seventies; because of its importance, the following chapter is devoted to it.

NOTES

1. It should be noted, however, that a number of plays and musicals not discussed
in Chapters 3 and 4 are touched on here. Works surveyed earlier will generally be
referred to without extended comment. Furthermore, because of space limitations,
many patterns are discussed here without mentioning each relevant work. The
appendixes in my forthcoming *Encyclopedia of the New York Stage, 1970-1980* list
all patterns with the plays that conform to them.

2. Actually, the term "biographical drama" is used loosely here to refer, not so
much to plays that tell someone's "life story," as to those in which dramatized
versions of real persons perform a central role, even if the events depicted are more
fiction than fact.

3. Donald Loeffler, *An Analysis of the Treatment of the Homosexual Character in
Dramas Produced in the New York Theatre from 1950 to 1968* (New York: Arno
Press, 1975), pp. 43-47D. This edition contains supplementary material covering the
period through 1975.

4. Leah Napolin and Isaac Bashevis Singer, *Yentl* (New York: Samuel French,
1977), p. 7.

5. Hans Kooning, "Films and Plays About Vietnam Treat Everything but the
War," *New York Times*, 17 May 1979, Sec. II, p. 23.

6. David Rabe, "If You Kill Somebody . . . ," *New York Times*, 12 December
1971, Sec. II, p. 3.

7. Erika Munk, "Cross Left," *Village Voice*, 23 April 1979, p. 89.

8. Mel Gussow, "The Time of the Wounded Hero," *New York Times*, 15 April
1979, Sec. II, p. 1.

★ 6 ★
REVIVALS

Among the most significant developments in the New York theatre of the seventies was the enormous number of revivals produced. The commercial managements increasingly looked back to the past for surefire shows, especially musicals, that would reduce their financial risks, while the non-profits continued to explore the great and not-so-great old plays as a means of keeping their subscribers happy. Broadway saw the work of many classic playwrights, including Shakespeare, Brecht, Chekhov, Ibsen, Shaw, Pirandello, O'Neill, and Molière, but these works normally emerged from the sheltered cocoons of institutions such as Lincoln Center, the Circle in the Square, and the Phoenix in productions that originated Off-Broadway or in the repertoires of visiting foreign groups. In terms of numbers, the true hotbed of classical revival activity was in the Off-Broadway companies. Broadway's commercial managements, while occasionally pulling off a box-office coup with star casting in a work like Pirandello's *Emperor Henry IV*, regarded such plays as economic suicide and searched instead for popular old musicals that could effectively be revitalized to attract nostalgia-craving audiences.

Despite the plethora of old plays filling stage space and turning the city into a veritable large-scale rep company, the majority of the revivals were decidedly second-rate. Some featured major stars supported by inferior companies, some lacked purposeful direction, others seemed dated, and yet others were shabbily produced. However, a few revivals, both dramatic and musical, made significant contributions and achieved historical stature by their originality of approach, perceptive production values, and memorable performances.

The average Broadway season offered a bit more than a dozen dramatic revivals, the peak coming in 1975-76 when twenty-one such plays were mounted, and the low arriving in 1977-78 when only five appeared (three at the Circle in the Square, whose annual program traditionally depends on revivals). Old musicals available went from the two of 1970-71 to the eight of 1976-77. Musical revivals were much less visible Off-Broadway, some seasons having none at all, and the entire decade presenting fewer than ten. Revivals of plays, however, were far more endemic to each Off-Broadway season than they were to Broadway; one season, 1979-80, had thirty.

DRAMATIC REVIVALS

Of all playwrights, living and dead, Shakespeare stands like a colossus, offering a canon of work that actors, directors, and producers never tire of presenting, and in which audiences express abiding interest. No other author received anywhere near as many stagings during the seventies. Thirty-two of the thirty-seven plays in the First Folio were given, some in multiple versions. *Hamlet* led with seven productions, featuring such actors as Sam Waterston, Stacy Keach, and William Hurt; one touring version even featured septuagenarian Dame Judith Anderson in the title role. Broadway productions of Shakespeare numbered ten, several of them born Off-Broadway.

The most admired Broadway productions of the Bard were Peter Brook's visiting Royal Shakespeare Company mounting of *A Midsummer Night's Dream* and A. J. Antoon's *Much Ado About Nothing*. In Brook's historically significant staging, influenced by Polish critic Jan Kott's *Shakespeare Our Contemporary*, all semblances of the traditional romantic approach to the comedy were excised in favor of a starkly modern, stripped-down, circus-like interpretation which tried to express the inner world of magic and sexuality in the writing. Brook had his actors, brightly costumed in pajama-like silks, cavort on a white-walled set (critics thought it looked like anything from a squash court to a rehearsal room), with action going on both on the stage and on trapezes. Beautifully spoken and inventively visualized, the production startled by its daring choices, which, naturally, did not satisfy all comers, some feeling that the play had been robbed of its romance. The consensus, however, was that the play came vividly to life in a way unknown in conventional productions. Critic Clive Barnes even wrote, "This is without any equivocation whatsoever the greatest production of Shakespeare I have ever seen in my life. . . ."[1]

Much Ado, which moved from Off-Broadway's Public Theatre, was thought by many to be brilliantly conceptualized, set as it was in a turn-of-the-century Teddy Roosevelt America, and using such realistic devices as a canoe, carousel horses, a jalopy, Keystone Kops, cigarettes, an oom-pah band, and straw boaters and blazers. The actors (Sam Waterston and

Kathleen Widdoes as Benedick and Beatrice) gave believable characterizations and natural performances that seemed easy and unforced and
helped make the show a popular one with the public. Its 136-performance
run was thought to have been cut short by a drop in attendance following
its national TV airing.

A controversial development in Shakespearean staging occurred in 1979
when Joseph Papp announced the formation of a troupe of Third World
actors to produce the Bard's plays at the Public under the aegis of British
director Michael Langham. With top black and Hispanic actors in the
company, *Julius Caesar* and *Coriolanus* were staged, but the reviews were
negative, mainly because of the actors' inability to speak Shakespeare well.
The company was soon disbanded.

Most Off-Broadway revivals of Shakespeare were cast in a conventional
mold, although there were several strikingly idiosyncratic, if unsuccessful,
versions at the Delacorte in Central Park, where Joseph Papp's New York
Shakespeare Festival offered free Shakespeare every summer. The most
respected American Off-Broadway Shakespeare productions (all except one
at the Delacorte) were *King Lear* with James Earl Jones, the *Hamlet*s of
Keach, Waterston, and Hurt (at the Circle Rep), *Henry V* with Paul Rudd,
and *The Taming of the Shrew* with Raul Julia and Meryl Streep. Of visiting
British mountings the most distinguished were the Royal Shakespeare's
Richard II, with Ian Richardson and Richard Pasco alternating nightly as
Richard and Bolingbroke, and *Henry V* with Alan Howard, also in an RSC
interpretation.[2]

Many other examples of classical and pre-modern drama were presented,
but these rarely attracted broad critical and/or popular enthusiasm. Of the
three Greek tragedies and one comedy (*Lysistrata* as a Broadway musical)
seen, only Andrei Serban's staging of Aeschylus' *Agamemnon* stirred
interest. Serban gave it a violently ritualistic manner, with masks, a text
made up of both English and ancient Greek, extensive use of athletic mime,
strange vocal contortions, and other original effects in order to convey the
savage frenzy he felt was an essential factor in the original performances.
He had earlier gained critical recognition for his highly provocative stagings
of Greek tragic materials in the Off Off-Broadway *Fragments of a Trilogy*.
Serban's theatricalist style was not for all tastes, but his work evoked considerable discussion as to its merits.

The Italian Renaissance was represented by a clever Off-Broadway staging of Machiavelli's *The Mandrake*, and the English Renaissance by four
passable stagings of Shakespeare's contemporaries, Middleton, Marlowe,
and Webster. It was the work of the post-Renaissance genius Molière,
however, that gained the most attention after Shakespeare. Molière had
nine revivals, six on Broadway. *The School for Wives* was given an
enjoyable staging by the Phoenix with Brian Bedford as Arnolphe in a
120-performance run. Britain's Young Vic company triumphed with *Scapino*

(based on *Les Fourberies de Scapin*), starring the irrepressible Jim Dale in an acrobatic performance of the title role. Another English production, the National Theatre's *Misanthrope*, had Alec McCowen and Diana Rigg in an intriguing version set in France under De Gaulle. John Wood, Tammy Grimes, and Patricia Elliott headed a fine revival of *Tartuffe* at the Circle in the Square. Other Molière productions fared less well.

Among other classical revivals of English works there were two Restoration comedies, four eighteenth-century comedies, and a very funny RSC staging of Boucicault's 1841 *London Assurance* with Donald Sinden. Only a small number of continental European classics was attempted, including two of Schiller's *Mary Stuart*; four of George Büchner's *Woyzeck*, one of them notable because it marked the return to acting of Open Theatre director Joseph Chaikin; a parody of *Camille* by the Ridiculous Theatrical Company; a well-received *A Month in the Country* by Turgenev with Tammy Grimes and Farley Granger; and an uninspired *Inspector General.*

The modern dramaturgical era rests on a foundation of realist and realist-symbolic plays by Ibsen, Strindberg, and Chekhov. Ibsen lovers had thirteen productions to visit, while Strindberg admirers had five and Chekhov fans eleven. Of the Ibsen revivals, the most distinguished included the two done in repertory by Claire Bloom and Donald Madden in 1971, *A Doll's House* and *Hedda Gabler*. Another *Doll's House*, starring Liv Ullman, boasted little more than the actress' luminous performance. Except for several fine performances in the leads by actresses such as Beatrice Straight and Vanessa Redgrave, the other Ibsen revivals were unmemorable.

Strindberg revivals were even more uninspiring. The only sparks caused by his plays flew when the *New York Times* published correspondence concerning the backstage tiffs between translator/adaptor Paul Avila Mayer and stars Rip Torn and Viveca Lindfors over what Mayer alleged was the star's mangling of his text of *The Dance of Death*.[3] Regardless of their claims and counterclaims, the critics settled the matter forever when they blasted the cast for their histrionic excesses.

Chekhov's plays received several important mountings. One was Mike Nichols' radiant incarnation of *Uncle Vanya* at the Circle in the Square with a brilliant cast including Lillian Gish, George C. Scott, Nicol Williamson, Barnard Hughes, Conrad Bain, Elizabeth Wilson, Julie Christie, and Cathleen Nesbitt. Scott and Williamson as, respectively, Astrov and Voinitsky, offered one of the best acting duels seen locally in years.

Another Chekhov revival proved even more epochal; this was Serban's revisionist staging at the Vivian Beaumont of *The Cherry Orchard*, a masterwork that several years previously had been given a controversial Public Theatre mounting with an all-black cast. The latter's reviews were mostly favorable, but a debate arose over the appropriateness of black actors doing Chekhov. The consensus was that the idea was acceptable, especially when applied to a humanistic masterpiece performed by a virtuoso ensemble that could reach beyond the specifically racial qualities depicted and emerge with a work of universal values.

In Serban's hands, *The Cherry Orchard* was given a revival that allowed it a place on the same shelf as Brook's *Midsummer Night's Dream*—as one of the most illuminating approaches to a play with which few thought something new could be done. There were dissenters, but most sided with Walter Kerr, who found this a "confidently daring, alternately vulgar and delicate, perverse, funny, deeply original and visually stunning event."[4] Serban and designer Santo Loquasto covered the vast expanse of the theatre's thrust/proscenium stage with white carpeting and only a highly selective assortment of furnishings; both indoors and out were seen simultaneously because the Ranevskaya home was shown without walls. Upstage stood an impressive cherry orchard, normally never shown in the play. The effect was a supercharged surrealistic theatricality, filled with dynamic images and tableaux, backed by an evocative Elizabeth Swados score and supported by an energetic, comedic acting style; all of this was undercut periodically by twinges of tragic insight. The sparkling talents of Irene Worth, Raul Julia, Michael Cristofer, Meryl Streep, and Priscilla Smith were employed to enormous advantage. No other Chekhov revival of the period remotely compared in effectiveness to this one.

Moving to the twentieth-century dramatists we note an abundance of revivals. From the Germans came generous helpings of Brecht and Wedekind, from the Italians Pirandello, from the French Anouilh, Feydeau, and Genet, and from the Russians Gorky and Isaac Babel. Moreover, there were revivals of Rumania's Ionesco, the Yiddish writer Ansky, South Africa's Fugard, Hungary's Molnar (including two productions of his *The Play's the Thing*), and Switzerland's Dürrenmatt. The English-speaking nations provided Ireland's Beckett, O'Casey, Wilde, Behan, Yeats, Synge, Joyce, and Shaw; England gave us Brandon Thomas, Patrick Hamilton, Coward, William Archibald, Deane and Balderston, Pinero, Rattigan, Barrie, J. B. Fagan, R. C. Sheriff, Maugham, and Pinter. Dominating the lot were America's own playwrights, the most amply represented being Williams, Miller, and O'Neill.

Six of Bertolt Brecht's plays were brought to new life on local stages, but, as in the past, only *The Threepenny Opera*, with its Kurt Weill score, made a notable dent. Avant-garde director Richard Foreman's Vivian Beaumont staging was a notable one, partly because of the new, earthy translation by Ralph Mannheim and John Willett, which was deemed closer to Brecht's corrosive style than Marc Blitzstein's older one. In Foreman's intensely theatricalized treatment, the actors moved and behaved like ice-cold mannequins, their scenes filled with bizarrely imaginative groupings, explosive energy, and ritualistic choreography. The decor resembled a dreary turn-of-the-century London railroad depot. Actors Raul Julia, Ellen Greene, Elizabeth Wilson, and the marionette-like Tony Azito were singled out for kudos. The show garnered 307 performances with another 27 added on when it was reopened at Central Park's Delacorte.

Luigi Pirandello was Italy's sole representative of the past, with four plays. Rex Harrison's performance of the title role in *Emperor Henry IV* was the principal bright spot among these revivals, and helped the piece to a successful run on Broadway and on tour.

Of plays by the French dramatists mentioned, several had competent productions, but none of major importance. However, established Russian dramaturgy saw interest shown in the work of Maxim Gorky, especially in the wake of several successful London revivals. In addition to a brief showing of *The Lower Depths*, there was a respected production of *Enemies*, never seen before locally, by Ellis Rabb at the Vivian Beaumont. Another Gorky play making its New York bow was *Barbarians*, but it did not truly come to life in this incarnation.

Ireland's playwrights were well represented, but the three whose works received the bulk of attention were Shaw, Beckett, and O'Casey. Shaw, whose talents were beginning to look less luminous to some critics, was nevertheless present in thirteen revivals, none of them superlative. Some suffered from miscasting, as in the otherwise commercially successful *Captain Brassbound's Conversion*, produced as a vehicle for Ingrid Bergman, or the roundly trashed *Mrs. Warren's Profession* with an out-of-place Ruth Gordon in the title role. Other Shaw failures ranged from a misconceived *Caesar and Cleopatra* with Rex Harrison and Elizabeth Ashley to a series of five adequate to less-than-adequate revivals by the Roundabout Company.

Samuel Beckett's plays have never been considered commercially attractive, but few dispute their importance in providing the modern theatre with a voice of profound despair tempered by an underlying optimism in man's ability to endure. Beckett's masterpiece, *Waiting for Godot*, was given three productions, the first by Alan Schneider, who had intended to introduce the play to Broadway in 1956 but got bumped during the play's disastrous Florida tryout. In his new Off-Broadway production, he scored very highly and the play ran for 277 performances, a Beckett record in New York. Another revival of the play was staged in German with German actors by the author himself, while a third was done in English but based on Beckett's own staging.

There were also three productions of *Endgame* and two of *Happy Days*, one with Jessica Tandy and the other with Irene Worth. In all, nine Beckett plays were revived.

O'Casey, the themes of whose plays bear some resemblance to the political troubles anguishing Ireland in the seventies, had three revivals, including two of *The Plough and the Stars*. The better was the one offered by Ireland's Abbey Theatre, with Siobhan McKenna and Cyril Cusack.

England itself gave New York only nineteen plays for revival in a total of twenty-five productions. Most commonly seen was the work of Harold Pinter, whose *Homecoming* had three revivals, none outstanding, along with one each of *The Caretaker* and *The Birthday Party*. Two Somerset Maugham plays were shown, and there was also a shoddy revival of that old workhorse *Rain*, based on a Maugham short story. Of the two Noël Coward revivals, only *Private Lives* with Maggie Smith had charm; the two showings of *Hay Fever* were dismal.

Of the remaining English plays in revival, few were exciting, although the critics did like Pinero's *Trelawney of the "Wells"* in an Off-Broadway production that was damaged by the actors' strike of 1970. Producer Joseph Papp liked the piece well enough to give it a second revival at Lincoln Center several years later, with Meryl Streep, John Lithgow, Marybeth Hurt, Mandy Patinkin, and other fine actors in a staging handled by A. J. Antoon. The most successful revival of a British play was Dennis Rosa's staging of *Dracula*, the vampire play originally written by Briton Hamilton Deane for its premiere London production but revised for American consumption by American John L. Balderston. It was this Balderston-Deane script that was revived in a delightful witch's brew with all the right ingredients to produce a highly sophisticated, slightly campy, gorgeously acted and designed *danse macabre* of Gothic mannerisms that became one of the smash hits of the decade, running 952 performances. With its creepy-funny black-and-white decor by illustrator Edward Gorey and a sensationally sexy performance of the thirsty protagonist by Frank Langella, *Dracula* was a "fun show" on every count.

It is only natural that the New York stage's revivals during the decade should have stressed the work of its own national dramatists. This is particularly true because America during these years was celebrating its 200th anniversary. The 1975-76 season was especially rich in American dramatic revivals. During the seventies nearly seventy-five familiar American plays were taken off the shelf, some of them within a decade of the demise of their original presentations. Examples of the latter are *P.S. Your Cat is Dead*, *The Basic Training of Pavlo Hummel*, *The Effect of Gamma Rays on Manin-the-Moon Marigolds*, *No Place to Be Somebody*, *The Runner Stumbles*, *Moonchildren*, and *Father's Day*. The only one that was a failure in its original but came back a winner in its resuscitation was *Moonchildren*.

Looking over the titles of the remaining American revivals one can find a number of older works that were commercially and/or critically unsuccessful in their first productions and that were restaged in hopes of reversing their fortunes. Of them, only Dale Wasserman's *One Flew Over the Cuckoo's Nest* and Paul Osborne's *Morning's at Seven* did the trick.

The Wasserman play (1,025 performances), which failed in 1963, became a hot Off-Broadway ticket in its new mounting with William Devane. *Morning's at Seven* (564 performances) which had achieved only forty-four performances in 1939, despite being chosen one of the Ten Best Plays of the

Year, returned in a magically unified ensemble production directed on Broadway by Vivian Matalon, with a company including David Rounds, Elizabeth Wilson, Teresa Wright, Nancy Marchand, Maureen O'Sullivan, and Gary Merrill, among others.

Familiar and unfamiliar dramas from America's pre-1920 past were rare. William Gillette's *Secret Service*, Edward Sheldon's *The Boss*, Booth Tarkington's *Clarence*, J. Hartley Manners' *Peg O' My Heart*, and, the most successfully revived of them all, Langdon Mitchell's 1906 *New York Idea* (at the BAM Repertory Company), tell almost the whole story. There was as well a new and moderately popular version of the 1845 *Fashion* by Anna Cora Mowatt, but in a musical rendition with all the men's roles but one played by women.

Temporarily leaving aside the plays of O'Neill, Williams, and Miller, we can gloss over the revivals of plays from the twenties through the sixties; all that came from the twenties were Sidney Howard's *They Knew What They Wanted*, George Kelly's *The Show-Off*, and George S. Kaufman and Edna Ferber's *The Royal Family*. The latter was given a hit rendition by director Ellis Rabb with Eva Le Gallienne, Sam Levene, George Grizzard, and Rosemary Harris. From the thirties there were Kaufman and Hart's *Once in a Lifetime*, Steinbeck's *Of Mice and Men*, Saroyan's *The Time of Your Life*, Luce's *The Women*, Rand's *Penthouse Legend* (originally called *The Night of January 16th*), the Spewacks' *Boy Meets Girl*, Rice's *Counsellor-at-Law*, Behrman's *Biography*, and Odets' *Awake and Sing*. None were outstandingly done. Only three American plays originated in the forties (Wilder's *The Skin of Our Teeth*, the Goetz' *The Heiress*, and Hellman's *Watch on the Rhine*), but the plays refused to come back to life. A slightly higher number of plays returned from the fifties, including McCullers' *The Member of the Wedding*, Inge's *Summer Brave* (a revision of *Picnic*), Odets' *The Country Girl*, Inge's *The Dark at the Top of the Stairs*, Masters' *Spoon River Anthology*, and Goodrich and Hackett's *The Diary of Anne Frank*. Finally, the sixties was the original decade for Albee's *Who's Afraid of Virginia Woolf?*, Anderson's *The Days Between*, Lowell's *The Old Glory*, Kilty's *Dear Liar*, Mosel's *All the Way Home*, McClure's *The Beard*, and Merriam's *The Coach with Six Insides*. Of these plays, the only one capable of jolting the critics was Albee's *Virginia Woolf*, directed by the playwright, with riveting acting by Colleen Dewhurst and Ben Gazzara as Martha and George. It seemed even better than the original.

The works of O'Neill, Williams, and Miller, America's three leading dramatists of the pre-seventies years, deserve to be surveyed in a section of their own. Their place in the American theatrical tradition could have no more pertinent testimony than the frequency with which they were revived during the decade. In almost every case, revivals of their work were events of importance, involving theatre artists of the first rank. Not all of the plays proved acceptable, of course, some because of weak productions, and others because of inherent dramaturgical defects. However, it is significant to note that the plays chosen for these numerous revivals struggled to depict the clash of social forces, the tragedy of misguided souls, and the search for ever elusive answers to the human dilemma; not one play by America's most commercially successful playwright, Neil Simon, was revived during the decade.

Except for two revivals of *Long Day's Journey Into Night*, all of the O'Neill plays were on Broadway. All five hours of *Mourning Becomes Electra*, starring Colleen Dewhurst, were given by the Circle in the Square as that theatre's first production in its new Broadway home. The Circle continued to lay claim to the title of America's foremost producer of O'Neill, although not all its revivals were good ones. They also gave us *The Iceman Cometh* with James Earl Jones a compelling Hickey, and a very poor *All God's Chillun Got Wings*. *The Great God Brown* failed, and *Anna Christie*, despite a brilliant Liv Ullman performance, seemed dated and awkward, but New York viewed a magnificent *Moon for the Misbegotten* with Jason Robards and Colleen Dewhurst (314 performances) and an excellent production of the one-act *Hughie* with Ben Gazzara. Also noteworthy was *A Touch of the Poet*, beautifully staged by José Quintero, who staged several of the other O'Neill revivals; this one featured Jason Robards, the quintessential O'Neill actor, Geraldine Fitzgerald, and Milo O'Shea. The O'Neill masterpiece, *Long Day's Journey Into Night*, had an honorable presentation with Geraldine Fitzgerald, Robert Ryan, and Stacy Keach, but when it was revived a few years later, with Robards directing as well as playing James Tyrone, it fared miserably.

Tennessee Williams, whose works received more revivals nationwide than any other native playwright during the decade, had eight plays done in nine New York revivals, whereas O'Neill, who experienced a comeback of sorts, had nine plays in ten local productions. The play many consider Williams' chef d'ouevre, *A Streetcar Named Desire*, had an exceptional production as the last play staged under the Jules Irving regime at Lincoln Center; director Ellis Rabb inspired a wonderful Blanche Dubois from Rosemary Harris and a fine Stanley from James Farentino. After 110 performances it was restaged for Broadway with a largely new company. There was also a successful *Cat on a Hot Tin Roof* with Elizabeth Ashley and Keir Dullea, an excellent coupling of Irene Worth and Christopher Walken in *Sweet Bird of Youth*, and a touching *Glass Menagerie* with Maureen Stapleton, Rip Torn, and Pamela Payton-Wright. *Summer and Smoke* earned a new look, as did Williams' revision of it, *Eccentricities of a Nightingale*, which proved to be better than the original. The one-act *27 Wagons Full of Cotton* benefitted from Meryl Streep's sexuality, and *The Night of the Iguana* had a respectable revival with Richard Chamberlain, Sylvia Miles, and Dorothy McGuire.

Arthur Miller is not so prolific a pillar of the theatre as O'Neill and

Williams, yet the five productions of his plays speak highly of the esteem in which he is held. *The Crucible* was well revived at Lincoln Center and proved a modern classic, but *All My Sons* floundered in its revival. *A Memory of Two Mondays* was interesting as an example of Miller's early work, and there was a very fine mounting of *The Price* which moved to Broadway for 144 performances after an Off-Broadway start. The greatest success accrued to Miller's best-known play, *Death of a Salesman*, in its first New York revival; George C. Scott directed and gave a tour-de-force performance as Willy Loman. Teresa Wright was Linda; Harvey Keitel, Happy; and James Farentino, Biff; black actors Arthur French and Chuck Patterson played Charlie and Bernard, roles traditionally acted by whites. It was a sell-out production and closed early only because it was a limited run.

MUSICAL REVIVALS

The big news in the 1970s revival business was the unearthing of nostalgia-laden old musicals, from the flapper-era razzmatazz of *No, No, Nanette* to the fifties sociological probing of *West Side Story*. If the Broadway theatre was in the business of making money, reproducing popular musical hits seemed the surest way to guarantee box-office profits. The music of old Broadway was familiar to millions of potential ticket buyers; with the scarcity of exciting new composers, lyricists, and librettists and the increasing dependence on rock music and plotless or bookless shows, audiences were starved for the rich scores and straightforward stories and characters of Broadway's golden oldies.

Once *No, No, Nanette* scored a fabulous success at the decade's outset, producers realized that musicals of the past, if prepared properly, could ensure long lines outside of theatres. Each season was to profit from this lesson, as anywhere from three to six major musicals were revived annually. If we include *The Threepenny Opera*, *Happy End*, and *Candide* (which might, on the other hand, be considered a new work), and exclude the various operetta revivals done by operetta troupes (such as the Light Opera Guild of Manhattan), the number of Broadway musicals revived in the period comes to thirty-eight. Only two, however, *One for the Money* and *Tip-Toes*, appeared on Off-Broadway stages.

Actually, the quality of a good number of Broadway revivals left much to be desired. Supporting casts were frequently made up of unknown and mediocre (or worse) performers, and the decor often seemed tatty and worn (from pre-New York touring). Too many shows opted simply to retrieve from the originals whatever had worked back then, and new ideas and interpretations were hard to find. The original designs, orchestrations, choreography, and direction were slavishly followed, as if time had stood still. The most flagrant aspect of this tendency was the casting of the original stars, despite the evidence of the ravages of time. Other shows reached back for old-timers whose presence was expected to juice up revenues even though they had no connection with the original production.

The American musical, like the American play, did not really become a world-shaking phenomenon until the 1920s. However, earlier examples often displayed the imagination, enthusiasm, and energy that led to the great shows of later years. Three such pre-Jazz Age shows came back to Broadway, each having been gone and nearly forgotten for over half a century. The first was *Irene* (604 performances), a 1919 show remembered chiefly for "Alice Blue Gown." It stumbled into New York after an arduous out-of-town tryout during which director John Gielgud had been replaced by Gower Champion and major revisions had taken place. In it, Debbie Reynolds, at forty, was making her Broadway bow. President Nixon had declared it a terrific show, but one that would be appreciated more by "out-of-towners" than by Big Apple dwellers. These nationally publicized remarks may have been part of the reason that the show chalked up its long run despite a severe critical drubbing.

Slightly older was the 1915 Jerome Kern piece, *Very Good, Eddie* (304 performances), the revival of which originated at the Goodspeed Opera House in East Haddam, Connecticut, home of some of the best new and old musicals of the decade. A year later the 1917 *Going Up*, also from Goodspeed, went down in 49 showings.

Four seventies revivals were from the twenties. The oldest was the biggest, the already mentioned *No, No, Nanette*. Its great success (861 performances) stemmed partly from its having lured from retirement the long-time favorite, tap dancer Ruby Keeler, having employed the services of veteran comedienne Patsy Kelly, also long absent from Broadway, and from having used the production ideas of famed choreographer Busby Berkeley, away from the stage for forty years. The direction, decor, and choreography as well as the slam-bang cast turned this lighter-than-air confection into one of the great theatre events of the decade.

Not all the twenties shows were so well received. Both *The Desert Song* and *Good News* were fatally punctured by their reviews. However, the last of the twenties revivals, *Whoopie!*, with Charles Repole in the old Eddie Cantor role, lasted 204 performances and received warm approval, even though its shallowness was obvious to everyone.

Lowest on the revival scale were the thirties, with only the Paul Green-Kurt Weill anti-war *Johnny Johnson* and the Gershwin classic *Porgy and Bess* being shown. The former was a dud, the latter a gem in a brilliant staging first done for the Houston Grand Opera. Performers alternated in the leading roles, but none was as widely acclaimed as gorgeous Clamma Dale. History was made in this production by its being the first to use the uncut Gershwin score.

With the 1940s, the number of revivals starts to grow. Five of them made their way to town: *Pal Joey, Oklahoma!, On the Town, Where's Charley?*,

and *Lost in the Stars*. The only one to make good was 1943's *Oklahoma!*
(293 performances), in its seventh revival, brought back with the look and
style of the original. Of the others there is not much to say, except that *Pal
Joey*'s production was something of a cause célèbre because its proposed
star, ballet dancer Edward Villella, who had never done a Broadway show,
found himself incapable of making the adjustment and dropped out during
rehearsals. He was soon followed by his co-star, Eleanor Parker. Her
replacement, Joan Copeland, was excellent; his, Christopher Chadman,
was not, and the show flopped.

*Guys and Dolls, The King and I, The Pajama Game, My Fair Lady, The
Most Happy Fella, West Side Story*, and *Gypsy*, shows that deserve a place
on any list of all-time greats, were all products of the fifties, perhaps the
greatest decade for classy musicals. They were brought back in the
melodically meagre seventies, in addition to a reworked version of *Kismet*,
now called *Timbuktu!*

The revival of *Guys and Dolls* (293 performances) chose to cast all the
Damon Runyon characters with black actors, to orchestrate the score in
black musical terms, and to change the entire emphasis to one that brimmed
with "soul." It did not really work, but the spirited production, with
Robert Guillaume as Nathan Detroit, pleased many.

Yul Brynner, the perennial Siamese monarch in *The King and I* (696 performances), returned with it in 1977, twenty-six years after he became
famous in the 1951 production. The opulent production in many ways
duplicated the brilliance of the original.

Kismet, the 1953 hit operetta of ancient Baghdad, underwent a sea change
to Africa where it was reborn as a black musical called *Timbuktu!* (221
performances) in an otherwise pedestrian production beautifully designed
and directed by Geoffrey Holder with Gilbert Price, Melba Moore, and
Eartha Kitt.

The Pajama Game remained delightful in its strangely short-lived revival
staged by octogenarian director George Abbott, who recreated his original
production, except for bowing to contemporary standards by racially
mixing the cast with black performers Barbara McNair, Cab Calloway, and
others in roles usually played by whites.

More fortunate was another 1954 show, *Peter Pan, or The Boy Who
Wouldn't Grow Up* (554 performances), in which Sandy Duncan proved an
exuberant, high-flying Peter and George Rose a devilishly likeable Captain
Hook.

Two 1956 shows tried their staying power. *My Fair Lady* achieved 377
performances in its copycat production based on the original, with Robert
Coote returning to play Col. Pickering, and with Ian Richardson and Chris-
tine Andreas as Higgins and Eliza. *The Most Happy Fella*, however, had
little luck.

The juvenile delinquents of 1957's *West Side Story* seemed in the show's revival like a fantasy of good boys gone wrong, but the great score and lyrics were as fresh as ever. It returned in a duplicate version (333 performances) directed and choreographed by Jerome Robbins, whose dances made the original explode like a musical bombshell.

Youngest of the fifties musicals was the 1959 *Gypsy*, staged by Arthur Laurents, its librettist, in one of the few truly effective original approaches to a musical revival. The keystone of the show was Angela Lansbury's beautifully acted Rose, which was, nevertheless, not vocally up to Ethel Merman's unforgettable performance. Many were surprised it did not last longer (120 performances).

Compared to the fifties, the quality of the following decade's musical output may have been lacking, but the twenty-four musicals that totalled over 500 performances each (counting shows that opened through June 1970) reveal a period replete with hits. Some of them played for several years into the seventies, but are not considered here, as they belong to the earlier period. Still, a couple of sixties shows that did close in the seventies were considered strong enough contenders to make their revival seem worthwhile only a few years after the passing of the originals. Two of them even had two separate re-stagings.

The oldest of the sixties shows, *A Funny Thing Happened on the Way to the Forum* and *Stop the World—I Want to Get Off*, date back to 1962. *A Funny Thing* came along in a hilarious production starring Phil Silvers as Pseudolus, a role he rejected in the original only to see it become a sensational vehicle for Zero Mostel. Despite excellent reviews the show closed after 156 performances, which was attributed to Silvers' illness. *Stop the World* had a limited engagement with Sammy Davis, Jr.; it was panned.

In 1964 both *Hello, Dolly!* and *Fiddler on the Roof* opened. *Dolly* returned five years after its 1970 closing, but with a mostly black cast led by Pearl Bailey (in 1968 one of the replacement Dollys for the original production). It became one of three seventies revivals (four if *The Pajama Game* is counted) to try this tack of creating new interest in a familiar show by means of changing the cast's race. The overall impression, however, was one of a tired road show. Two years later yet another *Hello, Dolly!* revival hit town, this time with the lead played by the very first Dolly, Carol Channing herself.

Fiddler also returned with its first star, Zero Mostel, in tow, and became a hot ticket for 167 performances. Once again, all the original trappings were revived. Mostel's Tevye was better than ever and the entire show was on a comparably high level of excellence.

The first star of 1965's long-running *Man of La Mancha*, Richard Kiley, was back on Broadway twice in the role of Cervantes/Don Quixote, first for 140 performances, and then for 124. Like James O'Neill and *The Count of Monte Cristo*, some major actors could not free themselves from roles with which they were indelibly linked in the public's eye.

Hair burst upon the scene in 1967 as a blast of fresh air and its success spawned many dubious imitations. The revolutionary show was revived but, regardless of the direction of Tom O'Horgan, recreating his original, *Hair* was balding and dated in 1977. A 1969 hit, *You're a Good Man, Charley Brown*, no longer seemed so special, and a 1969 flop, *The Canterbury Tales*, was a flop when revived. As for shows of the seventies themselves, *Purlie* and *Jesus Christ Superstar* were both put on again, but only for brief reincarnations.

Off-Broadway's musical revivals consisted only of John Gay's 1728 *The Beggar's Opera*; its sequel, *Polly*; a forties revue, *One for the Money*; a thirties revue, *Pins and Needles*; a sixties revue, *Jacques Brel Is Alive and Well and Living in Paris*; a 1926 Gershwin musical, *Tip-Toes*; the rock opera, *Joseph and the Amazing Technicolor Dreamcoat*; and the spoof of thirties movie musicals, *Dames at Sea*. The most successful was the Chelsea's production of *The Beggar's Opera*, which was granted a commercial run after its original version closed.

* * *

Revivals have become big business on Broadway; many fear that the economic picture will eventually lead more and more to Broadway's becoming just another road-show town for traveling musical revivals. This will prove ever more threatening to the survival of America's musical theatre tradition, which will suffer inordinately from the denial of opportunity to new shows in the rush to produce material that will offer a lower investment risk. The pattern begun in the seventies has continued thus far into the eighties, and shows no sign of slackening.

NOTES

1. Clive Barnes, "Theatre: A Magical *Midsummer Night's Dream*," *New York Times*, 21 January 1971, p. 27.

2. Many of these productions are described in my *Shakespeare Around the Globe: A Guide to Notable Postwar Revivals* (Westport, Conn.: Greenwood Press, 1986).

3. See Paul Avila Mayer, "Which One Had the Clout?" *New York Times*, 9 May 1971, Sec. II, p. 1; "Drama Mailbag," *New York Times*, 16 May 1971, Sec. II, p. 6; and "Drama Mailbag," *New York Times*, 23 May 1971, Sec. II, p. 11.

4. Walter Kerr, "A Daring, Perverse and Deeply Original *Cherry Orchard*," *New York Times*, 27 February 1977, Sec. II, p. 1.

★ 7 ★
Ploys,
Playgoers,
and
Playhouses

PLOYS

Broadway audiences are like old dogs still capable of learning new tricks. After several years of sulking in the doghouse as the treats offered them grew progressively less appealing, audiences began, in the early seventies, to gnaw with varying degrees of interest at several bones thrown their way by producers anxious to set them barking. Some ploys were limited in scope, like the few shows that increased their weekly matinees from two to four and cut their evening shows from six to four. For *Sugar* David Merrick offered his patrons free parking, while audiences at *Don't Bother Me, I Can't Cope* were given free cab rides home.[1] These lures stemmed largely from the producers' desire to allay theatregoers' fears of entering the supposedly threatening environs of Broadway after dark. One such idea, the 7:30 P.M. curtain, was industry-wide and incited a mild controversy during its brief existence.

The 7:30 Curtain

Broadway's curtains had been going up at 8:30 P.M. for as long as anyone could remember. But at the beginning of the decade, 8:30 was becoming a less and less desirable starting time. New York's widely publicized crime in the streets convinced thousands that they would be better off in front of their TV sets than going to a play and getting out after 11:00 P.M. when there was an appallingly good chance of getting mugged. The League of New

York Theatre Owners and Producers (LNYTP), concerned about the decline in attendance figures, agreed to try moving their curtain times up an hour to 7:30 P.M., allowing patrons to get home an hour earlier. An eight-week tryout for a 7:30 curtain had been made back in 1960, but only for Wednesday nights. The new system was for every night. Matinees were also moved up, from 2:30 to 2:00, so actors could have their accustomed rest between shows. The plan went into effect for all twenty-three Broadway shows in January 1971. A number of limited surveys over the next two years found the majority of theatregoers in favor of the earlier curtain, but a considerable number still wanted a later one, to give them a chance for a relaxed dinner. Many would have liked an 8:30 or even 9:00 opening on Saturday nights.

The stumbling block to the plans of the LNYTP was the restaurant business, which insisted that their dinner trade was being ruined. At first, some claimed that they made up the pre-show slack with after-show business; others tried out special dinner plans where you could eat your meal in two sittings, before and after the show.

The first producer to pull out of the agreement was the ornery David Merrick, who also had been the first to do so in 1960. Not being a member of the LNYTP, he ignored its protests and moved *Promises, Promises* to a compromise time of 8:00 P.M. Soon, other shows began to opt for 8:00. By October 1972 the LNYTP agreed to go for the 8:00 start with 8:30 Saturday nights if the restaurants would put up money for promoting Broadway shows, but this idea fell through. Nevertheless, by 1975 few shows started earlier than 8:00; matinees remained at 2:00. It was observed that the 8:00 curtain allowed marquee lights to remain on longer, more time was available for ticket sales, local businesses were given a chance to attract customers, and food emporiums had time to serve dinner.

Limited Gross

Another ploy, as unsuccessful as the 7:30 curtain but a good example of the way the theatre business was moving to correct the problem of empty seats, was the Limited Gross Contract. The idea was to stimulate production of unconventional shows that might fail to fill large Broadway houses by allowing them to play to smaller audiences of between 300 and 599. The productions had to agree not to gross more than $25,000 a week, although they could play in theatres that, when fully occupied, could draw much more. Full-sized Broadway theatres could have seating roped off to keep their seat totals and gross incomes within the allowable limits. Altogether, ten full-sized theatres and the several smaller Broadway houses of fewer than 600 seats (Off-Broadway houses then seated 299 or fewer) agreed to use the system, but the only full-sized theatre to actually produce a play under its provisions was the John Golden, for the ill-fated *Solitaire/ Double Solitaire*.

Audiences, it was hoped, would turn out in droves to the Limited Gross theatres (then called Middle Broadway theatres), because the plan required that seats be sold at no more than $5 each. The $25,000 maximum gross arrangement was expected to cut producers' weekly operating costs significantly, thereby lengthening a show's run and giving it more of a chance to pay off. Shows that had clear-cut hit potential could, if they wished, convert to a full-scale Broadway contract, increase their seating capacity, their prices, and, consequently, their operating costs and grosses. Presumably, a show that might have selected to go Off-Broadway would, under this plan, benefit from a Limited Gross production because it could offer even cheaper seats than the $7.50 currently being assessed most Off-Broadway playgoers.

The idea never caught on. Several shows tried it and all died swiftly. Gilbert Cates, producer of *Solitaire/Double Solitaire*, said afterwards that the provision allowing a potential Limited Gross hit to move to full Broadway status put the producer under pressure from those who wanted the show to make bigger money so that their own wages would increase.[2] This would have placed the producer in an uncomfortable position if he wished to keep running at the Limited Gross rates. As a result, it would have been hard to keep one's staff from leaving for better-paying jobs. As none of the shows trying the idea became hits, and since the danger of losing one's staff for better-paying jobs in a depressed theatre industry seems remote, this argument is open to suspicion. Cates also felt that the Limited Gross did little to reduce production costs. Only the operating costs were affected. The cheaper tryout period, said Cates, was the only advantage of this once-promising concept.

New Sales Methods

The 7:30 curtain and the Limited Gross may have failed to achieve their aims, but that could not be said of the new methods for buying tickets that Broadway inaugurated. Charge accounts were late in coming to the theatre scene, except for those who purchased their seats through brokers. In March 1972, however, anyone with an American Express card could order tickets and not have to carry cash to the box office. Personal checks were also being accepted. In the Spring of 1974 you could for the first time call the theatre on the phone and reserve seats by using any number of credit cards. Sales were boosted dramatically.

Computerized selling through firms like Ticketron with outlets throughout the city also spread during the decade. By purchasing your seats at these outlets you received an instant printout ticket for your preferred seating;

further, the box-office treasurer could know on the day of a show exactly how many seats for the performance had been sold this way. The Shuberts instituted their own nationwide computer system at the end of the decade, thereby enormously facilitating for people all over the nation the purchase of a ticket to one of their seventeen theatres.

No approach to selling tickets was as sensationally effective as the discount ticket office that opened in June 1973 on Duffy Square in the heart of Broadway. Known as the Times Square Theatre Center or TKTS, it was created to provide customers with tickets to Broadway shows on an as-available basis on the day of performance itself. The price was set at one-half of that at the box office, with a small service charge per seat.

TKTS was brought to fruition through the efforts of the LNYTP (with $20,000 of Shubert backing), the New York City Cultural Council, the Mayor's Office of Midtown Planning and Development, and the Theatre Development Fund (TDF); the last raised $85,000 for the project. Of the various TDF programs (built on funds provided by a number of private, public, corporate, and individual sources) TKTS was definitely the most exciting for the general public.

From June 25, 1973, to today, the TKTS architectural award-winning trailer with its red pipe scaffolding and white canvas walls proclaiming TKTS in bold red letters has been a Broadway fixture, operating every day of the week. (Eventually other branches opened elsewhere in the city, and the idea even spread to other cities with multiple entertainment outlets.) To oldtimers it brought back memories of Joe LeBlang's cut-rate ticket agency in the basement of Gray's Drugstore on Forty-third Street and Broadway, a landmark during much of the century's first half.

Ticket sales zoomed, reaching figures few had anticipated. As attendance figures began to rise, the average age of ticket buyers began to drop. A Fall 1973 study found that the median age of Broadway theatregoers had fallen to thirty from the thirty-nine of 1966, and that 63 percent of the buyers were willing to buy seats for another show if the one they most wanted was not available.[3] This meant that one of the theatre's long-lost customs was returning, i.e., impulse buying. For years audiences had been turning out only for shows that were certified hits and not bothering about the others. With TKTS around, people were coming to midtown just to see what was up on the board and often did not make up their minds until the very last minute.

In its early days some producers were reluctant to provide discount seats to the "pushcart," as it then was known in the business, because they did not want their shows to seem to be in trouble. Others refused on the grounds that it was not right to sell seats at half-price when their operating costs remained at full-scale. One company's artistic director was opposed to selling discount seats to his show because he felt it was a disservice to those who were paying full price at the box office. Those who did make use of TKTS sang its praises loudly. Many shows were kept alive by its presence, especially during the traditionally slow summer months. New audiences who would never otherwise have come to Broadway or Off-Broadway were showing up. An article in the *New York Times* in December 1973 noted that 34 percent of the people on the TKTS line had not been to a Broadway show for at least half a year. Nineteen percent had been to one once, and 12 percent twice. But since the booth had opened, 28 percent had attended more than once.[4]

Over 1 million tickets were sold by TKTS within its first two years. With four windows in operation, up to 2,000 tickets were sometimes sold in a single hour. Otis Guernsey reprints in *The Best Plays of 1977-78* the words of TDF's Hugh Southern, who announced that the organization, through TKTS and its various ticket selling measures, had made a great contribution in its

effective restoration of price/demand elasticity in the purchase of tickets by the public. Many producers offering tickets through these facilities have been able to adjust successfully to the changing levels of demand by offering more or fewer tickets for half-price sale. The effect has been to prolong the life of many productions. This, in turn, generates large increments of receipts through other channels of sale, and, of course, additional employment, royalties, theatre rentals, and revenues in restaurant, transportation, parking and other services within and around the theatre district.[5]

Another extremely valuable TDF contribution was its implementation of a voucher program for the Off Off-Broadway theatre. The program, begun in the 1972-73 season, allowed those on TDF's mailing list to purchase a sheaf of tickets to participating Off Off plays. One bought a set of vouchers for a low price and turned them in to the box office for what then amounted to a discount of $2 or more off the already low price of a ticket. Throughout the decade ads for these shows featured the now familiar words, "TDF vouchers accepted." Despite slight cost increases during the subsequent years, vouchers continued to represent one of the best theatre buys in town.

TV Commercials

If TKTS was responsible for selling millions of tickets that might otherwise have gone begging, television advertising did its share in making people know there was a theatre to go to. Until the seventies the largest share of most Broadway advertising budgets went for ads in the local newspapers, especially the *New York Times*. Stuart Ostrow, the producer of *Pippin*, was the first to recognize TV's great potential for reaching a mass audience that never reads the *Times*. Ostrow's *Pippin* commercial in 1973, featuring Ben Vereen and a chorus of voluptuous dancers wearing sexually enticing form-fitting armor and doing a syncopated Bob Fosse number, helped boost the

show into the financial stratosphere. Other producers followed suit, putting
the largest portions of their ad budgets into TV spots. Nothing reached so
many so easily. It was not long before some shows that would otherwise
have vanished quickly found entire new audiences through such electronic
salesmanship.

The most talked-about TV commercial-inspired success story was that of
The Wiz, which opened to a respectable if not overly enthusiastic press.
During its out-of-town tryout it received terrible reviews and lost money;
only the aid of the Shubert Organization was able to bail out the producer,
Ken Harper, whose main backing had been from 20th Century Fox. Fox's
feeling was that the show would be a flop. After three weeks on Broadway
of slow box-office activity, advance sales started to improve. Bernard
Jacobs, one of the two Shubert leaders, decided to gamble $100,000 on a TV
ad campaign in return for a half interest in the show. According to the *New
York Theatre Review*, Jacobs said that Fox "screamed." He further stated:
"They're out $1.2 million, and I want half the show for a hundred thousand.
But I told them plainly: 'This way you'll have 50% of something. The way
it is, you have 100% of nothing.' Well, they thought it over, and decided
that if we were willing to risk a hundred thousand, they would risk it."[6]

The ad campaign and a clever press agent who kept the show a hot item
in the media helped turn failure into success. By the end of a two-week
saturation of the air waves, *The Wiz* was becoming a sellout hit.

In the late seventies television ads for the entire Broadway season were
cooked up by the New York State Department of Commerce as part of its "I
Love New York" campaign, designed to increase city tourism. Broadway
shows were perceived as the biggest tourist draw of all, and commercials
using moments from top shows were concocted for widespread viewing
outside of the city (and, later, within it). One estimate put the increase in
Broadway's business resulting from this campaign (after a four week trial
period) at $2.87 million or 19.9 percent.[7]

PATRONS

The annual increment in audience totals during the last half of the decade
was in large part owing to the ploys just described, as well as to the avail-
ability of a healthy number of highly popular shows. Also responsible was
the huge influx of foreign tourists.

Variety only began to report paid attendance totals following the 1975-76
season. Its annual summations from that season through 1980 are:

1975-76	7.1 million
1976-77	8.8 million
1977-78	8.6 million
1978-79	9.1 million
1979-80	9.3 million[8]

These great increases (offset by the 1977-78 drop when only forty-six shows were done on Broadway), coupled with the rise in ticket prices, were what was pushing Broadway grosses to fantastic heights during this half-decade. One counting made by the LNYTP proudly declared that the attendance on Broadway was far in excess of the total attendance at home games of New York's nine big-league sports teams (baseball, hockey, soccer, football, and basketball).[9]

These theatregoers were certainly not all New Yorkers. Tourism to New York made great bounds forward late in the decade. Nor were New York's tourists simply out-of-towners. Worldwide economic problems had made the United States an inviting place to spend one's yen, pesos, pounds, marks, and francs; goods in this country were considered cheap by international standards. Foreign visitors made up an ever more sizeable chunk of audiences, having gone up from 1 million annually in 1968 to 2 million in 1978. Broadway shows, especially non-book musicals and revues with little dialogue, like *Dancin'*, were a must for sightseers from abroad. Some shows were said to be playing to audiences of up to 80 percent foreigners on weekends. *Oh, Calcutta!*, a popular show because of its racy material and nudity, provided audiences with free programs containing summaries of its sketches in five languages.

An article in *Playbill* in December 1980 counted 11 percent of the audience as foreign with 38 percent coming from Europe, 37 percent from the Western hemisphere, and 25 percent from Africa, Asia, and Australia.[10] On a country-by-country basis, Canada sent the most tourists to New York, followed by Great Britain, Israel, Italy, and Japan.

At the start of the decade it had seemed that no one wanted to come to the city, especially not conventioneers or international tourists. But with the inauguration of the "Big Apple" publicity campaign in 1971 New York's tourist industry blossomed vigorously enough to make it once more first in the world. In 1979 a record-breaking number of visitors came to the city, leaving $2 billion behind. The number of hotels was increasing, especially in the theatre district, and conventions were finding New York the city of choice among most participants.

With the great growth in attendance experienced during these years it was only fitting that an elaborate study be made to examine the makeup of the local audience. The *New York Times* reported on an $80,000 study completed in 1980 that compiled interesting statistics relative to the type of people who attend the theatre.[11] Spectators were analyzed in terms of age, income, education, and marital status. They were categorized as:

1. Traditionalists: true theatre-lovers who prefer plays to musicals and often go to Off-Broadway productions and view other performing arts. This mostly mature audience hailing chiefly from Manhattan, Queens, and the suburbs comprises 33 percent of the "typical" audience.

2. Theatre enthusiasts: people who are fond of musicals and plays with strong contemporary themes. Enjoyers of visual effects, romantic and nostalgic themes, and

famous stars, this group lives throughout the city, is mainly female, and relatively young. They account for 30 percent of a typical audience.

3. Entertainment seekers: this chronologically oldest group is largely suburban, enjoys escapist offerings, has been going to the theatre for many years, and occupies 24 percent of the seats at the shows it attends.

4. Dispassionate theatregoers: the youngest category, these people are not regular playgoers but choose only specific shows. Young marrieds with children, many of them live in Queens and enjoy light theatre experiences. They make up 13 percent of the audience.

Among other interesting findings were the following:

1. At least 1 million of all theatregoers had begun the habit in 1975; they represented 30 percent of the total.

2. Over half of all theatregoers were under thirty-five, reversing the trends of the early seventies towards older audiences.

3. The Broadway audience had risen by 4 million during the decade, 30 percent of the spectators coming from outside the city.

4. There is little difference in the tastes of the younger and older audience members, both groups enjoying light, escapist entertainment, with only slight differences in their specific tastes in types of shows.

The *New York Times* gave the following breakdown:

Age Profile

34 or younger: 57 percent

35 or older: 43 percent

Education Profile

High school or less: 34 percent

Some College: 24 percent

College or post-graduate: 42 percent

Income Profile

$15,000 or less: 22 percent

$15,000-25,000: 37 percent

$25,000 or more: 41 percent

Residence Profile

Manhattan: 14 percent

Other boroughs: 33 percent

New York and Connecticut suburbs: 26 percent

New Jersey suburbs: 27 percent

This survey did not make racial classifications, but it is well known that black audiences were growing during the period in response to the greater number of shows with black origins or orientation. These audiences were often brought to Broadway in large theatre parties, and their presence was a decided plus for the theatre. One reckoning made in 1977 pointed out that blacks made up about 10 percent of the Broadway audience.[12] Brooks Atkinson wrote in his book *Broadway* that black spectators often betrayed their lack of theatregoing experience by coming in late, discarding their stubs before locating their seats, and wearing obtrusive hats throughout the performance.[13] However, their appreciation of material reflecting their interests was immense, and they could often electrify a show by the fervor of their reactions.

Broadway became a home for more black plays and musicals during the seventies than during any previous decade. Black shows, however, had to appeal to racially mixed audiences to survive. As black actor-director-producer-playwright Douglas Turner Ward realized, black audiences for black theatre are "finite."[14] He said that the first true drama on Broadway to draw a largely black audience was *The River Niger*, which played to houses over 90 percent black, but these could only keep the show breathing for nine months.

One audience that is still largely untapped on Broadway is the Hispanic. Many small Hispanic theatre groups have proliferated, but these play mainly in Spanish. Broadway tried to reach this vast audience with only one big show during the seventies, *Zoot Suit*, a play-with-music about the Chicano subculture in Los Angeles. It not only failed to attract Hispanics, it failed with most New York audiences. One reason for its lack of appeal to local Latins may have been its West Coast types and basic differences between Chicano and New York's Hispanic (predominantly Puerto Rican) culture. There may also have been an ineffective publicity campaign among the city's Hispanic communities: a piece in the *New Yorker* noted the disagreement between the Shuberts and the show's original producer, Gordon Davidson, about how that campaign should be waged.[15] When a show comes along that can effectively draw the Hispanic population to Broadway the way *The Wiz* did the black, Broadway will be able to say it is truly representative of all New Yorkers.

Perils of Playgoing

One potentially discouraging side of New York theatregoing was alluded to in Chapter 1. The fear of muggings and purse snatchings was ever constant, despite beefed-up and improved police vigilance. Merely walking through Times Square and certain Off- and Off Off-Broadway neighborhoods could make theatregoing an ordeal. Some disasters, however, were beyond human control.

Free Shakespeare in Central Park long has been one of summertime's happiest occasions for lovers of the Bard. After waiting on line all day for admission there could be few occurrences as disturbing as a sudden downpour causing this open-air event to be cancelled. It was adding injury to insult when, in August 1979, a group of wet and disappointed playgoers were leaving a rained-out performance in the park only to see a taxicab careen crazily out of control into their midst, killing one and seriously injuring five others. And even if the night were fine in Central Park, there was no guarantee one would get through it safely. Consider the plight of Lulu May Wolfe: as she was enjoying *As You Like It*, someone in the park — a considerable distance away, it was believed — fired a gun; the bullet lodged in the poor Shakespeare fan's wrist.

Bullets are bad but bombs are worse. Broadway had at least two bomb scares in the decade; in August 1979, for example, the entire audience and company of *A Chorus Line* had to be evacuated from the Shubert Theatre for a half-hour until it was determined that it was safe to return.

Could the threat of a bomb have come from an unhappy actor, someone who couldn't get a part? No one knows, but a disgruntled actor was among the suspects sought in a series of "bombings" that began to plague pedestrians on Forty-seventh Street around the corner from the Palace Theatre in April, 1980. Within a year four people had been hit by pieces of construction material tossed off rooftops onto the street; one person died and the others were seriously hurt. The "Phantom" of Forty-seventh Street was never caught.

Blackouts are often an effective way to end a scene quickly and with point. No blackout, however, has ever been as surprising as the one that hit New York stages at 9:34 P.M. on July 13, 1977. This one, courtesy of a city-wide Con Ed power failure, forced most shows to ring their curtains down prematurely, but some shows valiantly kept going even in the dark. At the Vivian Beaumont in Lincoln Center the cast of *The Cherry Orchard* borrowed a load of candles from the repertory company's other production, *Agamemnon*, and played out its remaining third to an audience that gave it a standing ovation. At *The Wiz* a disturbed spectator began kicking up a ruckus about getting an instant refund until actress Ella Mitchell, the Wicked Witch of the North, admonished him, "Let's not be rude, darling. . . . You've seen most of the show anyway."[16] At *Anna Christie*, as the audience stumbled blindly for the exits, actor John Lithgow played his guitar for them for half an hour while Liv Ullman kept a flashlight on his face in lieu of a spot. The backstage darkness at *Oh, Calcutta!* prevented the naked cast from getting to their street clothes so they borrowed garments from the spectators and returned them to the theatre the next day for their owners to retrieve.

As some of these examples demonstrate, actors are often quick thinkers and frequently have prevented panic situations from arising. The outstanding instance of a true trouper's courage and wit occurred at the Billy Rose Theatre during a performance of Peter Brook's revolutionary version of *A Midsummer Night's Dream* on January 23, 1971. The actors were deep into the play, at the point just after the "mechanicals" have presented their "Pyramus and Thisbe" to the court, when a flash fire broke out backstage. As smoke billowed over the white squash-court-like walls of the set, Alan Howard, playing Theseus, had only to say his lines, for they bore a surprising pertinence when properly emphasized:

> Say, what abridgement have you for this evening;
> A very tragical mirth, merry and tragical
> That is hot ice and wonderous strange snow.

John Kane as Puck came in with, "You were saying, my Lord?" and Howard replied, "It made my eyes water," at which the cast and audience burst into laughter.[17] A moment afterwards, the smoke seemed to grow more threatening, and Kane ran backstage to return instantly with news of the sprinklers being on, to which there was an enthusiastic response. The flames were soon under control.

Several other theatres were threatened with or damaged by fire in the seventies (the Truck and Warehouse, 1971; the Mercer-O'Casey, 1971; the Winter Garden, 1976; the T. Schreiber Studio, 1976), but only one other flared up while an audience was in attendance. This was *Over Here!* on April 18, 1974, at the Shubert. The show didn't miss a beat, and the flames were quickly doused, but several front-row patrons dashed for the rear of the house when the acrid fumes burned their eyes.

PLAYHOUSES

The Case of the Vanishing Playhouses

Though fire broke out in several theatres, only the T. Schreiber Studio, an Off Off theatre, was ruined totally. The Truck and Warehouse blaze was serious enough to end the run of *The House of Blue Leaves*, but the theatre was later rebuilt. Similarly, the Mercer-O'Casey was reconstructed after its fire put an unconventional version of the traditionally unlucky *Macbeth* out of business. This fire appears to have been the only one in which arson was suspected.

Aside from deliberate demolition, fire is probably the commonest means of removing playhouses from existence. The seventies, however, did see several local theatres vanish for other less conventional reasons. Take the case of the South Street Theatre, for instance. In the summer of 1973, this Off Off company was running a production of *Spoon River Anthology* in a large tent theatre at its Fulton Street seaport location. Came a violent thunderstorm in the early hours of a July morning and down went the tent, a thing of shreds and patches.

If the South Street Theatre company was surprised to discover its home gone with the wind (it later relocated), one can only guess at producer Harry Joe Brown's chagrin at seeing his property disappear. Brown had purchased a church on East Thirteenth Street with plans to rebuild it as a theatre. In 1975 he returned from a trip to Europe to find an empty lot where once he had envisioned a stage with actors. Brown had been having bureaucratic difficulties with the Departments of Health, Fire, and Buildings since buying St. Mary's Catholic Church in 1969, but no determination as to the city's possible action regarding the site had been taken when he left for overseas. Not only did he return, as if from a lost weekend, to find the church missing, but the city, which had razed the place, billed him close to $13,000 for the job. Brown, who never had been told of the impending wrecker's ball, sued the city—and eventually won his case.

True, the transformation of St. Mary's to a theatre was still just an idea, but that was not the case of the Mercer Arts Center, a multitheatre complex located in one of the city's oldest and most historic hotels, the Universal (Broadway Central in recent years), on the fringes of Greenwich Village behind New York University. This combination Off-Broadway/Off Off hive of activity, renovated in 1971 at a $300,000-plus cost, included the Mercer-Hansberry Theatre, the Mercer-O'Casey, the Mercer-Shaw, the Kitchen Theatre, the Oscar Wilde Cabaret Theatre, and the Mercer-Brecht, as well as the Gene Frankel Workshop. Playing there on August 2, 1973, were the hits *El Grande de Coca-Cola*, *One Flew Over the Cuckoo's Nest*, and *The Proposition*, and a newer work, *The Interview*. On that day, the 102-year-old structure, now mainly occupied, aside from the theatres, by welfare clients, began to show signs of terminal illness as its sides bulged and its walls cracked, audibly and visibly. A day later, death tremors set in as bricks started tumbling and crumbling, and the Police, Fire, and Buildings Departments arrived to stand humbly by and administer last rites. At 5:10 P.M., with a sound resembling an explosion, the Broadway Central succumbed to the inevitable and collapsed, taking with it several residents who failed to get out in time.

Interestingly, not all of the hotel gave up the ghost, and the part containing the theatre enclave was only partly ruined. It was considered too dangerous, however, to allow the theatres to resume operations, and the four shows were forced to transfer to other homes.

Off-Broadway theatres generally have shorter lives than those on Broadway, but only rarely do they face the wrecker's ball when running a hit show. This fate, alas, befell the New Theatre on East Fifty-fourth Street in 1973 when *Oh Coward!* had to be moved so the building could be torn down to make room for a bank.

Broadway was graced briefly by a new theatre that lived not quite two years during the period. An old, disused playhouse near Lincoln Center was renovated for dance companies and opened as the Harkness. The Harkness operated under a Broadway contract though technically not in the theatre district (like its neighbor, the Vivian Beaumont). From 1975 to 1977 it housed a repertory season of the Acting Company and several commercial productions before being sold to and gutted by developers.

"Save the Theatre" Campaigns

Theatres were occasionally pestered by the threat of demolition, conversion to other purposes, or foreclosure, but were saved by groups of concerned theatre workers and "civilians." Fights to prevent removal from the landscape of several popular playhouses occupied large numbers of people throughout the decade. Even Off Off theatres figured in these debates. One example was St. Clement's Church on West Forty-sixth Street, which was at the eye of a hurricane when it was threatened with an untimely death because of a $20,000 debt. Various schemes to save it were broached; perhaps the most memorable effort was that of director Tom O'Horgan and playwright Megan Terry, who created a fund-raising event called *St. Hydro-Clemency, or a Funhouse of the Lord* which charged over 500 people $5 a head for the pleasure of immersing themselves in a two-hour "happening" within the space. The theatre survived.

No Off or Off Off theatre menaced by impending loss or levelling received as much print space as Joseph Papp's New York Shakespeare Festival Theatre on Astor Place. A landmark building, the 1848 Italianate-style Astor Place Library had been converted in 1967 into a home for several theatres; soon collectively christened the Public Theatre, this enclave became one of the most productive theatre centers in town. Nevertheless, in 1970 the complex faced apparently insuperable financial difficulties, which Papp tried to short-circuit by convincing the city's Board of Estimate to buy the place and lease it back to him for a nominal annual sum.

Papp undertook an extensive campaign to convince Mayor John V. Lindsay and the Board of his idea's feasibility. The Public was being threatened by foreclosure at the hands of the construction company, which thus far had not been paid $400,000 for renovations to one of the building's new theatres. Papp lowered his asking price from $5.1 million to $2.6 million, explaining that the original figure included the price of planned improvements.

Important arts figures formed a special committee to support Papp's idea. The Board seemed on the brink of acceding when Papp, inflamed by a remark made at a meeting by Queens Borough President Sidney Leviss, stormed out angrily, thereby inciting a shouting match. The final vote came on March 26, 1971, with Papp in attendance backed by fifty supporters whom he rallied by reciting Henry V's speech at Agincourt. Like Henry, he romped home free, winning by a unanimous vote which agreed to lease him the Public at $1 per annum.

Papp was peripherally involved in the next major playhouse dispute, in 1971, which centered on the idea of converting the smaller of the two Lincoln Center playhouses (then called the Forum) into three small movie theatres, a screening room, offices to administer the film archives of Henri Langlois, and a film museum. The plan, put forward by the City Center, a non-profit performing arts institution which would be in charge of the new space, called for the Forum to be rebuilt in the vast storage areas behind the Beaumont.

The Lincoln Center Board of Trustees was seeking a way to alleviate the financial problems incurred by the Lincoln Center Repertory Theatre, a company whose annual $750,000 deficit was not eased by the twenty weeks each year during which the Beaumont was dark. The Board sought to make use of what it deemed wasted storage space, originally planned for the needs of a true repertory company, which the present occupants were not. The City Center plan called for that institution to rent the Beaumont to the repertory company for its usual season and to outsiders for the remainder of the year, thus increasing productivity.

A hornet's nest of conflicting opinions developed. Many parties were convinced that it would be a sacrilege to disturb the gem-like perfection of the intimate Forum. Few, including the place's original co-designer, Jo Mielziner, believed it could be duplicated in the space suggested. Among the outraged opponents of the plan was critic John Simon, who fulminated, "I consider it a cultural and moral scandal, an act of organized vandalism."[18] On the other hand, critic Stanley Kauffmann argued that the plan was economically viable, that film had every right to co-exist at Lincoln Center with opera, theatre, and dance, and that the repertory company's work there was nothing of which to be especially proud;[19] the latter diagnosis had few opponents, even though the surgery seemed extreme.

Among the many plans offered as alternatives was Papp's, who said that the Beaumont should be sold to the City Center for $5 million and the money used to subsidize the repertory company for another decade. It was Papp himself who would eventually take over the task of creating a Lincoln Center company of his own—and give it up when it grew too unwieldy even for his Herculean powers.

In October 1971, Richard Clurman, representing the City Center, admitted defeat, claiming surprise at the vehemence of the public's outburst over his attempts to do something positive for the Lincoln Center situation. The decisive blow came when the repertory company's artistic director, Jules Irving, spoke at a hearing and denounced the City Center plan as "a big lie, but—above all—a tragically ironic lie" that he had been "forced" to believe in.[20] Nearly a month later, the Rockefeller Foundation granted the Forum $100,000 to develop an experimental theatre program; the Foundation denied any connection with the controversy, however. The publicity generated by the fracas drew to the repertory company large enough contributions from various donors to enable it to meet its deficit and survive a bit longer without City Center backing.

The longest-raging playhouse controversy had not yet been put to bed when the decade ended. Three Broadway theatres were involved, and all were eventually demolished. They were the intimate Bijou and the full-sized Morosco, next door to one another on West Forty-fifth Street, and the Helen Hayes, around the corner on West Forty-sixth. All stood on a site chosen by Atlanta builder and architect John Portman for a new luxury hotel. When, in 1972, the *New York Times* first discussed the potential new structure, it mentioned only the possibility of razing the Hayes, a 1911 playhouse seating 1,139. Few protested the idea, nor was there a public outcry as later years saw the other playhouses added to the list. The New York Drama Critics Circle voiced its distress, and Actors Equity later claimed that it did, too, though no major public outlet for its views was provided. The LNYTP put its muscle behind Portman because it saw the planned fifty-five-story hotel (the final version had fifty stories) as a potentially powerful economic force for the redevelopment of the Broadway area. A Forty-fifth to Forty-sixth Street hotel with more than 2,000 rooms would bring with it thousands of jobs as well as millions of hotel guests who would be a ready market for theatre tickets. To those who bewailed the loss of three old Broadway theatres, the LNYTP and others would point to the 1,500-seat theatre included in the blueprints. Theatregoers who had visited the new, hangar-like Uris and Minskoff Theatres were not elated by the news.

Through most of the seventies, the Portman project was involved in raising funds and working its way through the morass of red tape so extensive an undertaking requires. Late in 1979, however, virulent public protests against the building began to be heard as theatre workers and theatre lovers decried the dilution of the city's theatrical heritage by the fat-cat real estate interests. Equity was now fighting vigorously on behalf of the protestors. The LNYTP argued that enough movie theatres originally used as legitimate playhouses could be found in the Broadway area to offset any foreseeable theatre shortage caused by the planned razing. Local businesses were also pro-Portman as they recognized the hotel's value in upgrading the neighborhood and bringing it more dollars.

For the city, the hotel would mean a substantial windfall. At 1979 tax rates the city raked in a paltry $700,000 annually from the buildings on the site. With the hotel standing there—an edifice whose estimated cost of over $240 million (its final cost was $450 million) would make it the world's most expensive hotel—taxes of $8 to $10 million a year would be funneled into the city's money chests. A $15 to $20 million impact on the city's economy was forecast as well.

On the side of the protestors was the non-economic but all important cultural and artistic question: could New York City afford to deny its historical and architectural past for the sake of financial advantages? To the hundreds of actors and other theatre folk who rallied and picketed against the hotel in 1980 the answer was a resounding "No!" Their feeling was that the Portman interests should either find another nearby location that would not endanger the theatres, or build the hotel over and around the theatres. The latter suggestion, offered by Equity, was rejected as impossible by the engineers involved.

By March 1982 the battle was over. Distinguished theatre people had been arrested, ringing speeches had been made, there was mass media attention to the problem, but nothing availed, for in that month demolition began on the Morosco, Hayes, and Bijou. In September 1985 the hotel, named the Marriott Marquis, opened its doors to the public.

Return to the Ranks

While some theatres were pulled down and others threatened with extinction, a number of playhouses were given new leases on life after years of standing empty or being used as movie theatres and broadcasting studios. Others, in use throughout the period, were extensively renovated and redecorated. The Shuberts, for example, after several highly profitable years of business, spent a large sum near the decade's end to have all their theatres brought up to snuff. The stories recounted here concern some of the better-publicized refurbishings of the period.

Off-Broadway's major renovations included those at One Sheridan Square, the Roundabout, and the Delacorte in Central Park. There were also important architectural innovations at the Public Theatre's Newman, the Queens Playhouse on the site of the Flushing World's Fair, the Brooklyn Academy's Le Percq Space, the Chelsea Westside Theatre (situated in an old church on West Forty-third Street), and the queen of Off Off-Broadway theatres, La Mama, ETC. Space permits brief discussion of only two of these theatres.

The Delacorte is widely known to Shakespeare lovers as the home of free classical theatre every summer. In 1971 producer Joseph Papp oversaw some major design changes in the seating arrangements, revising them from a fan shape to a horseshoe shape, thus aiding audibility and sight lines. He really wanted to tear the place down (it had been built as a temporary edifice) and put up a new theatre. A few years later, TV commercials began to inform the public about the deteriorating state of the Delacorte; donations were sought for reconstruction. Papp's desire to move the Delacorte to another site in the park had irritated the public in 1971; now, in 1974, when he sought a city grant of $1 million to build a concrete playhouse, he met with even stiffer resistance. The entire park budget was $4.5 million, noted the *Times*, which thought the cost wildly excessive and the concrete inappropriate.[21] Papp's consequent fund-raising efforts netted him $780,000 for the extensive renovations needed. The publisher after whom the theatre was named, George Delacorte, had already provided a matching grant of $200,000. The new Delacorte proudly opened in late June 1977 with improved seating and a larger stage on concrete foundations.

The new Roundabout and La Mama theatres represent the practice of converting a nontheatrical space to playhouse uses. In 1974 the Roundabout, for years bursting at the seams in its tiny basement theatre on Chelsea's West Twenty-sixth Street, opened a larger space on West Twenty-third, in the disused RKO Cinema. The new house was dubbed Roundabout I (later changed to the Susan Bloch Theatre), the old one Roundabout II, and the company kept both active into the eighties. The movie conversion cost about $100,000 and created the largest open stage in the city, measuring 93 feet by 50 feet. Unhappily, the Roundabout lost the lease in 1984, and the Susan Bloch was reconverted to a multiplex movie house while the Roundabout moved to a new theatre on the East Side in 1985.

The most exciting Off- and Off Off-Broadway theatre construction news revolved around the Theatre Row development. This project, which blossomed into a group of theatres that neighbor one another on the south side of West Forty-second Street between Ninth and Dyer Avenues, began inauspiciously. When the Playwrights Horizons company (then an Off Off, now an Off-Broadway group), was evicted from its former home, its artistic director, Robert Moss, spent four months searching for a suitable location; he feared loss of $44,000 in grants if his company failed to establish a permanent new address. In desperation, he examined a row of dilapidated buildings on Forty-second Street where X-rated shows, massage parlors, and book stores plied their trades. Moss nervily rented two buildings—one for offices, the other for a theatre—on a six-month lease, intending to use the time to search for better quarters.

From the moment of occupancy on January 1, 1975, Playwrights Horizons was back in the production business. Audiences flocked to the new theatre, Moss extended his lease, and the decision was reached to make the entire block a theatrical one. Assisting in the project were the Forty-second Street Redevelopment Corporation, which originally wanted to turn the space into a park, and the New York State Urban Development Corporation, owner of most of the property.

In June 1976, when 416 West Forty-second Street, which still had burlesque signs standing in front of it, was closed down for failure to pay its electric bills, Moss and a group of actors took occupancy of it for Playwrights Horizons, while their theatre at Number 422 was taken over by the

Lion Theatre Company. Their next neighbor was the Nat Horne Theatre. A joyful celebration was held on August 31, 1977, with various dignitaries in attendance, to mark official inauguration of the block. Other tenants now included the South Street Theatre, the Actors and Directors Lab and its Harold Clurman Theatre, the Harlem Childrens Theatre, the Black Theatre Alliance, and INTAR (International Arts Relations, an Hispanic cultural center); together with a new French restaurant nine tenants occupied the former sex-for-sale real estate. A bilingually staffed central ticket office was created to service all productions.

In May 1978 the nearly completed Theatre Row celebrated its formal opening with ceremonies presided over by Vice President Walter F. Mondale and his wife. Two and a half hours of free entertainment were provided for the 15,000 celebrants who showed up. Theatre Row flourished artistically in the ensuing years, but serious financial problems arose as well, threatening the Row's very existence, which remained precarious throughout the early eighties.

Better known to the average theatregoer were the renovations on view at uptown theatres. Over the years, a number of Broadway's playhouses dropped out of the legitimate theatrical business and were converted to cinema grind houses, often for pornography, or else were used as radio and TV stations. One such theatre, the Ritz, built in 1921, had had a spotted history before returning to the fold in 1971 with the musical *Soon. Soon* soon closed, porno returned, and then another flop play was produced there. Two more shows tried the ill-fated theatre before the decade ended, and there was also a period in 1973 when it was run as the Robert F. Kennedy Theatre for Children. This latter concept was crushed when Equity, discovering that its producer had been asking the actors he hired to return their paychecks to him, disallowed him from hiring any more of its members. It was no longer considered a Broadway theatre by the decade's end, but it was attempting yet another comeback in the mid-1980s.

Another formerly much-used theatre, the Cort, had been a TV studio since 1969; it was freshened up in 1972 and played out the decade by serving in the function for which it originally had been designed; *The Magic Show* enjoyed a long run there.

An even longer-lasting success story was that of the Little Theatre, also known as the Winthrop Ames Theatre; a 1912 edifice, it had become a TV studio in the sixties; for one day in the seventies it was taken over by a purveyor of gay porno, but the ensuing hue and cry of neighboring theatre interests led to its being padlocked. Plays returned not long after, and the hit *Gemini* found the Little a comfortable home for years. In the eighties, its name was changed to the Helen Hayes in the wake of the demolition of the original Hayes.

More prolific in the seventies was another intimate Broadway house, the Bijou, now a victim of John Portman's wrecking ball. Erected in 1917, it had been showing films for years, only rarely shutting off its projectors for a drama. In 1971, when the porno people had their eyes on it, it managed to keep itself clean and go legitimate, after undergoing a $30,000 dressing up. Of its various productions, the Swiss mime show *Mummenschanz* was the longest lived.

A couple of Broadway theatres underwent name changes in an effort to revive their sagging fortunes. The Billy Rose on West Forty-first Street, Broadway's southernmost theatre, began to decline seriously in the mid-seventies; a 1975 storm damaged the stage area severely. Bad luck plagued the place for another couple of years until the Nederlander firm made it the seventh in their string of Broadway playhouses in 1978. In partnership with a London company, the Nederlanders hoped to make the house specialize in British imports, therefore naming it the Trafalgar. A year and a half later it was rechristened the Nederlander, which name it retains today.

A former West Forty-eighth Street nightclub, the Latin Quarter, was converted to a small theatre in 1979, after a few years of porno movies. Its new name was the 22 Steps Theatre (there were that many steps to climb from the street-level entrance). In 1980, after a series of unsuccessful shows, it changed its name once more, to the Princess Theatre. Today, it operates as a nightclub *cum*-disco under its original name.

Another landmark nightclub, West Forty-sixth Street's Billy Rose's Diamond Horseshoe, had closed in 1951. Sonja Henie tried running an ice-skating school there in 1961, and the same year saw it used as a theatre, the Mayfair. A cabaret moved in two years later, but theatre was back in 1975 with *Dance With Me*. The 299-seat house struggled to survive with several other shows, was again renovated, was christened the Century, and played host to new plays through the end of the decade.

No theatre conversions were as exciting for Broadwayites as those sponsored by the Brandt Corporation just before the turn of the decade. These movie-theatre landlords undertook to return several historically significant theatres to legitimate use after years of grind-house service. All the theatres were located on or around the corner from the most notorious street in the city, Forty-second Street between Seventh and Eighth avenues. Once the proud home of more legitimate playhouses than any other thoroughfare, it had long since been transformed into a row of grimy movie theatres, "adult" book stores, and massage parlors, with curb-to-storefront crowds of hookers, pimps, drug dealers, and other midnight cowboys.

Broadway's late-seventies booking jams created a need for new theatres; the Brandts figured that they could benefit financially by converting several film palaces back into legitimate playhouses. They aimed to work on the Apollo, built in 1910 as the Bryant, the Lyric, constructed in 1903, and the Selwyn.

The only one actually to be changed over was the Apollo, called the New Apollo to avoid confusion with the Apollo in Harlem. The Lyric was cleaned up but no producers chose to book anything there. The New Apollo's last legitimate show had been *The Blackbirds of 1933*, following which it was a burlesque house and then a movie theatre. The New Apollo opened in February 1979 with *On Golden Pond*, and its audience was shielded from the Forty-second Street sleaze by being granted access from the original entrance on Forty-third Street (the Forty-second Street entrance had been added, for prestige, in 1920). A new marquee designated the long-disused entrance. A $350,000 renovation put playgoers back into its 1,161 seats. The New Apollo faced bad times in the eighties, however, and was fated to return to the ranks of the grind houses.

Equally ill-fated was one other Brandt Corporation movie theatre conversion, that of the Rialto, changed to the New Rialto when it opened as a legitimate playhouse in February 1980. This theatre, on the west side of Seventh Avenue just north of Forty-second Street, was on a site once occupied by the 1899 Victoria Theatre, which began showing films in 1915. In 1935 it was torn down and rebuilt as the Rialto; its 1980 incarnation was as a 499-seat Art Deco playhouse. A string of failures forced its owners to reconsider its potential as a venue for live theatricals.

New Theatres

If the seventies had known only conversions and redevelopments, the evidence would suggest a minor boom in reconstruction. But theatres new from the ground up were also very much a part of the picture. In fact, the first new Broadway playhouses in close to half a century were erected during the period. It was Mayor John V. Lindsay's administration that saw the potential danger posed to the future of the legitimate playhouses by a current office-building boom in the theatre district. To stimulate new theatre construction in an area where the last ones to have been built were the 1928 Ethel Barrymore and Craig Theatres, the administration legislated zoning ordinances according to which builders were granted meaningful concessions in the amount of rentable floor space they were permitted if they included theatres in their designs. Thus, all four of the decade's new theatres were contained within skyscrapers: the Uris and the Circle in the Square in the Uris Building, the Minskoff in One Astor Place, and the American Place in the J. P. Stevens Building. Two of these were large-sized musical houses, and two were small theatres suitable mainly for plays.

The first to open, in December 1971, was the American Place at 111 West Forty-sixth Street, near Sixth Avenue. It was built to house productions of the seven-year-old American Place Theatre (APT), a non-profit organization devoted to new plays; it had formerly occupied St. Clement's Church further west on the same street. Unlike the other theatres, the APT was really not in an office building, but was built as a separate unit adjoining one. This up-to-340-seat theatre, designed by scenic artist Kurt Lundell and architect Richard D. Kaplan, is an architectural beauty containing a thrust stage. Situated forty feet below street level, it is reached by stairs or escalator. Costing over $1 million, it was rented to the APT for a nominal $5-a-year fee. Because of its size, the APT is officially classed as an Off-Broadway house.

A few months after the APT opened, two truly Broadway-size theatres neared completion, both in the same building straddling the block from Fiftieth to Fifty-first streets between Broadway and Eighth Avenue. Older Broadwayites remember the elaborate Capitol movie palace that stood on the same site. The Uris, named for builder Harold Uris (but since renamed the Gershwin), is a cavernous 1,900-seat house for large-scale musicals. It occupies six stories in the Uris Building. Controlled by James Nederlander and Gerald Oestreicher, this $12.5 million theatre designed by Ralph Alswang was equipped with a fully automated hydraulic rigging system containing eighty-five sets of lines; when the time came to use the system for the opening production, the ill-fated science-fiction musical, *Via Galactica*, it malfunctioned disastrously.

The Uris entranceway is an arcade-like underpass that cuts through the block, allowing cars to drop off passengers without tying up street traffic. One can park one's car, see the show, and eat dinner in the same building. The lobby and interior are in Art Nouveau style, all of which was designed by Alswang, who was given the freedom to create every inch of space without interference. Housed on an upper floor is the Theatre Hall of Fame, a display area given its first home here. Escalators move audiences from the street level to a lofty balcony.

Playbill's Louis Botto surveyed the Uris and observed such features as "dark proscenium panels that serve as light towers that are removable if the production demands it; a flexible stage floor that can be taken apart like a Tinker Toy . . . or that can be extended like a thrust stage; and—for the first time in any theatre—a water curtain instead of asbestos in case of an on-stage fire."[22]

Despite excellent audience sight lines, the house proved too vast for comfort and tended to dwarf all but the most splashy or spectacular of shows. Balcony spectators complained of remoteness from the action. Only the efforts of brilliant acoustical engineers working with amplified sound could make the actors heard.

Next door to this immense playhouse was the clumsily named Circle in the Square-Joseph E. Levine Theatre (usually called by only the first half of this title), another basement project. The Circle in the Square, New York's oldest continuing company, headed by Theodore Mann and Paul Libin, was entrenched in a 299-seat theatre on Bleecker Street when the Lindsay administration asked it to consider moving uptown to the Broadway area as part of the city's plan to rejuvenate Times Square. But Mann and Libin, unable to see how a 299-seater could succeed on Broadway, convinced the planners that the idea would work only if 650 seats were provided (it can actually hold up to 681). The Circle in the Square bore no responsibility for building the theatre, only for filling it and making it work. Foundation support enabled them to make their move and the decade soon saw Broadway possessed of a permanent non-profit company devoted to limited runs of standard and new plays with leading players of the day. It opened in November 1972.

Like the American Place, the Circle in the Square, designed by Allen Sayles, has a street-level lobby area. One must descend a steep staircase or escalator to reach its spacious lower lobby carpeted in red and gray checks. The theatre itself is a functionally simple, U-shaped arena surrounded by the audience on three sides or four depending on the play's scenic needs. When necessary, the open part of the U is either filled in with seats or used as a scenic background. The sides of the U have seven rows of seats and the lower curve has ten, making visibility easy no matter where one is situated. This design is based on that of the downtown playhouse which the organization still maintains for productions put on by independent managements. Critics have complained, however, that the U shape is not a good one since its extended acting space creates uncomfortable problems of blocking and acoustics. The theatre has excellent trapdoor facilities, enough overhead space for flying, and an overhead grid which allows technicians to move about with ease.

The huge Minskoff Theatre presented its first show in 1973. Costing between $7 and $8 million, and designed by the firm of Kahn and Jacobs for the fifty-five-story Sam Minskoff Building at One Astor Place on Broadway between Forty-fourth and Forty-fifth streets, it features a "processional" entry route taking spectators to its Grand Foyer, thirty-five feet above Broadway, by twin escalators. Even those who have criticized the Minskoff for its less-than-perfect acoustics and sight lines have praised the marvelous view of the Great White Way through the immense glass window hovering over the Broadway glitter and litter. Other novel features include a variable proscenium opening and a fly gallery on the upstage wall instead of in the side wings. As at the Uris there are no opera side boxes, and the seating provides plenty of legroom.

Early in its career, the Minskoff was faced with a need for architectural revisions when, during the run of *Irene*, its first show, dancers regularly sustained injuries because of the too-rigid stage flooring. Extensive repairs had to be made in the face of threats by the actors' union to disallow the dancers from continuing in the show. The Minskoff faced such serious financial problems during its first decade that one of its highest officials stated that if he had it to do over again, he would not include a theatre on the premises.

It appeared for a while after these theatres were built that Broadway had made a grave error in erecting three new structures at a time when the already existing theatres were hard put to find new attractions. What was once viewed as a shortage of theatres now seemed like a glut. This phase did not last long, and booking jams helped almost all the theatres find waiting customers; however, the eighties saw a return to the depressed situation of the early seventies, and an uncomfortable number of Broadway theatres once more stood like ghosts of their former selves.

In 1970 there were thirty-three theatres of varying size on Broadway (including the Vivian Beaumont at Lincoln Center). In 1980 there were forty-two (not including the American Place). In Table 7.1, List A names all theatres active at the start of the decade; List B includes all those that returned to live theatre or were built during the decade.

Table 7.1
Broadway Playhouses of the Seventies

List A: Theatres Active
in 1970

Alvin Theatre (renamed the Neil Simon Theatre, 1983)

Ambassador Theatre

ANTA Theatre (renamed the Virginia Theatre, 1981)

Belasco Theatre

Biltmore Theatre

Booth Theatre

Broadhurst Theatre

Broadway Theatre

Brooks Atkinson Theatre

Edison Theatre

Ethel Barrymore Theatre

Eugene O'Neill Theatre

Forty-sixth Street Theatre

Helen Hayes Theatre*

Imperial Theatre

John Golden Theatre

Longacre Theatre

Lunt-Fontanne Theatre

Lyceum Theatre

Majestic Theatre

Mark Hellinger Theatre

Martin Beck Theatre

Morosco Theatre*

Music Box Theatre

Nederlander Theatre (Billy Rose)

Palace Theatre

Playhouse Theatre

Plymouth Theatre

Royale Theatre

St. James Theatre

Shubert Theatre

Vivian Beaumont Theatre

Winter Garden Theatre

List B: Reversions, Conversions, and New Theatres

Bijou Theatre*

Century Theatre (Mayfair)

Circle in the Square Theatre

Harkness Theatre*

Minskoff Theatre

New Apollo Theatre

New Rialto Theatre

Princess Theatre (22 Steps)

Ritz Theatre

Uris Theatre (renamed the George Gershwin Theatre, 1983)

---

*Subsequently razed.

NOTES

1. Among other inducements, not discussed here, which remained in effect once instituted were the addition of Sunday matinees and the licensing of theatres to serve alcoholic beverages to their patrons.

2. Cited by Lewis Funke, "Was It All in Vain?" *New York Times*, 17 October 1971, Sec. II, p. 33.

3. Sharon J. Fujioka, "Discount Ticket Center Found to Be a Theatergoing Stimulus," *New York Times*, 11 October 1973, p. 57.

4. Lewis Funke, "I Love the Theater, Man, But Those Prices," *New York Times*, 16 December 1973, Sec. II, p. 3.

5. Otis Guernsey, *The Best Plays of 1977-78* (New York: Dodd, Mead and Co., 1977), p. 44.

6. Tom McMorrow, "The NEW Shuberts: Schoenfeld and Jacobs," *New York Theatre Review*, Premiere Issue (Spring/Summer 1977): 14.

7. "Shows Register Strong Profits," *New York Times*, 5 November 1979, Sec. IV, p. 2

8. Hobe Morrison, "Legit Season Posts New Record," *Variety*, 4 June 1980, p. 1.

9. Carol Lawson, "News of the Theatre," *New York Times*, 19 December 1979, Sec. III, p. 23.

10. "In League for International Audiences," *Playbill*, December, 1980, p. 40.

11. Richard F. Shepard, "A New Portrait of the Broadway Theatergoer," *New York Times*, 16 March 1980, Sec. II, p. 1.

12. "Personal Investing," *Fortune*, May 1977, p. 148.

13. Brooks Atkinson, *Broadway* (New York: Macmillan, 1973), pp. 502-3.

14. Mel Gussow, "Negro Ensemble Find Hit Play Poses Problems," *New York Times*, 7 February 1973, p. 30.

15. "Talk of the Town: Conference in Shubert Alley," *New Yorker*, 19 February 1979, pp. 30-31.

16. Frank J. Prial, "New York Theaters Bouncing Back Faster Than Its Restaurants After the Blackout," *New York Times*, 15 July 1977, p. 14.

17. Henry Raymond, "Shakespearean Actors Keep Audience Calm in Fire," *New York Times*, 24 January 1971, p. 66.

18. John Simon, "The Seizers at the Forum," New York Magazine, 5 July 1971, p. 50.

19. Stanley Kauffmann, "Drama at Lincoln Center," *The New Republic*, 23 October 1971, p. 20.

20. Howard Taubman, "Beaumont Takeover Now Seems Doomed," *New York Times*, 14 October 1971, p. 56.

21. "Too Solid Concrete," *New York Times*, 6 September 1974, p. 32.

22. Louis Botto, "A Walking Tour of Three New Theatres," *Playbill*, December 1972, p. 17.

★ 8 ★
ACTORS, DIRECTORS, AND CRITICS

THE ACTORS

In New York it sometimes seems that everybody and his brother is an aspiring actor. The cabbie who shuttles you about, the waitress who brings you your eggs and coffee, the substitute teacher who covers your class, and the letter carrier who delivers your mail may very likely be spending their non-driving or serving or teaching or delivering hours taking acting classes, going to auditions, sending out pictures and resumes, or—if very lucky— rehearsing for a production. Of course, the chances of a professional actor's actually landing a role—paying or non-paying—are, as they always have been, dismally slim. Early in the seventies, David Weinstein wrote in *The Nation* that

from all available statistics, the income and employment prospects of an Equity member are not nearly as good as those of a poor black, recently arrived in a big-city ghetto from a Southern dirt farm. Unemployment in the theatre, in years when the rest of the economy is booming, averages around 80 per cent. Most actors work less than ten weeks a year, so that out of a membership of 15,000 or 16,000, maybe 13,000 on any given day are walking the streets looking for a sale on hot dogs.[1]

By the decade's end, Weinstein's figures had barely altered, but still the lemming-like influx of young theatre hopefuls went on. And while most were absorbed into the sea of non-theatrical employment, never—or rarely ever—to experience the sweet smell of theatrical success, some did manage to parlay their wherewithal into overcoming the incredible obstacles and becoming that paragon of paragons, the "working actor." And of this select group, a few succeeded in making notable contributions to the history of the New York stage. Later in this chapter, some of the more conspicuous of these players will be isolated for a brief look at their major achievements.

As is too well known, the life of even a successful actor, for all its superficial glamour, is one of constant hard work, frustration, and low pay. Although Broadway and Off-Broadway salaries were greatly increased during the decade, the number of actors receiving them was, compared to the total acting pool, minuscule, and the chances of continuing to earn one's salary in a long-running hit were as unlikely as a drought-free Ethiopia. Yet the urge to perform and the desire to work in their profession was so strong for thousands of thespians, novices and veterans, that they readily accepted these conditions, and were willing to be cast in Off Off-Broadway showcases where they would be glad to earn even enough for carfare to and from the playhouse. From the ranks of such perennially struggling artists came some of the finest and most respected young talents of the decade.

Acting could not only be a sometimes depressing, starvation-level occupation, it could also be a dangerous, even painful one for those with jobs. There is a good reason for Equity's requirement that actors receive hazard pay for risky assignments, as demonstrated by some of the mishaps involving actors of the period. In addition to the fires, bomb threats, and blackouts that have been described earlier, actors experienced a range of onstage disasters.

Barry Bostwick, for example, the rakish leading man of *The Robber Bridegroom*, had to swing across the stage on a rope like Tarzan; at a final preview, with about 600 people in the audience, he fell so precipitously from a thirteen-foot height that some thought he had been killed; the resilient actor bounced back for the opening five days later, his fractured elbow and wrist in a sling, his swashbuckling style undiminished, and his performance of Tony-winning caliber. In another play, *Modigliani*, when actor Jeffrey DeMunn was unable to go on in the title role, understudy Tony Lampisi sought to make the most of his opportunity. In one scene Modigliani was required to slash a group of paintings; Lampisi's slashing was so enthusiastic that he badly cut his finger and had to keep staunching the wound with makeshift bandages throughout the remaining forty minutes, refusing to stop the show and seek help in mid-performance. A standing ovation greeted his heroic efforts. In the nearby Public Theatre, three actors were involved in a single accident during Tina Howe's *The Art of Dining* when the liquid used to ignite a dish of crepes suzette flared up and sent a shower of blazing brandy on the nearest persons. Actress Dianne Wiest suffered severe burns on her arm and shoulder, and all three were immediately taken for treatment to the hospital; the crepes were cut from future performances.

Sometimes the most immediate danger came from one's fellow actors, as chorus member Jim Litten learned when, during the curtain calls one night for the musical *Rex*, star Nicol Williamson took offense at something Litten had done and slapped him in the face before the shocked audience and cast. Williamson was later forced to apologize to the other actor. Only one actor, forty-eight-year-old veteran Arnold Soboloff, actually died in the midst of a seventies New York stage production; it was *Peter Pan*, in which Soboloff played Smee, Captain Hook's sidekick. Following an especially vigorous scene, the actor walked offstage and proceeded to collapse of a heart attack in the wings. In the best show business tradition, Soboloff's understudy, also playing the role of Cecco, kept the show going by assuming Smee's lines in addition to his own; the audience left the theatre never knowing of the tragedy that had transpired.

There were other reasons that being a New York stage actor during the period could be tough. Actors have always had to shed their inhibitions to be effective, but the looser moral attitudes of the seventies meant that actors would frequently have to shed their clothes as well. Production after production required its actors to display breasts, buttocks, and balls, and often to engage in simulated sex acts (these could be homosexual, heterosexual, or autoerotic). The most obvious examples were in sex-oriented shows like *Oh, Calcutta!* and *Let My People Come!*, where the actors were mostly eager unknowns, but there were also distinguished stars who revealed their privates, sometimes in plays of serious import. British actors Diana Rigg and Keith Michell who peeled off their costumes for a love scene in the medieval romance, *Abelard and Héloise*, were said to be the first of world-class caliber to perform in the nude on Broadway. Much of this artistic exposure led to journalistic exposure, and to a few legal entanglements as well. In a lighter instance of the latter an actress in *Oh, Calcutta!* was allowed a $445 tax deduction in 1979 because of expenses incurred in purchasing body makeup. Much more was at stake when the Village Gate had to wage a time-consuming and costly fight against the State Liquor authority which tried (unsuccessfully) to deprive it of its liquor license for serving drinks during performances of the sexually explicit *Let My People Come*.

In addition to acting in the raw and simulating sex, performers in the new plays were sometimes asked to do things that might have provoked reluctance in even the most liberated actors. For example, in Arrabal's *And They Put Handcuffs on the Flowers* a character who was hanged had to empty his bladder on cue at every performance, while in *Ulysses in Nighttown*, a leading actress had to do considerable emoting while enthroned on a commode. Words and images that only a handful of years earlier would have been cause for public outrage if expressed on the stage, were now sharing the stage fifty-fifty with the rest of the vocabulary. Indeed, playwrights like David Mamet were being elevated because, among other reasons, their ear for the nonstop vulgarity of certain characters was so uncanny that the result was like a new form of "poetic" prose.

In another area of concern, actors of the increasingly technological seventies were occasionally the target of those who deplored their growing reliance on the electronic amplification of their voices. Actors in musicals—particularly those with most of their training in films and TV—too often seemed incapable of projecting audibly in Broadway's theatres, especially when rivaled by a blaring orchestra. Whereas once the actor's powers of projection had been the badge of his stage prowess, the new breed of performer knew that even with a puny, paper-thin voice he could be heard in the distant balconies through the magic of a tiny body-mike. No one wanted to pay high admission prices and then have to struggle to comprehend the lyrics or dialogue; instead, audiences had to pay the price of uneven and mechanical amplification in return for increased audibility; the innovation unarguably began to eat away at one of the theatre's most precious assets, its "aliveness." In 1972 Walter Kerr lamented that audiences had become so accustomed to the "dehumanization" of miked performances that they could not do without them. "We've been earwashed," he said.[2]

Related to this problem was that of Liza Minnelli when she appeared in *The Act*. Among Minnelli's many numbers in this musical were several that required simultaneous dancing and singing of a particularly strenuous nature. After complaints were registered it was reluctantly revealed that the star was lip-synching parts of two of these difficult numbers and all of another one. Had the words not been pre-recorded, she would never have been able to project them as effectively. The practice was regrettable, if understandable. Minnelli was a recognized singing talent, so the disappointment registered at this revelation could be understood. However, technology had not yet been invented that could make a non-singer sing well, at least by Broadway standards, although several such performers must have wished it could. One who might have wished so was Swedish actress Liv Ullman, when she struggled with the title role of Richard Rodgers' musical *I Remember Mama*. When Martin Charnin, fired as the show's director, commented publicly on his low opinion of her singing voice, a brouhaha erupted because Ullman's feelings were so hurt that she threatened suit against the famed lyricist-director.

The headaches of hunting for a role could be unendurable, but the pain was exacerbated for minority actors. There were more black acting jobs than ever before, and the old practice of hiring a white to play a black would, if attempted, have resulted in a good old-fashioned riot. Those most concerned were the Asian Americans, who commenced the decade by picketing *Lovely Ladies, Kind Gentlemen* for employing a mere twelve Orientals when close to forty were needed, and for failing to consider an ethnically appropriate actor to play the lead. Equity and the League of New

York Theatre Owners and Producers attempted to work out a racially equitable casting plan for future productions, but problems similar to those of *Lovely Ladies* continued for several years. The key story in this regard was related to the Lincoln Center regime under Jules Irving, when actors of Asian ancestry failed to figure in productions of *Narrow Road to the Deep North* and *The Good Woman of Setzuan*. Irving could not adequately defend himself against charges of discriminatory casting policies and in 1973 a unanimous vote of a State Human Rights Appeal Board, overturning an earlier ruling that had exonerated him, found the producer's company guilty of discrimination against Asian Americans in giving too many Oriental roles to non-Orientals. Such casting, it was declared, tended to perpetuate white racist stereotypes. Ironically, a few years later, when Hal Prince decided to cast *Pacific Overtures* exclusively with Asian actors, he had trouble finding them in the numbers he desired and had to resort to extensive doubling, with nineteen actors playing sixty-one roles. One explanation from the Asian-American community was that many performers had dropped out of the business because of constant discouragement.

Related to these controversies were two focusing on producer Joseph Papp, whose liberal, pathbreaking, interracial casting policies had been almost solely responsible for the breakthroughs seen in dozens of classical and modern plays since the 1950s. In 1973 Papp was accused of discrimination against Latins and even received threatening letters ("Muera [death to] Joe Papp!" read one). The dispute, sparked by the Puerto Rican Actors Guild (which disclaimed any connection with the letters), grew from Papp's having fired actress Edith Diaz from the road tour of *Two Gentlemen of Verona*. He explained, with reference to theatrical precedent, that the firing was because of the actress' limitations, not because of her ethnic background. The affair blew over, but in 1979 Papp again figured at the eye of a racial-casting hurricane, this one whipped into action by the Asian Americans who picketed his theatre with the aim of spurring him to cast their group more equitably than they claimed he had in the past. When the small number of Asian Americans employed by the Public during the decade was noted, Papp promised to hold a series of auditions to create a core of talented actors for the development of new scripts in which their ethnic backgrounds could be reflected. Papp ultimately did produce several well-received Asian-American scripts and thereby brought actors such as John Lone and playwrights such as David Henry Hwang to public attention.

Actors were involved in several other important developments during the period, but space permits only a passing reference to the more prominent of them. One problem which continued to disturb relations between producers and performers concerned the hiring of British actors for (mostly) British plays, a practice greatly frowned upon by Equity except in the instance of stars with international reputations. Since British Equity placed similar restrictions upon the use of American actors, little progress was made in this important area, despite its being given considerable attention. The inability of leading American actors to convincingly portray British characters was evident in many productions, which clearly were hurt by the restrictions on their casting. However, while plays such as *Betrayal* and *The Norman Conquests* might have achieved greater success with authentic English players, there were several London imports, such as *The Changing Room*, which were played by American companies with accents only a Henry Higgins could find fault with.

Few established New York actors, of course, made their livings solely by working in the local theatre; most were forced to supplement their incomes from TV shows and commercials and from films; others took suitable employment at the nation's numerous regional theatres. Still, the New York stage in the seventies shone with a galaxy of acting lights whose names, if they were recorded with their credits, would fill the rest of this chapter and leave no room for other matters. The talent on New York's stages ranged from octogenarian grande dames such as Eva Le Gallienne to juvenile newcomers such as Andrea McArdle, from world-class masters such as John Gielgud, George C. Scott, and Katharine Hepburn to brilliant younger ones such as F. Murray Abraham, Kevin Kline, Raul Julia, and Meryl Streep. Rather than simply list the approximately 200 leading players of the decade, a survey is offered of that select group who were the recipients of the Broadway theatre's most prestigious—if sometimes disputedly so—award, the Tony. To be sure, this arbitrary selection omits those who won awards from other sources, notably the Obies, Off- and Off Off-Broadway's principal sign of recognition. Similarly, it acts as a tacit acknowledgement of the appropriateness of such awards, which is an impression that it would be preferable to avoid. Nevertheless, citation of the Tony winners does serve as a pair of binoculars to focus on many of the decade's highlights and provides a convenient frame for managing an otherwise sprawling subject. It should be borne in mind, however, that nearly all the Tony-winning performances cited here had one or more outspoken detractors.

The award designations changed slightly from year to year, as indicated below, but there were eight annual acting awards presented, for leading and supporting players in straight plays and musicals. The annual Tony ceremony was held in the late spring near the end of the season that was usually considered to have begun in June of the preceding year. Primary attention is given here to the Best Actor and Best Actress designations, first for plays and then for musicals. Award-winning supporting players are noted without further comment.

In 1971 the choice for Actor, Straight Play was Brian Bedford, the British-born star of a Molière revival, *The School for Wives*, never previously produced on Broadway in English. Bedford played Arnolph, the crazily jealous old husband of a beautiful young wife. Bedford offered, said Douglas Watt, "a smashing comedy performance" in which "he seizes the part and plays it as the young Charles Laughton might have done, but in his own special style."³ Although active elsewhere, Bedford had only one other Broadway performance of the decade—in *Jumpers*—which received mixed reviews.

A year later the award was called Best Actor—Play and went to Cliff Gorman for his dazzling impersonation of controversial comic Lenny Bruce in *Lenny*. Gorman's energetic performance was touted as one of the most notable in years, and stood out in a play which many dismissed as unfulfilled. Like Bedford, Gorman reappeared on Broadway only once more during the decade; projections of his imminent superstardom were inaccurate, as his role in *Chapter Two* was in support of Judd Hirsch.

Winner of the Best Actor—Play award for 1973 was Britain's Alan Bates for his remarkable portrayal of a seedy, alcoholic, quick-witted, and sadistic bisexual university professor—onstage throughout—in the black comedy *Butley*, the only play Bates appeared in locally during the decade.

Michael Moriarty copped the 1974 Best Actor—Play award for his work in John Hopkins' candid *Find Your Way Home*, about a middle-aged husband who deceives his wife, not with another woman, but with a young homosexual hustler, played by Moriarty. The actor's involvement in this production led to a much-publicized squabble with his producer when Moriarty allegedly reneged on a commitment to the play by leaving it for another engagement. During the seventies, Moriarty was a frequent presence in the New York theatre, both because of his performances and because of his leadership of a young Off Off-Broadway Shakespearean troupe called, oddly enough, the Potter's Field Theatre Company. He figured strongly in eight productions ranging from Broadway to Off Off, including a decidedly offbeat interpretation of the title role in *Richard III*.

The next recipients of the Best Actor—Play award were a pair of actors, John Kani and Winston Ntshona, two black South Africans who surprised Broadwayites with their extraordinary performances in the mini-repertory of *The Island* and *Sizwe Banzi Is Dead*, which they assisted Athol Fugard in writing. In *The Island* the pair played close-knit political prisoners faced with separation when one's release is arranged. These were the actors' only local performances of the period.

In 1976 British classical actor John Wood was named Best Actor for his pyrotechnical portrayal in *Travesties* of a role written especially for him, that of Henry Carr, a minor British consular official who, declining into senility, fondly but distortedly remembers his experiences in Zurich in 1917. Wood was one of the most notable presences on seventies Broadway stages with his dominating performances as Sherlock Holmes in the play of that name, as Tartuffe in the play of that name, and as the mystery writer-wife murderer in *Deathtrap*.

Al Pacino, at the peak of his film career, returned to his theatre roots to become a Best-Actor Tony-winner in 1977 for his performance of the eponymous hero in the revival of *The Basic Training of Pavlo Hummel*, about a hapless young dogface who meets his meaningful fate in the meaningless morass of Vietnam. Pacino had first played the role for the Theatre Company of Boston in 1972 (William Atherton had originated it in New York), and it was the same company that handled this revival. Pacino's earthy, naturalistic mannerisms disturbed some, but he managed to limn a disturbingly potent portrait that most found devastatingly effective. Pacino was seen locally once more at the end of the decade when he headed a somewhat sourly received version of *Richard III*.

The 1978 prize was won for Outstanding Performance by an Actor in a Play, a new designation that made the award sound more impressive but was not necessarily more significant. The recipient was veteran character man Barnard Hughes, whose dependable abilities were recognized in one production after another during the decade. Despite a lengthy career, Hughes first tasted real stardom with his award-winning performance in the Irish drama *"Da."* In this play, he appeared as a ghost, the deceased father of a middle-aged author who cannot exorcise his memories of his blustery, mendacious parent. At other times during the decade, Hughes played in Shakespeare, Chekhov, Shaw, and such moderns as Simon and Schisgal, appearing in at least a dozen productions on and Off-Broadway.

A year after Hughes' achievement, British actor Tom Conti was awarded the Tony for his distinguished performance in *Whose Life Is It Anyway?* as Ken Harrison, the sharp-witted, paralyzed victim of a car crash who uses every mental wile to convince his doctors to let him die in peace. Conti's role required him to lie in bed immobilized except for his head. Conti nearly did not get to play the role in New York when Equity sought to intervene in his employment because he was not an American. As mentioned in an earlier chapter, when he had to leave for another commitment, the producers closed the production but later reopened it with Conti's role rewritten for a woman; Mary Tyler Moore earned a special Tony for her achievement as Claire Harrison.

The decade's final Outstanding Performance by an Actor in a Play award went to John Rubinstein for his role as James Leeds, the earnestly idealistic young teacher of the deaf in *Children of a Lesser God*, a demanding role in which he had to perform many of his lines both verbally and in sign language. Rubinstein, the son of the famed pianist Arthur Rubinstein, appeared in New York only twice during the decade, but his two roles were well chosen, the first one having been as the title character in the hit musical *Pippin*.

Four of the above Tony Award actors were British-born, two (sharing a single award) were South Africans, and five were Americans. Of the award-winning actresses, however, two were British-born, but, like Brian Bedford, resident in America (or Canada), while two, Irene Worth and Constance Cummings, were Americans who owed a tremendous portion of their success to their work in England. Thus, although a number of English actresses were nominated, none, in the Bates/Wood/Conti sense of visiting stars, were actually granted the award.

The first of the decade's Actress, Straight Play awards was bestowed upon Maureen Stapleton, an actress with a lengthy list of Broadway credits, for her incisive performance as Evy Meara, the middle-aged, alcoholic, nymphomaniacally inclined, wisecracking singer of *The Gingerbread Lady*. The tone of many reviews suggested that Stapleton was winning the Grand Prix at the wheel of a jalopy. Stapleton continued to give glowing performances during the seventies, going on to offer a memorable Georgie in a revival of *The Country Girl*, a campy movie buff in *The Secret Affairs of Mildred Wild*, and a touching Amanda in *The Glass Menagerie*, and to serve as an excellent replacement in the Jessica Tandy role in *The Gin Game*.

Another middle-aged star, the versatile Sada Thompson, was considered by many the sole reason to see George Furth's *Twigs*, for which she won the Tony in 1972. The actress' scope was stretched to the limits to play four roles, three daughters and their Irish virago of a mother, in what was essentially a program of related one-acters. Although several critics prayed that she would go on blessing Broadway's stages, Thompson appears not to have found another role of comparable challenge, and her only other local appearance during the decade was in the flop production of the Neapolitan comedy, *Saturday Sunday Monday*.

For 1973 one of America's best-loved stage stars, Julie Harris, was the Best Actress—Play award winner, for her portrayal of Mary Todd Lincoln in the critically panned drama, *The Last of Mrs. Lincoln*. The role required her to cover the seventeen years following Lincoln's death. Harris' devotion to the living theatre was borne out by her seven Broadway roles of the decade, among the highest number accumulated by a major star. Unfortunately, despite her own achievements, most were critical and commercial failures; she had a moderate success, however, in Rattigan's *In Praise of Love*, in which she co-starred with Rex Harrison, and a sizable one in the one-woman *The Belle of Amherst*, in which she played the reclusive nineteenth-century poet Emily Dickinson and for which she received her second Tony of the decade in 1977. In a monodrama that moved freely backwards and forwards through time, mingling poetry, letters, and imagined conversations—some thought it more a "reading" than a play—Harris, dressed in white and with her hair parted in the center, a bun at the back, captured the eccentricities, passions, aspirations, and genius of her character.

When she wasn't winning Tonys, it was likely that Julie Harris was being nominated for them, as was also true of 1974's winner, Colleen Dewhurst, another of Broadway's most durable stars. Dewhurst's Tony recognized her accomplishment as the big-bodied "earth mother" of a farm girl, Josie Hogan, in a lauded revival of *A Moon for the Misbegotten*, co-starring Jason Robards. Dewhurst appeared locally in a total of nine productions during the seventies, two more than Harris. Her range took her from older classics such as *Hamlet* to modern classics such as O'Neill's *Mourning Becomes Electra* and the play that led to her award.

For 1974-75 the Best Actress—Play award went to the performer who subsequently was elected head of the actors' union, Ellen Burstyn, for her role in the smash-hit two-character comedy, *Same Time, Next Year*, which required her to play the same character as seen at six five-year intervals from 1951 to 1975. Despite her ultimate position as head of Equity, Burstyn was more prone to exercise her opportunities as a member of the Screen Actors Guild during the seventies, her one other local appearance being as Masha in *The Three Sisters* as produced by the Brooklyn Academy of Music's repertory company.

The year 1976 witnessed the receipt of the Tony by one of the modern theatre's most dedicated and respected artists, Irene Worth, who, while dividing her time between films, TV, and the stage, and between England and America, managed four times to make her distinguished mark locally during the decade. First came her Tony-winning, bigger-than-life realization of the fading actress in a revival of *Sweet Bird of Youth* that played both at the Brooklyn Academy of Music and at uptown Broadway's Harkness; then came her memorable performance as Madame Ranevskaya in Andrei Serban's provocatively idiosyncratic interpretation of *The Cherry Orchard*; this was followed by her portrayal of the mysterious Elizabeth in Albee's *The Lady from Dubuque*; and finally, Worth presented a splendid Winnie in Beckett's *Happy Days* at the Public Theatre.

The award-winner in 1978 was another one of the theatre's leading lights, the inimitable Jessica Tandy. Tandy and her actor husband, Hume Cronyn, may not be the Lunts—to whom they are occasionally compared —especially since Cronyn's talents, for all their exceptional qualities, do not have the breadth nor the romantic disposition of the late, great Alfred's; however, along with Eli Wallach and Ann Jackson, the Cronyns represent a tradition of American husband-and-wife acting teams (Cronyn is actually Canadian and Tandy British-born) that suggests the theatre at its finest. Of the four seventies plays which profited from Tandy's presence—*Home, All Over, Noël Coward in Two Keys*, and *The Gin Game*—the latter pair offered the Cronyns the chance to play together in blissful harmony. In the two-character *Gin Game*, Cronyn and Tandy were two embittered residents of a run-down home for senior citizens who act out their emotional frustrations through the rivalry they develop while playing a series of gin rummy games. There were no distractions from other actors, and playgoers were able to see these peak-form veterans marshall all their accumulated skills to present a tour-de-force demonstration of what great acting is all about.

The year 1979 saw the unusual expedient adopted of granting two actresses the Tony; unlike the double award to John Kani and Winston Ntshona, the award did not go to actresses appearing in the same play.

Carole Shelley snared it for her work as Mrs. Kendal in *The Elephant Man*, while Constance Cummings shared it for her portrait of a stroke victim in *Wings*. Shelley, British by birth but continuously employed in America and Canada since 1965, is an accomplished classical actress, with a penchant for high comedy. She brought her tall, attractive, bird-like presence to six productions during the seventies; her plays included revivals such as *Hay Fever*, *The Devil's Disciple*, and *The Play's the Thing*—the latter two while a member of the Brooklyn Academy of Music company—and new plays such as *Absurd Person Singular*, *The Norman Conquests*, and *The Elephant Man*, each of them sharing her British ancestry. In the latter, she had to compete against Philip Anglim's exceptional portrayal of John Merrick, the grossly disfigured title character whose deformities were suggested solely by posture and movement; her sensitive picture of the actress brought to Merrick by Dr. Frederick Treves (Kevin Conway) was affecting.

Constance Cummings, born in Seattle and ultimately granted the distinction of CBE (Commander of the British Empire) for her contributions to the English stage, on which she first appeared in 1934, had last appeared locally in 1969. In *Wings*, her only New York assignment of the decade, she tackled an awesomely difficult role, that of aviatrix Emily Stilson, who, felled by a stroke, must battle her way back to mental clarity. Cummings presented a wrenchingly accurate impression of the puzzled but struggling character.

The award for 1980 went to a young actress who had never appeared in New York before, and who was both deaf and incapable of speech. This was Phyllis Frelich, who was in large part the inspiration for *Children of a Lesser God*, in which she played Sarah, a born-deaf woman who demands to be granted the liberty to communicate in her own expressive signing way without being forced to satisfy the demands for speech and lip-reading of the hearing world.

In the Best Supporting Actor and Actress categories of the Tony Awards (called Best Featured Actor and Actress beginning in 1976 and Outstanding Performance by a Featured Actor and Actress from 1977), the achievements of the following actors were rewarded: Paul Sand for *Story Theatre* (1971); Vincent Gardenia for *The Prisoner of Second Avenue* (1972); John Lithgow for *The Changing Room* (1973); Ed Flanders for *A Moon for the Misbegotten* (1974); Frank Langella for *Seascape* (1975); Edward Hermann for *Mrs. Warren's Profession* (1976); British actor Jonathan Pryce for *Comedians* (1977); Lester Rawlins for *"Da"* (1978); British veteran Michael Gough for *Bedroom Farce* (1979); and David Rounds for *Morning's at Seven* (1980).

Actresses in this group include Rae Allen for *And Miss Reardon Drinks a Little* . . . (1971); Elizabeth Wilson for *Sticks and Bones* (1972); Leora Dana for *The Last of Mrs. Lincoln* (1973); Frances Sternhagen for *The Good Doctor* (1974); Rita Moreno for *The Ritz* (1975); Shirley Knight for *Kennedy's Children* (1976); Trazana Beverley, the only black performer in a straight play to win a Tony during the seventies, for *For Colored Girls* . . .

(1977); Ann Wedgeworth for *Chapter Two* (1978); English visitor Joan Hickson for *Bedroom Farce* (1979); and Dinah Manoff for *I Ought to Be in Pictures* (1980).

Almost every actor on this list of supporting players performed regularly on Broadway and Off during the seventies; the only exceptions were Paul Sand, the young Dinah Manoff, the two British actors, and Trazana Beverley.

Broadway confers awards not only on the actors in its dramatic plays but on those who combine acting and musical skills in the production of musical theatre. The decade's first Tony for Actor, Musical, as the award was then called, went to Hal Linden, the lead in *The Rothschilds*, a historical musical about the famous banking family. Linden played the family's eighteenth-century patriarch, Mayer, for which he donned caftan and beard to disguise his youthful thirty-nine years. Linden achieved stardom with the role after a series of fourteen Broadway shows in fifteen years during which he was normally a standby for someone else. Linden returned to Broadway for the short-lived straight-play revival, *The Sign in Sidney Brustein's Window*, and a revival of *The Pajama Game*, but most of his time during the seventies was devoted to TV acting.

In 1972 the Tony for best musical actor was taken by one of America's favorite clowns, the irrepressible sixty-one-year-old Phil Silvers. Silvers had rejected the role of the wily freedom-seeking slave, Pseudolus, in the original Broadway production of *A Funny Thing Happened on the Way to the Forum*, and then watched Zero Mostel make an enormous hit in it. Silvers played Lycus in the film version, but he finally got to do the lead—and win a Tony for it—in the well-received 1972 revival. Silvers, a Broadway hand since 1939, had one other Broadway job in the period, when he appeared in Alan Ayckbourn's tepidly reviewed British comedy, *How the Other Half Loves*.

A relative newcomer to Broadway, Ben Vereen, was voted Best Actor, Musical in 1973 for his emcee-like role of the sardonic Leading Player in *Pippin*. Vereen's Broadway debut had come only a couple of years earlier as Judas in *Jesus Christ Superstar*, which brought him considerable acclaim. In *Pippin*, this flashy black song-and-dance man had a tailormade role; he dressed—despite the show's medieval setting—as a spiffy nightclub-type entertainer, with rakish straw hat, bow-tie, and white gloves. Many thought that Vereen was the glue that held the problematical show together.

Linden, Silvers, and Vereen were undisputedly dyed-in-the-wool musical theatre actors, but the seventies saw a considerable number of outstanding musical performances by actors who had established their reputations almost entirely in the realm of non-musical theatre. A major example was Christopher Plummer's dazzling title-role performance in *Cyrano*, based on Rostand's late nineteenth-century romantic classic about the long-nosed swordsman-poet. Plummer, a Canadian whom some consider the finest native-born classical actor in the Western hemisphere, was visible in one other Broadway play of the decade, *The Good Doctor*, and one Off-Broadway, *Drinks Before Dinner*.

Any short list of the first-rate leading men of the seventies who could both sing outstandingly and act with distinction would have to include John Cullum. The tall, angular-faced, fair-haired, big-voiced Cullum won the 1975 Tony for his *Shenandoah* role of Virginia farmer Charlie Anderson, a widower who gets drawn against his will into the Civil War; the role was first played by James Stewart in the movie of the same title from which this show was adapted. Cullum's abilities led numerous critics to consider him the most impressive singing/acting talent in the American theatre. Although he worked fairly frequently, Cullum did not get as many opportunities to display his marvelous skills as Broadway audiences would have liked. His local performances included another Tony-award performance in 1978 for *On the Twentieth Century*, in which he was a wonderfully flamboyant Oscar Jaffe, a thirties Broadway producer trying to get screen star Lily Garland to sign a contract while they hurtle across the country on the streamliner the Twentieth Century Limited. A considerable part of Cullum's excellence stemmed from the accuracy with which he incorporated suggestions of John Barrymore's personality, the Great Profile having played the role in the movie based on Hecht and MacArthur's original play. During the seventies, Cullum also served as an important replacement in the casts of *Vivat! Vivat! Regina* and *Deathtrap*. Moreover, he worked as a director in several workshops and in one Off-Broadway situation.

Some might argue that the leading male role in *My Fair Lady* is Henry Higgins, and that Alfred P. Doolittle should be classified as a supporting role, no matter how important or how excitingly performed. Such a discrimination, however, did not disturb the Tony committee when they presented the Best Actor, Musical prize to 1976's Doolittle, George Rose, a vastly experienced, classically trained English character actor who had developed his career in the United States since the early sixties, although he appeared on Broadway with the Old Vic as early as 1946. Rose's show-stopping, sooty, bibulous Cockney edged out his Tony-nominated co-star, Ian Richardson. Rose was one of the workingest actors on Broadway and Off in the 1970s, several times appearing in the roles of dryly witty, prissy, aging homosexuals. Three of his nine local credits were for roles in revivals at the Brooklyn Academy of Music.

Theatre awards go alike to outstanding veterans and to dazzling newcomers. Thus, it was no surprise for George Rose to pass on the baton to the young Barry Bostwick, a tall, dashing actor who brought his youthful panache to a string of Broadway and Off-Broadway roles, musical and dramatic. Having made a great splash as Danny Zucco in the hit musical *Grease*, Bostwick rose to Tony-winning prominence for his robber bridegroom in *The Robber Bridegroom*, a musical set in the backwoods of Mississippi. The role had been played locally the year before for another company's production by Kevin Kline, and Bostwick was generally considered superior to his predecessor. He snared the Tony even though, as mentioned earlier, he had to play the first couple of weeks with his arm in a sling as a result of a serious fall suffered in a preview performance. An all-around performer, Bostwick graced local stages in another two musicals and three dramas, including *The Screens* and *They Knew What They Wanted*.

Len Cariou is a Canadian whose virile presence and powerful voice put him soundly in the tradition of forceful leading men capable of playing Shakespeare or Sondheim. It was Sondheim who provided Cariou with the role that landed him the Tony, that of the eponymous homicidal hero of *Sweeney Todd*, which, in center-parted wig and ghoulish makeup, he played opposite the Tony-winning performance of Angela Lansbury. Distinguishing himself as one of the decade's most respected players, Cariou came on strong in one work after the other, from his replacement role in a sixties holdover, *Applause*, to the mystery thriller *Night Watch*, to the one-man Peter Handke piece *A Sorrow Beyond Dreams*, at the American Place, to the Bergmanesque *A Little Night Music*, to the Broadway version of *Cold Storage*.

The decade's final Tony for a leading actor in a musical went to Britain's Jim Dale, for a masterful display of showmanship in the title role of *Barnum*. Dale did acrobatic tricks (including walking the tightrope), sang, danced, and in general gave his audiences a roaring good time in this musical about the nineteenth century's master of humbug. Dale's unusual virtuosity had earlier astounded local playgoers in two rumbustious British import versions of comic classics, *Scapino*, adapted from Molière, and *The Taming of the Shrew*.

Leading the decade's array of Tony winners for best musical actress was the petite Helen Gallagher, one of the modern musical theatre's most versatile performers, playing the soubrette role of Lucy Early in an extremely popular revival of the twenties hit, *No, No, Nanette*. Gallagher nightly stopped the show in a dance number shared with Bobby Van in which a variety of Jazz Age dance styles were displayed, and she also thrilled audiences with her rendition of the "Where-Has-My-Husband-Gone Blues." A veteran Broadway performer known before *Nanette* for her demure appearance in bangs, Gallagher radically changed her image to play the vampy Lucille. She appeared with additional images in the decade's succeeding years, showing up in both dramas, musicals, and revues. None, however, came anywhere near matching her memorable effect in *Nanette*.

Succeeding Gallagher in this noteworthy-performance category was the strikingly glamorous Alexis Smith, an actress with extensive film star credits, but with no New York stage experience—and not much of note elsewhere—before enacting the role that garnered her the Tony. Smith played former showgirl Phyllis Stone in *Follies*; her performance stood out among other standouts, especially when she delivered her show-stopping song-and-dance number, "The Story of Jessie and Lucy." Some critics found her more exciting, beautiful, and charming than in her movies. Smith graced Broadway stages later in the decade with performances in *The Women*, *Summer Brave* (a revision of Inge's *Picnic*), and the big musical flop *Platinum*.

Glynis Johns, a British thespian with absolutely no reputation in musicals, won the Tony in 1973 for her performance as the middle-aged and worldly-wise but still desirable actress Desirée Armfeldt in the operetta-like *A Little Night Music*. Although several critics noted the foggy-voiced performer's musical drawbacks, she introduced "Send in the Clowns," which became the most popular song ever written by Stephen Sondheim. Johns, who had appeared on Broadway as early as 1952, did not do so again for the remainder of the seventies.

The 1974 winner was Virginia Capers, who played Lena, the matriarch of the Younger family, in *Raisin*, based on *A Raisin in the Sun*. In the role made memorable in the original play by Claudia McNeil, the hefty Capers seemed warm, earthy, and maternally touching, reminding some of Ethel Waters. Even more than for her acting, Capers was admired for a trumpet-like voice that tore the house down when she sang, her biggest number being the gospel-style "Measure the Valleys." For all the excitement generated by her performance, Capers did not become a Broadway regular; her one other local appearance of the decade was in an Off Off workshop production of *Sister Sadie*.

Throughout the sixties and the seventies, Angela Lansbury rose to a position as one of the most versatile and respected performers on the American stage. The British-born star, whose stage career began on Broadway in 1957 when she was already thirty-one and a Hollywood veteran, won the Tony for 1966's *Mame*, for *Dear World* (1969's musical adaptation of *The Madwoman of Chaillot*), again for 1975's revival of *Gypsy*, in which she played Rose, and yet once more when she played Mrs. Lovett in 1979's *Sweeney Todd, the Demon Barber of Fleet Street*. Most critics agreed that Lansbury's singing gifts, though adequate, fell considerably short of those possessed by the great Ethel Merman, the creator of the *Gypsy* role, whose Rose was the highlight of a brilliant career. Few, though, disputed the effectiveness of Lansbury's thoroughly well-rounded acting. Lansbury's star remained undimmed throughout the period. Following *Gypsy*, she served as a temporary replacement for Constance Towers, starring opposite Yul Brynner in a revival of *The King and I*. Then she returned to Tony luminescence in *Sweeney Todd*, in which, her wig twisted into two horn-like tufts, she played the melodramatically wicked proprietor of a nineteenth-century London meat pie shop who stuffs her victuals with human flesh.

For 1976 the Best Actress, Musical award went to a quadruple-talent,

Donna McKechnie, who could not only sing, dance, and act, but was also stunningly attractive. Audiences who saw her vibrant performance in *A Chorus Line* as Cassie—the never-quite-a-star dancer who auditions for a chorus role being cast by a director she once lived with—could attest to that. Despite the ensemble nature of the production, McKechnie was singled out by most critics. It was observed, however, that she was particularly first-rate in her big dance number, "The Music and the Mirror (and the Chance to Dance)," performed for the director to prove her earnestness in seeking a chorus job after a failed stab at Hollywood stardom. Despite her recognized abilities, McKechnie, like Cassie, did not quite achieve the stardom she was entitled to. She had earlier in the decade been an important part of such Main Stem shows as the revival of *On the Town* and the revue *Music! Music!* After *A Chorus Line* she disappeared from Broadway; her final performance of the decade came as one of the five women in a weakly received Off-Broadway play from Norway called *Wine Untouched.*

Nineteen seventy-seven was the year the multi-Tony-winning musical *Annie* opened; two of the show's performers were nominated for Best Actress, Musical—Dorothy Loudon for her role as the wicked orphanage director, Miss Hannigan, and Andrea McArdle, the child actress who played the title role. As the heavy-drinking, child-abusing Miss Hannigan, Loudon undercut the show's overall sentimentalism with a refreshingly nasty tone and won the coveted award—as well she might have, given her distinguished career as a Broadway regular since 1962. Prior to *Annie*, which brought her her greatest fame, Loudon had appeared in *The Women*; after *Annie*, she was the female lead in the much-anticipated *Ballroom*, which was a major flop.

One of the surest ways to attract a seventies audience to a Broadway show was to star Liza Minnelli in it. Minnelli appeared at the head of her own one-woman revue, *Liza*, supported by four dancers, in what was essentially a concert performance; she won a "special" Tony for her efforts. She reappeared to acclaim as a brief replacement for Gwen Verdon in *Chicago*, then returned at the head of *The Act*, for which she won the Tony, and made one brief local appearance, reading Lillian Hellman's famous letter to the House Un-American Activities Committee in *Are You Now . . . . The Act* was criticized as being too much like a Las Vegas production, but there were few negative comments for Minnelli's Michelle Craig, a washed-up movie star hitting the comeback trail via a glitzy nightclub act; she is seen from age sixteen to thirty-two. As mentioned earlier, Minnelli's performance was at the heart of a controversy when it was revealed that at least one of her more strenuous numbers was lip-synched.

The last actress of the seventies to be named Outstanding Actress in a Musical was the youthful Patti LuPone; she began the decade as a student in Juilliard's theatre program, became a founding member of the Acting Company—a touring troupe originally created by John Houseman to give

Juilliard graduates professional acting opportunities, appeared locally with them in fourteen productions, mostly classics, and then moved through three non-Acting Company productions before hitting the jackpot with *Evita*. As the glamorous wife and then widow of Argentine dictator Juan Perón, who, in her turn, became the nation's ruler before dying in her early thirties, LuPone had a role custom-made for stardom. The bookless, essentially operatic, format employed a continuous score with no dialogue. LuPone wore a blond wig pulled straight back into a bun at the rear, and an assortment of stylish gowns. LuPone's other roles of the seventies, in addition to her Acting Company work in such plays as *The School for Scandal* and *Measure for Measure*, included *The Water Engine, Working*, and an experimental workshop staging of Israel Horovitz's *The Quannapowitt Quartet Part 3: Stage Directions*.

As indicated by several of the names of those awarded Tonys as best musical supporting or featured player, the distinction between leads and supports was often not so much a matter of the relative importance of a role as it was of the billing the actor got when the show opened. If , for example, any two roles could be considered the leads in *The Best Little Whorehouse in Texas*, they would be those of Miss Mona and the sheriff, roles taken in the film version by superstars Dolly Parton and Burt Reynolds; in the Broadway show, however, the actors in these roles were both awarded Tonys, but in the supporting category.

The list of exceptional "supporting" players in musicals who won Tonys includes a wide assortment of talents, many of whom were among the finds of the decade, while a few were oldtimers who came into their own when they met up with the right role. The winners were Keene Curtis in *The Rothschilds* and Patsy Kelly in *No, No, Nanette* (1971); Larry Blyden in *A Funny Thing Happened on the Way to the Forum* and Linda Hopkins in *Inner City* (1972); George S. Irving in *Irene* and Patricia Elliott in *A Little Night Music* (1973); Tommy Tune in *Seesaw* and Janie Sell in *Over Here!* (1974); Ted Ross and Dee Dee Bridgewater in *The Wiz* (1975); Sammy Williams and Carole (Kelly) Bishop in *A Chorus Line* (1976); Delores Hall in *Your Arms Too Short to Box With God* and Lenny Baker in *I Love My Wife* (1977); Kevin Kline in *On the Twentieth Century* and Nell Carter in *Ain't Misbehavin'* (1978); Henderson Forsythe and Carlin Glynn in *The Best Little Whorehouse in Texas* (1979); and Mandy Patinkin in *Evita* and Priscilla Lopez in *A Day in Hollywood/A Night in the Ukraine* (1980). The decade's powerhouses among this lot, in terms of overall New York theatre contributions, were Curtis, Hopkins, Elliott, Irving, Tune, Baker, Hall, Kline, Forsythe, Lopez, and Patinkin, most of whom first found stardom during these years.

The forty-odd Tony winners mentioned only scratch the surface in trying to identify the decade's most significant contributions among performers. Moreover, the New York presence of some of those listed was fleeting, while others who continued to find sustenance in and respect for their stage acting did not win Tonys (although they may have been nominated or won other awards) and so are regretfully omitted from this catalogue.

DIRECTORS

The life of a stage director is even more precarious than that of an actor. Not only are there fewer jobs, but the pay is often negligible. Since most directors earn a straight fee of several thousand dollars for a Broadway show, and then see nothing else from it regardless of its ultimate success, a director may conceivably be responsible for a major hit from which he earns no more than his initial fee. Directors with clout, of course, can demand a contract which allows them a share in the profits. Like actors, directors can be summarily dismissed by anxious producers; state-of-the-art directors whose heads rolled in the rehearsal and tryout phases of major Broadway productions during the seventies included such illustrious figures as Harold Clurman, John Gielgud, Julie Bovasso, Paul Sills, and Franco Zeffirelli. If even these distinguished figures could be dismissed or—to save face—allowed to tender their resignations, it is obvious that novices felt the threat even more; too often, the director stayed with a show in name only, while the producer hired another director or playwright—known in this context as a "play doctor"—to apply the required remedies to the script or staging before the official opening. Thus, while one individual may have received credit for a show's direction, it was not unlikely that the touch of an outsider was ultimately responsible for an eventual success (Gower Champion's work on *The Act* is a notable example). Of course, the formula could just as easily backfire, and a director's work be ruined by outside meddling. The difficulty faced by critics and audiences in assessing the named director's contributions only made the issue more confusing.

Despite the cloudiness involved in evaluating the contributions of an artist whose work is often said to be most effective when most invisible, a number of seventies directors proved their worth by compiling impressive track records that demonstrated, among other facets of their art, the level of their conceptual imaginations, ability to draw excellent performances from actors, and interpretive insight.

During the seventies many New York directors had at least one important success, but few struck sparks on a regular basis. A number were recognized as important artists, but the irregularity of their local presentations makes it difficult to establish their significance. One of the most successful of the lot, for example, was Michael Bennett; he was responsible for five shows, and on several he shared directing and/or choreographic reins with collaborators, so a precise determination of his own contributions is not entirely possible. Bennett's works of the decade included his co-choreography and co-direction of *Follies* (he shared the musical direction Tony with Hal Prince), his direction of the straight play *Twigs*, his co-choreography and direction of *Seesaw*, his collaborative work on *A Chorus Line* (he won the Tony as director and shared one with Bob Avian for his work as choreographer), and his direction and co-choreography of *Ballroom*. Bennett's participation in the highly regarded *Follies*, *Twigs*, and *Seesaw*, capped by his key show of the decade, *A Chorus Line* (described in Chapter 4), led many to believe him a Broadway wunderkind who would go on to do even bigger and better shows. However, Bennett's involvement with *A Chorus Line* led in the years that followed to an intense preoccupation with the preparation of the show's numerous national and international companies. When he finally returned with a lavish new show, *Ballroom*, its serious failure was an extreme letdown to the theatre world at large, and Bennett had to wait until the early eighties to polish up his temporarily tarnished image.

In addition to Bennett, the best known musical directors of the seventies were Gower Champion, Bob Fosse, Tom O'Horgan, and Hal Prince. Very close behind them were such figures as Vinnette Carroll, Martin Charnin, Michael Kidd, Tom Moore, Geoffrey Holder, Burt Shevelove, and Elizabeth Swados. Champion, who in addition to his film career had been directing and choreographing on Broadway since the late forties, entered the decade as one of the musical theatre's giants. He had an up-and-down career in the seventies, participating in six Broadway productions but scoring strongly only with *Sugar* and *Irene*, the latter in the capacity of replacement director for John Gielgud; it was the only musical he did not also choreograph. His excitingly theatrical ideas for *Mack and Mabel*, set in the silent-movie era, were a powerful inducement for attending, and the show was one that later developed a large following among buffs because of its fine score, but it flopped. Champion followed with another disappointing work, the Shakespearean musical, *Rockabye Hamlet*. It was well known that Champion was the "doctor" on call for Liza Minnelli's vehicle, *The Act*, and helped shape it for success, although the original director he replaced, Martin Scorcese, took the credit in the billing. Finally, Champion was credited with "supervision" of the one-night flop *A Broadway Musical*. His Broadway career seemed very tenuous, but he returned with a powerful hit, *42nd Street*, at the onset of the following decade, only to pass away on the very day of the opening in one of the most poignant show-biz stories of the time.

Bob Fosse, another of the great director-choreographers whose innovative total-theatre approach helped to change the very nature of the Broadway musical, was represented by four shows, three of them major musicals indelibly marked by his unique style. They were *Pippin*, which garnered him a Tony, *Chicago*, and *Dancin'*, in addition to the Liza Minnelli revue, *Liza*. The year that brought him the Tony for *Pippin* also saw him capture

an Academy Award and an Emmy for direction, the first time such a feat
had been accomplished. Fosse's energies remained at full charge, despite
open heart surgery undergone during the decade.

Fosse's seventies shows invariably turned to the theatre as a metaphorical
framework for their workings. He employed all the rhythm, glitter, slick-
ness, and sensual appeal associated with American show business at its glos-
siest, and developed choreographic techniques—angular, even eccentric,
movements; white-gloved dancers manipulating derby hats and canes;
curvaceous chorus girls—that immediately signaled his special touch. The
weakest element in a Fosse show was the book, normally little more than an
excuse for his dazzling staging and dances.

Early in the seventies, Tom O'Horgan looked as though he were going to
become one of the most influential figures in the Broadway theatre. This
veteran of tiny Off Off-Broadway coffeehouse theatres had four Main Stem
shows running simultaneously at one point, but a series of debacles turned
Broadway's back on him and he spent much of the second half of the era
back in cozier East Village confines. O'Horgan was one of the new breed of
conceptual directors who moved easily back and forth between musicals
and straight plays, and his credits for the decade show about an equal
amount of participation in both. His most important Broadway shows were
Lenny, a drama about Lenny Bruce, and *Jesus Christ Superstar*. The flops
soon began to plague him, however, and even a revival of his great 1960s
hit, *Hair*, failed to reestablish his reputation. O'Horgan's productions
invariably incorporated spectacular, sometimes vulgar, imagery; popular-
ized versions of Off Off-Broadway "ritualism"; nudity; and gigantic props.
Visual effects usually predominated over character and story line. His
productions frequently stirred controversy, perhaps none more so than
Jesus Christ Superstar, which he developed from the score for a record
album into a sensationalistic but decidedly original stage work that was
both praised to the sky and damned to perdition.

The prince of seventies directors (and producers) in the musical theatre
was the aptly named Harold Prince, who won an unprecedented five Tonys
for his direction of *Company* (awarded for the 1970-71 season although it
actually opened at the end of what this book considers the 1969-70 season),
Follies (co-directed with Michael Bennett), *Candide*, *Sweeney Todd*, and
Evita, five of the most innovative, pathbreaking "concept musicals" of the
period (see Chapter 4 for a definition of concept musicals). In the latter two
shows, the book element became progressively less visible as the works
took on operatic dimensions; *Evita* actually had no words except those in
the lyrics. Prince was intimately associated with the work of composer-
lyricist Stephen Sondheim, who wrote the scores for three of these shows,
contributed lyrics to the revival of *Candide*, and composed the words and
music for *A Little Night Music* and *Pacific Overtures*, both of which Prince
also staged. As these works indicate, Prince's stylistic range was great, and

each contributed new ideas to what a Broadway musical could achieve. Moreover, Prince directed another vastly appreciated musical, *On the Twentieth Century*, which served to solidify his position at the pinnacle of contemporary musical directors for his ability to select and brilliantly realize the most unconventional material. Prince also tackled four straight plays during the decade, including revivals of *The Visit*, *The Great God Brown*, and *Love for Love*, but his work on these was strangely lacking the sense of originality and insight he demonstrated in the musical theatre.

The diversity and seriousness of the subject matter in Prince's musicals, and the means he selected to make them work, could easily fill a book; from the central conception of ghostly Follies girls coexisting with their mature selves within the ruins of a once-glorious theatre, to the turn-of-the-century ambiance of a Swedish estate with the personae from a classic Bergman film, to the environmental playing and seating arrangement used to stage Voltaire's great novel, to the employment of Japanese theatrical techniques for a work set in 1850s Japan, to the manipulation of a spectacular Art Deco train, to a bloody nineteenth-century Grand Guignol blend of comedy and horror: Prince's contributions display a fulfilled eclecticism unmatched by any other musical director of the time.

Selecting the most significant directors from among those primarily involved with straight plays is a touchy business, as so many fine contributions were made in this area. One director's importance to the decade's New York theatre might stem from a single outstanding production, such as Peter Brook's *A Midsummer Night's Dream*, while another's might be related to a more regular demonstration of skills. One might be notable primarily for revivals, another for new plays. To narrow the discussion, the ten mainstream directors briefly surveyed below (leading experimental directors are discussed in Chapter 2) each staged at least four works—new or old—of critically and popularly acknowledged magnitude. They are A. J. Antoon, Gordon Davidson, Frank Dunlop, Robert Kalfin, Marshall W. Mason, Mike Nichols, Ellis Rabb, Alan Schneider, Andrei Serban, and Douglas Turner Ward. The inherently arbitrary nature of such a selection means that the work of other major directors, such as Arvin Brown, Melvin Bernhardt, Liv Ciulei, John Dexter, John Houseman, Vivian Matalon, Austin Pendleton, Edward Berkeley, José Quintero, Frank Corsaro, Gerald Freedman, Peter Hall, Michael Kahn, Robert Moore, Tom Moore, Edwin Sherin, Gilbert Moses, Stephen Porter, Gene Saks, Mel Shapiro, and Peter Wood, can receive no more than tacit recognition.

At the decade's start, young director A. J. Antoon quickly became a critics' darling for his sequence of acclaimed productions for the New York Shakespeare Festival. He had preceded this involvement with an Off Off-Broadway presentation in Story Theatre style in 1971, his first professional assignment. For the Festival he directed Robert Montgomery's surrealistic impression of Dostoevsky's *The Idiot*, titled *Subject to Fits*; followed this with an eccentric version of Shakespeare's rarely seen *Cymbeline* in Central Park; had a smash hit with the realistic all-male drama, *That Championship Season*, at the Public and then on Broadway; and then made Shakespeare-production history with his turn-of-the-century, post–Spanish-American War conception of *Much Ado About Nothing*, Off and on Broadway. Subsequent Antoon stagings included Strindberg's *Dance of Death* at Lincoln Center, Simon's *The Good Doctor* on Broadway, a revival of Pinero's *Trelawney of the "Wells"* at Lincoln Center, a new play by Susan Miller, *Nasty Rumors and Final Remarks*, done in workshop, and Tina Howe's *The Art of Dining* at the Public. Antoon's only bona fide hit was *That Championship Season*, which gained him the Tony. If any common thread can be drawn from this eclectic list of productions, it is that Antoon usually chose scripts with a strong blend of theatrical and literary qualities that offered actors excellent opportunities for ensemble acting. The performances in his plays were generally considered outstanding.

Gordon Davidson, a native New Yorker whose career has been tied since 1966 to the Center Theatre Group of the Mark Taper Forum in Los Angeles, where he has served with distinction as artistic director, was represented locally by six productions, all of them originally seen at his California theatre. Unlike the work of directors who seem primarily oriented toward providing exciting productions exclusive of extratheatrical concerns, all of Davidson's choices had a social or political thrust in addition to striking theatrical ingredients. Judging from his productions, Davidson had the most consistent *commitment* among seventies directors. His first New York play of the decade was the controversial *Trial of the Catonsville Nine*, a powerful Theatre of Fact reenactment of the trial of a group of anti-war protestors accused of pouring napalm on Selective Service records; it was produced Off-Broadway in a church before being moved to Broadway. This was followed by O'Brien's drama of international political intrigue focusing on Patrice Lumumba and Dag Hamarskjold, *Murderous Angels*; *The Shadow Box*, about cancer patients facing death, for which he won a Tony; a showcase presentation of *Savages*, a British play set in Brazil and dealing with Marxism, imperialism, and the desecration of an Amazonian tribe by a modern government; *Zoot Suit*, about racism toward Chicanos in 1940s wartime Los Angeles; and *Children of a Lesser God*, about the struggle for normalcy of a deaf-mute, with deaf actors in leading roles.

Frank Dunlop, a British director with a penchant for revivals of the theatre's more lighthearted old plays, made his New York debut with three London imports offered by the Young Vic Company of the National Theatre at the Brooklyn Academy of Music: *The Taming of the Shrew*, *Scapino*, and Rattigan's *French Without Tears*. *Scapino*, a Molière adaptation given a wild *commedia dell'arte* interpretation in a contemporary Italian setting with the versatile Jim Dale making his local bow in the lead, was later seen at Broadway's Circle in the Square. Not long afterwards came another

Dunlop/National Theatre import, his smashing production of that old warhorse, *Sherlock Holmes*, played 95 percent straight, the other 5 percent with its tongue placed ever so gently in its cheek. Dunlop soon became a New York mainstay, with productions of Allan Bennett's British comedy *Habeas Corpus, Joseph and the Amazing Technicolor Dreamcoat, The Three Sisters, The New York Idea, The Devil's Disciple, Julius Caesar,* and *The Play's the Thing.* The latter six—all revivals except for *Joseph*, which Dunlop had originally staged in England in 1972—were seen at the Brooklyn Academy of Music, where for two years Dunlop struggled unsuccessfully to develop a first-class repertory company with some of the best-known stage actors of the day.

Robert Kalfin also knew how difficult it was in the seventies to establish a world-class theatre at the venerable Brooklyn Academy, for it was there—in an upstairs loft—that his esteemed Chelsea Theatre Center labored valiantly for years with some of the era's most challenging new scripts. Kalfin's tastes ran largely to serious new European writing, and his contemporary selections came from Russia, France, England, and Switzerland, as well as from America. Had it not been for Kalfin's play choices, in terms both of those works he staged himself and those he produced in his role as the Chelsea's artistic director, local representation of important new European plays would have been practically nonexistent. Distinguished revivals of rarely seen works were also part of Kalfin's repertoire. The Chelsea, which eventually moved to Manhattan's West Side—witnessed his mountings of such plays as Alan Ginsburg's *Kaddish*, based on his poem about his mother's battle with mental illness. For its production Kalfin made considerable use of video effects blended with live action. He also directed Isaac Babel's 1928 Russian play, *Sunset*; Christopher Hampton's *Total Eclipse*, about the homosexual love affair of Rimbaud and Verlaine; Ibsen's *The Lady from the Sea* (at Off Off's New Repertory Company); Isaac Bashevis Singer's Polish folk-comedy, *Yentl*, which moved to Broadway and made Tovah Feldshuh a star; a revival of Gay's *Polly*, the unfamiliar sequel to *The Beggar's Opera*; Brecht and Weill's *Happy End* (codirected with Patricia Birch), which moved to Broadway; Kleist's early nineteenth-century *The Prince of Homburg*; Romulus Linney's new play, *Old Man Joseph and His Family*; Swiss author Max Frisch's *Biography: A Game* (codirected with Lynne Gannaway); the Russian play-with-music, *Strider*, another Broadway transfer; and *Monsieur Amilcar*, a contemporary French comedy by Yves Jamiaque. In staging these plays and producing others for the Chelsea, Kalfin constantly sought new audience-actor relationships; the environmental staging ideas current in the avant-garde theatres of the day found effective realization in his rearrangements of stage and auditorium space in the company's small loft theatre.

Marshall W. Mason is another director who came to prominence principally as a result of his work with a single company, in his case the Off-

Broadway Circle Repertory Company (CRC) which began life in the late sixties as an Off Off loft theatre, and captured national attention in the early seventies. The chief factor behind the company's acclaim was its brilliantly crafted realization of resident playwright Lanford Wilson's dramas. The style of acting and directing required by these lauded reflections of Americana was what Mason calls "lyric realism," a type of performance that suggests both an illusionistic impression of reality and a veneer of poetic sensitivity. A large number of the CRC's productions were in the vein mined by Wilson in such Mason-directed works as *The Hot l Baltimore*, *The Mound Builders, Serenading Louie, Talley's Folly*, and *Fifth of July*, and several one-actors. *The Hot l Baltimore* went on to become one of the longest-running hits in Off-Broadway history, and both *Talley's Folly* and *Fifth of July* moved to Broadway for extended runs. The great majority of the close-to-thirty plays directed by Mason during the decade were by contemporary American writers, although he did do a few revivals, including *The Three Sisters* in his early Off Off period, and *Come Back, Little Sheba* and *Battle of Angels* somewhat later. At the end of the decade Mason tried his hand at the classics, directing *Hamlet* and *Mary Stuart* in repertory, using the same basic costumes and set for both productions. The approach to these plays resembled that of his more realistic works and had some interesting effects but ultimately deprived the plays of the scope needed by their expansive language. At the CRC Mason helped develop a number of outstanding actors who formed a company nucleus over the years, among them William Hurt, Conchatta Ferrell, Tanya Berezin, Judd Hirsch, Jeff Daniels, Lindsay Crouse, Jonathan Hogan, and Trish Hawkins. Mason directed such important new plays as Edward J. Moore's *The Sea Horse*, Jules Feiffer's *Knock Knock* (which moved to Broadway and during its run experienced a controversial switch to a new director and cast), and Albert Innaurato's *Ulysses in Traction*. He also staged Ron Clark and Sam Bobrick's *Murder at the Howard Johnson's* directly for Broadway, where it flopped.

Operating as a free-lance director, Mike Nichols was less prolific and more selective than Mason; his choices, even when they (rarely) failed to click commercially, were among the best that the New York theatre had to offer. Nichols—the only director of the ten surveyed here who shared his talents with Hollywood—staged such Broadway plays as Neil Simon's *The Prisoner of Second Avenue*, Trevor Griffiths' bitter British comedy, *Comedians*, a limited-run, star-studded revival of *Uncle Vanya*, and Coburn's *The Gin Game*, the first and last being highly profitable hits; Off-Broadway profited from the Nichols touch in *Streamers* and *Drinks Before Dinner*, the latter perhaps the least-well-liked play he worked on. His most apparently commercial venture was the Simon comedy, but all the others were challenging and provocative dramas which demanded directorial sensitivity and intelligence as well as superlative acting skills. Essentially a

Stanislavskian (as filtered through the Actors Studio, where he studied for several years with Lee Strasberg), Nichols adds to his psychological perceptions a perfect sense of timing and a keen ear for the rhythms and inflections of dialogue, skills polished by his years as a writer/comedian in a famous act with Elaine May. Actors and playwrights who have worked with him consider him a genius because of his insight, patience, and respect for their artistry.

Although several of the other directors described here have done some acting, the only one of them to epitomize the dual talents of actor-director is Ellis Rabb. Rabb's credits reveal a taste for the classics, of which he is generally considered one of the nation's foremost interpreters, despite an occasional tendency to seek oddly unconventional approaches. His *Merchant of Venice*, for example, was set in a present-day Venice—on the order of *La Dolce Vita*, Antonio and Bassanio's relationship was decadently homosexual, and Belmont was Portia's yacht. Rabb's lengthy artistic directorship of the now-defunct APA Repertory Company equipped him to handle such other seventies assignments as *Twelfth Night*, Marlowe's *Edward II*, and Shaw's *Caesar and Cleopatra*, as well as revivals of more recent works such as *The Royal Family*, the 1927 hit which he freshened up for renewed Broadway popularity, and *A Streetcar Named Desire*, which he successfully directed in a colorful and touching version. New works with his name on the credits included *Veronica's Room*, an Ira Levin thriller, and *Who's Who in Hell*, by Peter Ustinov; both failed. He also staged with mastery a New York premiere of an early twentieth-century play by Maxim Gorky, *Enemies*. This, *Streetcar*, and the Shakespeare plays were seen at Lincoln Center during the Jules Irving regime.

Veteran Alan Schneider, killed in 1984 in a tragic accident in London, where he was staging a new play, had a Broadway career going back to 1948. During the succeeding years he gained an outstanding reputation for productions faithful to their authors' intentions. He staged a wide variety of plays, commercial, classical, and controversially experimental, and possessed a widely acknowledged genius for the work of Samuel Beckett whose chief American interpreter he became. Removed from command of the original U.S. production of *Waiting for Godot*, he revived the play to acclaim in the seventies, and also showed New York audiences his Beckett technique in *Happy Days, Act Without Words, Krapp's Last Tape, Not I*, and *Play and Other Plays*, all in Off-Broadway versions. Schneider's other local work of the period was consistently of the serious, essentially uncommercial type: Bond's provocative *Saved* was done Off-Broadway; a questionably received revival of Hansberry's *The Sign in Sidney Brustein's Window* was on; so was Weller's *Moonchildren*, modestly well reviewed but a box-office catastrophe until revived by another director Off-Broadway not long afterwards. On Broadway, Eli Wiesel's *Zalman, or the Madness of God* sought more than it could achieve; what came into New York as the most highly touted American work of the decade, Preston Jones' *A Texas Trilogy*, seen on Broadway on three consecutive nights, met with enough critical coolness to put it into the deep freeze; and Schneider's revival of Brecht's *Mother Courage* for the touring Acting Company was not around long enough to give many New Yorkers a chance to assess it. However, just before the decade ended Schneider directed *Loose Ends*, a play by Michael Weller, with whom he had opened the period; done at the Circle in the Square, it dealt with romance, marriage, and divorce among the disillusioned, aging *Moonchildren* generation; the play was the most successful of his new-play stagings and ran for close to 300 performances in its non-profit theatre. Schneider's commercial success during the period was nil, while his artistic contributions were generally of the highest caliber.

The most exciting and talked-of new director of the decade was a young Rumanian, Andrei Serban, whose early efforts were nurtured in the Off Off-Broadway domain of La Mama, ETC. Serban brought to the New York mainstream theatre the type of conceptual, imagistic directorial imagination associated with the modern European tradition of turning familiar plays inside out to reveal hitherto unrealized facets. Working with the most creative and forward-thinking new designers and composers, Serban expended his artistry on a wide assortment of demanding scripts, mostly classics. He sought to reignite the flames of Dionysiac exaltation in his strikingly unconventional Off Off-Broadway Greek revivals, collectively titled *Fragments of a Trilogy*, a large portion of which was spoken in a newly minted theatrical language, with the audience standing about in a darkened room lit by torches as the action practically caromed off the walls around them. He also turned Brecht's *Good Woman of Setzuan* into an Off Off exercise in total theatre; startled Lincoln Center's fashionable audiences with a thoroughly reconsidered, energetically comedic *Cherry Orchard* played on a huge, white-carpeted stage without walls; put a masked *Agamemnon* onto the Vivian Beaumont's stage with onstage bleacher sections that moved during the performance into new positions and with language half-English and half-gibberish; transformed a charming film, *The Umbrellas of Cherbourg*, into an even more charming musical theatre event at the Public; and performed equally unusual directorial magic Off-Broadway on an adaptation of Bulgakov's novel, *The Master and Margarita*, and Off Off on Shakespeare's *As You Like It* and Brecht's *Caucasian Chalk Circle*. Serban was totally committed to theatrical experiment, and did not work at all in the commercial arena.

The outburst of black theatre activity in the sixties and seventies led to the emergence of a number of excellent black directors. Among them were Michael Schultz, Vinnette Carroll, Lloyd Richards, Gilbert Moses, and Douglas Turner Ward. Ward, a playwright and actor of distinction in addition to being a noted director, is a cofounder of America's leading black theatre group, the Negro Ensemble Company, which he continued to head throughout the decade and for which he staged close to a dozen plays.

Three of these—Joseph Walker's Tony-winning *The River Niger*, Leslie Lee's *The First Breeze of Summer*, and Samm-Art Williams' *Home*—moved to Broadway. Ward's productions were all related to black subjects, and most of them were essentially naturalistic, although several plays, such as *Home* and *The Great MacDaddy*, allowed him to play with more theatrical-ist effects; *Home*, for example, had two actresses who played a wide assort-ment of characters in the life of the central character. Through Ward's work as a director and producer for the NEC, the best new black playwrit-ing found a congenial outlet with the highest professional standards of acting and production.

It should be remarked that with the exception of Vinnette Carroll, the ab-sence of women among the group surveyed is a reflection of the difficult times they had in gaining recognition as directors. Several did begin to make in-roads in the field, and a couple were able to claim records equal to many top men directors, but for most a lack of opportunities prevented them from gain-ing the acclaim granted to their male counterparts. Many were able to work regularly only by heading their own nonprofit companies. Women who managed to develop reputations as directors in the mainstream included Lynne Meadows, artistic director of the Manhattan Theatre Club, whose close to a dozen Off and Off Off works included the lauded *Ashes* and *Catsplay*; Julianne Boyd, whose *Eubie!* nearly achieved hit status on Broad-way and who toiled consistently in the groves of Off Off's showcase theatres; Vinnette Carroll, of the Urban Arts Corp., who staged at least twenty works, most of them Off Off but several going to Broadway, including *Don't Bother Me, I Can't Cope* and *Your Arms Too Short to Box With God*; Sue Lawless, who worked Off and Off Off, mostly on musicals and revues; Novella Nelson, whose black-oriented work was seen Off and Off Off; Shauneille Perry, very active Off and Off Off for her black theatre productions, notably *Black Girl* and *The Prodigal Sister*; and Elizabeth Swados, composer and director, who staged several distinctive pieces, including Broadway's *Runaways* and Off-Broadway's *Haggadah*, *Nightclub Cantata*, and *Dispatches*. Important women directors who worked almost exclusively Off Off included JoAnne Akalaitis, associated with the Mabou Mines; Tisa Chang, whose Pan-Asian Repertory Company pioneered in the production of Asian-American scripts; Miriam Colon, who headed the Puerto Rico Traveling Theatre; Linda Mussman, an experimentalist who was busy with her Time and Space Limited Theatre Company; and Barbara Loden, well known actress and wife of leading director Elia Kazan, who directed nearly half a dozen new plays in workshop situations.

THE CRITICS

In 1973 *New York Magazine*'s John Simon, reviewing Peter Keveson's Off-Broadway play *Nellie Toole & Co.*, wrote: "It stars Sylvia Miles, a sort of middling Bette Midler without music, better known as one of New York's leading party girls and gate-crashers, whose very acting technique is a kind of gate-crashing. Miss Miles has a devoted following among the gays, whose squeals suggested that the show might do better at the Continental Baths."[4]

Miles, confronting Simon shortly thereafter at a party, did not hesitate to dump a plate of pasta in his lap, an act which, when reported, must surely have sent a vicarious thrill of vengeance through the many artists humiliated by the Yugoslavian-born critic's scathing style. In two sentences Simon had ruthlessly smeared Miles' personality, private life, and talents. Although few other performers had the guts or the opportunity to express —either through verbal eloquence or primitive retaliation—their frustration and pique at such perverse criticism, the role and power of the critics were a steady source of heated public and private debate throughout the decade.

In terms of power, the position of the *New York Times* reviewer as the ultimate arbiter of whether a show would succeed or fail became ever more evident during the sixties and seventies as the number of New York's daily newspapers shrank to three, the *News*, the *Post*, and the *Times*. Since most regular theatregoers read the *Times*, its reviews came to have an undue influence on box-office sales, and a *Times* pan was usually enough to send the members of a theatre company scurrying to find new jobs. Aside from a few noteworthy exceptions, such as *Godspell* and *The Wiz*, the effect of positive reviews in the other dailies, in such weekly sources as *New York*, *The New Yorker*, the *Village Voice*, *Time*, and *Newsweek*, or on TV news shows, was rarely sufficient to overturn the negative impact of even a moderately negative *Times* review. Nor did it matter who the reviewer in question was, provided he was writing for the *Times*.

During most of the decade the chief daily reviewer for the *Times*—and also its dance critic—was British-born Clive Barnes (who once described his critical function as being "the intelligent tick on the backside of genius. Hopefully.").[5] Walter Kerr wrote second opinions for the paper's Sunday edition, a role he undertook in 1967 when he turned over the daily job to Barnes. Once one of the city's most influential critics, Kerr soon realized that his new capacity put him in an after-the-fact situation that robbed his reviews of any significant consequence. Barnes' tenure at the *Times* lasted until 1977, during which time he became the butt of many attacks by angry actors, producers, and playwrights. His response was to insist that no worthwhile play was ever really killed by a reviewer and that truly good plays survived despite bad notices. "Critics do not close plays," he claimed. "Producers close plays."[6] In 1977 the *Times* relieved him of his drama duties (soon afterwards he was hired as dance and drama critic by the *Post*), whereupon foreign correspondent Richard Eder, a man with little formal training as a critic, took over the post.

Eder lasted two years, during which he too became a target for dissatisfied members of the profession. Playwright Neil Simon went so far as to suggest on national television's *Today* show that Eder was unqualified for his position. For most of 1979-80 Walter Kerr returned to daily reviewing, sharing the load with Mel Gussow—the *Times'* long-time second-stringer, and before the season was out turned the first-string job over to Frank Rich, who still holds it today. All along, the *Times* drama desk was staffed by a succession of second- and third-stringers, chief of whom was Gussow, who continues to be the main backup man. Thus, many *Times* critics came and went, but the paper's reputation for integrity and excellence gave all their reviews a cachet of distinction to which they were often not entitled.

Considering the power of life and death held by the critics over not only specific productions but the careers and livelihoods of so many people, it is no wonder that they were so open—if not actually vulnerable—to attack from interested parties. Those regarded as the more churlish of the fraternity—Martin Gottfried (first for *Women's Wear Daily* and then for the *Post*) and John Simon best fit the description—were periodically forbidden complimentary tickets to shows produced by those whose earlier works they had attacked; Joseph Papp and Arthur Cantor were among the producers who thought this an appropriate way to slap a critic on the wrist. However, as no producer could stop a critic from purchasing a seat to a production, exclusionary tactics could result in nothing but a Pyrrhic victory. As most theatre people did not have Neil Simon's access to the airwaves, they resorted to sending grumbling missives to newspaper and magazine editors, in which they freely abused the critics for perceived weaknesses. (Papp was also likely to call a critic up in the middle of the night to rail about an unfavorable notice.) For example, John Simon was despised for his nasty physical descriptions of actors he found unattractive (Liza Minnelli was a prime target); Barnes was deemed incapable of appreciating American comedy (many respected American theatre artists professed to be insulted that the *Times* had hired a British critic), and was assailed for writing ungrammatically (a fault fellow-critic Simon loved to dwell on), for hating George Bernard Shaw, and for falling asleep at opening nights; Gottfried and Simon were mocked for their inability to sit through shows they hated—the former's reviews, especially, are filled with admissions that he left after intermission; and T. E. Kalem, reviewing *A Touch of the Poet*, was caught plagiarizing his *Time* predecessor, Louis Kronenberger, who had covered an earlier staging of the play in 1958.

Producers and others—among them the Dramatists Guild—continually sought to defuse the power of the critics. Their concerns were, of course, primarily business-oriented, and the ideals and values of perceptive criticism played little part in their agitations and cogitations. They suggested that the *Times* print more than one review; that a box score—such as one finds in the trade weekly *Variety* and which the *Times* itself used to print but discontinued early in the decade—be published to demonstrate the total critical reaction; that black plays be reviewed by a black critic as well as a white; that the critics make their comments right after the opening, to the audience, be forced to defend themselves, and then see the entire debate printed in the next day's papers; and so on. Nearly every one of the suggestions could be shown to be impractical, but the arguments persisted.

Several producers went further than speaking out at forums or through letters. In 1970 Barnes, reviewing a new musical, wrote: "Oh, dear! I come to bury *Lovely Ladies, Kind Gentlemen*, not to praise it,"[7] an example of the kind of hurtfully witty phrase that popular reviewers loved to turn. Producer Herman Levin, agreeing with Barnes' right to pan the show, nevertheless claimed that he had abused his authority by such "cruel and . . . obnoxious"[8] writing, and a brouhaha evolved leading to the *Times'* being picketed by over fifty actors and technicians.

No other incidents of picketing a critic were heard of; a number of shows, however, tried to avoid even having critics to picket by the simple expedient of not announcing an opening night. The concept of "previews"— generally several weeks of reduced-price performances prior to the official opening, during which a show was pulled into shape—had been in operation for years. Presumably, a show could advertise and fill seats indefinitely without facing the dangers of critical exposure. This tack was taken by several major shows in the seventies, thereby annoying the press, who felt that it was their responsibility to report new theatrical productions to the paying public. The press and the producers debated the ethics involved, but ultimately most such shows were attended and reviewed by the critics—usually led by the *Times* and *Variety*—at the expense of their employers; a prime factor in driving the critics to these shows was that they were charging the same prices that would have been in effect if they had officially opened. The critics therefore made it clear that any future attempts to bar them while a show was in actual production would not be tolerated. The most important of such shows were Off-Broadway's *Let My People Come*, and Broadway's *Sarava* and *Beatlemania*. Reviews for the first two were poor to middling, but only *Sarava* was seriously hurt by its tepid reception. *Beatlemania* never did have a press opening, having begun performances on May 26, 1977, although one of the *Times'* stringers covered it less than a month later. *Variety* did not see it until February 1978. Still, it managed to run for almost three years.

The atmosphere surrounding the critics' power being what it was, it was not unreasonable to expect that additional devious means would be found to provide relief. One practice that had been going on for some time and that reached a peak in the seventies was the producers' reprinting only the more positive phrases and words from reviews that, when read in full, were actually condemnatory. This practice led in 1971 to urgent attempts by the city's Commissioner of Consumer Affairs to have an ordinance passed forbidding such deceptive quoting out of context. Considerable steam was generated by the move, but the steam faded when it became clear that ad surveillance would constitute a violation of First and Fourteenth Amendment rights. And so the matter continued to stand.

There were various other debates and contretemps surrounding the intrinsically controversial work of New York's theatre critics. The critics sometimes defended themselves or offered outlines of their critical methods, but these did not and could not mitigate the response their negative reviews were bound to elicit. Nor could there be any proof that their occasional attempts to describe their principles were anything other than self-justifications by writers whose ultimate purpose was to attract and sustain a regular readership. After all, their job required the employment of fundamentally subjective skills for a task of ostensibly objective evaluation. In closing, then, a handful of the critics' own remarks on their view of what their work entails are offered without further comment:

Clive Barnes: I enter the theatre as its friend and its servant. I am not an adversary. I am an interpreter and a guardian—an interpreter of mysteries it did not know needed interpreting and a guardian of treasures that closed on Saturday night.[9]

T. E. Kalem: I consult my own entrails as I leave the theatre. I then proceed like a lawyer with his brief, marshaling the arguments as strongly as possible pro and con.[10]

Richard Eder: A good critic . . . is that one person that more or less goes forward on behalf of that abstract but real entity called the "intelligent audience," and comes back as if he were an explorer coming back to say "Here in the jungles of Brazil I have found this."[11]

John Simon: The critics [sic] function . . . is triple: to write as well as any writer, to educate the readers, and to use the critical platform also for broader speculations about art and life. The ideal critic, then, is an artist, teacher, and philosopher.[12]

Douglas Watt (News): The primary function of the theatre critic is to describe an event as clearly as possible as it's mirrored through him to his readers in terms of his opinions, background and interests.[13]

NOTES

1. David Weinstein, "Actors' Equity: Do You Call That a Union?" *The Nation*, 20 September 1971, p. 242.

2. Walter Kerr, "Take a Tip: Put Your Money in Tootsie Rolls," *New York Times*, 9 January 1972, Sec. II, p. 1.

3. Douglas Watt, "Bedford Shines in Fine New *School for Wives*," *New York Daily News*, 17 February 1971.

4. John Simon "Sick Transit," *New York Magazine*, 8 October 1973, p. 90.

5. Clive Barnes, "Further Confessions of a Drama Critic," *Playbill*, February 1978, n.p.

6. Clive Barnes, "My Life and the *Times*," *Playbill*, March 1973, p. 7.

7. Clive Barnes, "Theater: *Lovely Ladies, Kind Gentlemen* Opens," *New York Times*, 29 December 1970, p. 38.

8. Herman Levin, "Drama Mailbag," *New York Times*, 10 January 1971, Sec. II, p. 5.

9. Barnes, "Further Confessions of a Drama Critic."

10. T. E. Kalem, "The Visceral Response," *Playbill*, January 1980, p. 6.

11. Quoted in Bernard Carragher, "New Man on the Aisle," *Playbill*, October 1977, n.p.

12. "What They Said: On the Critic's Function," *New York Theatre Review*, 1 (November 1977): 15.

13. Ibid. An ambitious, but sometimes questionable, attempt to assess all the major critics of the period is Lehman Engel's *The Critics* (New York: Macmillan, 1976).

★ ★
EPILOGUE

One question haunts me as I complete this book; can the successful and unexpected turnaround undergone by the New York theatre of the seventies be repeated? In spite of the upward arc of activity and profits experienced in the decade's second half, the euphoria proved short-lived when the eighties arrived.

After several seasons of diminished production and considerable loss, Broadway in the mid-eighties is depressingly reminiscent of conditions in the early seventies. Some of Off-Broadway's subsidized theatres are thriving (Joseph Papp reported that his 1984-85 season at the Public was his best since he moved in in 1967), but the quality of most Broadway presentations—directorial, design, and performance aspects aside—have sunk to an artistic nadir. The musical theatre, Broadway's bread and butter, is moribund, and not a single smash-hit musical opened on Broadway during 1984-85; the competition for the Tonys among what remained was embarrassingly weak. Throughout the Broadway district, theatres are again standing unused; on September 18, 1985, as the new season was gearing up to begin, a total of twenty-one Broadway theatres were dark. Tickets remain forbiddingly expensive, averaging $29.06 for 1984-85, compared with $17.97 for 1980-81. Attendance figures have been falling precipitously from the all-time high of 1980-81 with its 10,822,324 tickets sold; in 1984-85 the number had shrunk to 7,156,683, even lower than the 7,181,898 of 1975-76, the year *Variety* first began reporting these figures. The life seems once more to have been drained from the theatre district, and the prognosis for the future is dreary indeed.

Will some new scheme to cut prices be introduced to draw spectators back to the Great White Way in the numbers registered in the late seventies? Two potentially important new developments need time before their impact can be assessed: one is producer Morton Gottlieb's scheme to cut costs by a method similar to that of the Limited Gross Agreement that failed in the early seventies; the other is the cost reductions allowed by the new royalty-payment provisions of a contract agreed upon after years of litigation between the Dramatists Guild and the League of American Theatre Owners and Producers (the new name of the League of New York Theatre Owners and Producers). A small number of works were produced under these arrangements. If successful, they will be employed on a wider scale and result in significantly lowered ticket prices to many Broadway offerings. But lowered prices, for all their importance in inducing audiences to attend, will have to be coupled with a strong and steady increase in the quality of the material produced. So, inevitably, this book must close with a big question mark as to the future; it also ends with a prayer that some miracle drug will be administered to once more revive the "fabulous invalid" and bring it roaring to its feet. It happened before; can it happen again?

★ ★

Notes
on
Sources

Because of the recentness of the period with which this work deals, few books have been published dealing with its theatre. Most books of specific pertinence to the decade have been cited in the notes to the various chapters. Important ones among them are Stephen Langley's *Producers on Producing* (New York: Drama Book Specialists, 1976), Lehman Engel's *The Critics* (New York: Macmillan, 1976), and Brooks Atkinson's *Broadway* (New York: Macmillan, 1974), each of which deals with the seventies only in part. In addition, the interested reader would be well advised to read Gerald Berkowitz's *New Broadways: Theatre Across America 1950-1980* (Totowa, N.J.: Rowman and Littlefield, 1982). Berkowitz provides a concise thirty-year perspective on the major developments in American theatre; although concerned principally with the American theatre as a whole, he nevertheless touches briefly on many issues also examined in the present book.

A worthwhile reference book on the black theatre of the century, with entries on nearly all the black plays of the seventies, is Allen Woll's *Dictionary of the Black Theatre: Broadway, Off-Broadway, and Selected Harlem Theatre* (Westport, Conn.: Greenwood Press, 1983). Jan Weingarten Greenberg has written an interesting book on *Theatre Business: From Auditions through Opening Night* (New York: Holt, Rinehart and Winston, 1981) which examines some of the areas presented in *Ten Seasons'* early chapters. A good portion of the musical theatre of the period may be read about in the updated version of Abe Laufe's *Broadway's Greatest Musicals* (New York: Funke and Wagnalls, 1977), in Gerald Bordman's comprehensive *American Musical Theatre: A Chronicle* (New York: Oxford University Press, 1978), and in Martin Gottfried's coffee-table volume, *Broadway Musicals* (New York: Harry N. Abrams, 1979).

The history of Broadway's theatres has been comprehensively treated in two vital books: in Mary C. Henderson's *The City and the Theatre* (Clifton, N.Y.: James T.

White, 1973) and, rather more colorfully, in Louis Botto's *At This Theatre* (New York: Dodd, Mead and Co., 1984). For an excellent descriptive overview of the leading American avant-garde artists and companies, many of whom were active locally in the decade, Theodore Shank's *American Alternative Theatre* (New York: Grove Press, 1982) is available. Shank's bibliography is a good source for further reading in this area.

As a general study of the experimental theatre, Margaret Croyden's *Lunatics, Lovers and Poets: The Contemporary Experimental Theatre* (New York: McGraw-Hill, 1974) is interesting, but its date of publication prevents it from covering much material of relevance to the seventies. This can be rectified by reference to various periodicals that focused on the experimentalists, most importantly *The Drama Review* and *Performing Arts Journal*, which first began publication in mid-decade. *Performance*, which appeared briefly early in the period, had similar purposes. First-rate background on both the avant-garde and the mainstream theatre may also be discovered in such scholarly and critical publications as *Theatre* (formerly *Yale/Theatre*) and *Theatre Journal* (formerly *Educational Theatre Journal*).

I have found a number of other regularly published sources of particular value. One is the annual *Best Plays* series, edited throughout the seventies by Otis Guernsey, Jr.; these tomes offer enormous amounts of valuable information, among them the most thorough available statistics on each theatre season, and a detailed essay on the season's achievements from both an artistic and economic point of view. John Willis' annual *Theatre World* series is Guernsey's major competition, and all who wish to learn about the statistical details of a New York season should consult both sources; however, Guernsey and Willis often differ in such figures as lengths of runs and in what constitutes a Broadway, Off-Broadway, or Off Off-Broadway work. I have opted to follow Guernsey's decisions in this book but am not impugning Willis' superb work; in fact, I have occasionally noticed errors in both. Willis is especially important because of the pictorial record he supplies of every local production and of hundreds elsewhere in the country.

A comprehensive pictorial overview of American theatre through the decade is Daniel Blum's *A Pictorial History of the American Theatre, 1860-1980*, 5th ed. (New York: Crown, 1985); by "American Theatre" Blum really means New York. Important statistical data on the non-profit theatres in New York and elsewhere appeared fairly regularly in the *Theatre Profiles* series published by the Theatre Communications Group. The *New York Times*, which reports nearly all the mainstream theatre news that's fit to print, was of inestimable assistance as were the files of the weekly trade journal, *Variety*, whose thorough coverage of all business-related aspects of the "legitimate" is not duplicated anywhere. The *Times* has since the early seventies been publishing bound volumes (*The New York Times Theater Reviews*) of all its annual reviews, which make for far more convenient reference than microfilm. Those who write for the *New York Daily News* and the *New York Post* have also been gleaned for information, as has Long Island's excellent paper, *Newsday*, which reports on New York productions. The weekly New York magazines printed numerous helpful articles and interviews, in addition to their reviews. For background on the experimental work of the decade, the *Village Voice* proved most helpful, as did the now-defunct *Soho News*, while *New York Magazine*, *The New Yorker*, *Nation*, *Saturday Review*, the *New Republic*, *Time*, *Newsweek*, and several others played a significant role in providing useful information and criticism. Some of the regular critics for these periodicals, such as Walter Kerr, Harold Clurman, Stanley Kauffmann, and John Simon have published collections of their theatre essays and reviews. Business magazines such as *Forbes*, *Fortune*, and *Business Week* were also helpful on occasion.

New York did not have the services of a national theatre magazine for most of the decade, but in 1977 *The New York Theatre Review* was founded to rectify the situation. This glossy monthly—aimed at both a popular and a professional audience—lasted only about two years, financial burdens having proved overwhelming. It provided some valuable data and ideas, but was in no way as attractively designed or as imaginatively edited as such outstanding magazines of the past as *Theatre Arts* and *Theatre Magazine*. Somewhat longer-lived was *Other Stages*, a weekly theatre newspaper distributed free in Off and Off Off-Broadway theatres, and concerned primarily with the work done in such places. It came out in 1979 and lasted five years, so only one year of its life was of immediate value for *Ten Seasons*. A regular theatrical publication which dates back to the nineteenth century and which, in recent years, has become a rich source of theatre stories, is *Playbill*, the free program distributed at Broadway theatres. *Playbill* offshoots are found in Off-Broadway houses under a variety of names and also occasionally provide useful information, in addition to cast lists and Who's Whos.

INDEX

Dates appearing in parentheses following the titles of plays are given only for productions given in New York during the 1970s. Although a play may have had multiple productions during the decade, dates are provided only for those mentioned in the text. In cases where an Off Off-Broadway work was later moved to Off-Broadway or Broadway, the date given is normally that of the latter production.

About the Author

SAMUEL L. LEITER is Professor of Theatre at Brooklyn College, City University of New York and at the Graduate Center, City University of New York. His earlier works include *The Art of Kabuki: Famous Plays in Performance* and *Kabuki Encyclopedia: An English Language Adaptation of Kabuki Jiten* (Greenwood Press, 1979), and numerous articles in journals such as the *Educational Theatre Journal, Players,* and *Drama Survey.* He is the editor of *Encyclopedia of the New York Stage, 1920-1930* and *Shakespeare Around the Globe* (Greenwood Press, 1985, 1986).

747